THREE AMERICAN LITERATURES

Essays in Chicano, Native American, and Asian-American Literature for Teachers of American Literature

Edited by Houston A. Baker, Jr.

With an Introduction by Walter J. Ong

The Modern Language Association of America
New York   1982

"An Introduction to Chinese-American and Japanese-American Literature" is copyright © 1972, 1973, 1974 by Jeffery Paul Chan, Frank Chin, Lawson Fusao Inada, Shawn H. Wong. Reprinted by permission of the authors. Earlier versions of this essay have appeared in *Bulletin of Concerned Asian Scholars*, Special Issue on Asian America, Vol. 4, no. 3 (Fall 1972), edited by Victor Nee, Brett Nee, Connie Young Yu, Shawn H. Wong; *Yardbird Reader*, Vol. 2 (1973), edited by Al Young; and *AIIIEEEEE! An Anthology of Asian-American Writers*, edited by Frank Chin, Jeffery Paul Chan, Lawson Fusao Inada, Shawn H. Wong (Howard Univ. Press, 1974; rpt. in paperback by Doubleday-Anchor Books, 1975).

A revised version of Dorothy Ritsuko McDonald's essay appeared as the introduction to The Chickencoop Chinaman *and* The Year of the Dragon: *Two Plays*, by Frank Chin (Univ. of Washington Press, 1981).

Library of Congress Cataloging in Publication Data
Main entry under title:

Three American literatures.

Includes bibliographical references.
1. American literature—Minority authors—History and criticism—Addresses, essays, lectures. 2. American literature—Mexican American authors—History and criticism—Addresses, essays, lectures. 3. American literature—Indian authors—History and criticism—Addresses, essays, lectures. 4. American literature—Asian-American authors—History and criticism—Addresses, essays, lectures. 5. Minorities in literature—Addresses, essays, lectures. 6. United States—Literatures—History and criticism—Addresses, essays, lectures. I. Baker, Houston A.
PS153.M56T5   810'.9'920693   82-6342
ISBN 0-87352-353-9   AACR2
ISBN 0-87352-352-0 (pbk.)

Published by The Modern Language Association of America
62 Fifth Avenue, New York, New York 10011

Contents

Preface

Literature offers representations of experience. The literary traditions of numerically and ethnically defined minority groups in the United States offer representations of the sui generis cultural and historical experiences of the groups from which they derive. On the strength of James's dictum that experience, for the refined sensibility, is never limited and never complete, one can construct an eloquent case for reading and teaching the literatures of various minority groups. Since Walter Ong's introduction to the present volume makes such a case and joins the published efforts of a sizable group of critics who have spoken in behalf of minority literatures in recent decades, there is no need to take up in this preface the question of whether minority literatures are worth teaching or should be taught. From almost any perspective in the current universe of discourse surrounding literary creation and study in the United States, the salient concerns vis-à-vis minority literatures seem to be what literary works from various traditions might be included in, say, a general survey course in American literature and how instructors and students should approach such works.

The present collection is governed by the belief that most teachers of American literature would welcome a single-volume work offering overviews of the literary traditions of selected minority groups. The essays that follow provide not only broad overviews but also detailed analyses of specific folk tales, poems, novels, dramas, and other literary forms that constitute significant aspects of three traditions. The entire collection is designed to be read cover to cover. Yet, the depth of analysis that characterizes the essays will, we hope, induce teachers and students to return to individual essays (or to the volume as a whole) on many occasions. Though the collection is not intended as an exhaustive reference source, its readers may find that it offers a range of information that guarantees its long-term usefulness.

The decision to focus on Chicano, Native American, and Asian-American literatures in the volume was based on several general and pragmatic considerations. First, all three literatures have received increasing critical and theoretical attention in recent years. Hence, a body of scholarship and an identifiable group of scholars are now concerned with the three traditions. This made the job of securing contributors a relatively easy task. Second, a number of major works in all three traditions are written in English and are thus accessible to most teachers and students of American literature. Finally, a clear recognition that Chicanos, Native Americans, and Asian-Americans are far more than "invisible minorities" played a decisive role in constructing this collection. The histories of all three groups are rooted in the culture of the United States and are far more extensive than traditional accounts allow. Without a sound knowledge of all three, one cannot arrive at a just assessment of the distinctive character of American social and intellectual history.

Obviously, the literatures of other minority groups also deserve study; that they are not represented in the present volume does not diminish their claim to critical attention. Editing is, by definition, a selective enterprise. The curious economy of academic life, combined with the considerations already mentioned, made the selection of Chicano, Native American, and Asian-American literatures seem a wise choice from a range of possibilities. The choice implies a necessary selectivity and should not be construed as an evaluative assessment of literatures that are not treated in the following essays.

The work of editing this collection has proceeded under the auspices of the Modern Language Association's Committee on Teaching and Related Professional Activities. I want to thank the committee for its support in the endeavor. To acknowledge the efforts of others who have helped bring the work to its conclusion would be an enormous undertaking involving the history of the work's origin in the proceedings of the MLA's Commission on Minority Groups and the Study of Language and Literature (now the Commission on American Literatures) and many other laborious details. Given the temporal and spatial constraints that should mark a preface, perhaps it will be sufficient to thank one key figure, Alfonso Ortiz, for his advice and counsel, and to say a word of sincere gratitude to my wife and son, who have lived with the idea of this project for several years. It is my hope that the guiding assumption of the project—that teachers and students of American literature will welcome a volume devoted to the literary traditions of selected minority groups—proves justified.

Houston A. Baker, Jr.
University of Pennsylvania

Introduction: On Saying We and Us to Literature

Walter J. Ong

The literatures of minority groups in the United States have been attracting more and more attention in recent years for several reasons. First, the literatures themselves are growing. Second, ethnic diversity is felt more and more to be a good thing, not the threat that it once appeared to be, whether to the majority ethnic group or to minorities themselves. Third, courses in American literature and American studies are multiplying, and it appears to many that such courses, at least in principle, should present a true cross-section of culture in the United States.

Minority cultures of surprising diversity exist in the United States and continue to produce distinctive literature here, by far the greater part of it now in English. This literature is a tremendous asset to everyone in a country where most of the population of over 200 million persons share a highly standardized culture—perhaps the most highly standardized that a group of such size has ever known. Literature is organized experience and consciousness. Since cultures organize experience and consciousness variously, the study of the literature of another culture opens new vistas both into the exterior world and into the human heart. Mainstream education in the United States has been mostly ethnocentric and fairly homogeneous, deriving primarily from European culture transmitted in English, diversified only here and there by irregular study of other languages and literatures. Attention to minority literatures can enrich the mainstream and make everyone's sense of the total culture of the United States more real.

A minority literature often mixes what is unfamiliar to the majority culture with what is familiar. It thus provides not only an organization of experience different from that of the majority culture (and of other minorities) but also an interactive organization. A minority literature often negotiates for its own identity with the majority culture and constantly redefines itself, ultimately bringing the majority culture to define itself more adequately, too. Cultures, whether majority or minority, are remarkably like persons, born both to isolation and to community. All of us want to realize ourselves as distinct persons, but we also want others—lots of others—to know that we are our own distinct selves. We do not want to be unique all alone. Hence we negotiate. And so do cultures.

The present volume should promote negotiation. It treats three of the principal minority literatures in the United States: Chicano, Native American ("Indian"), and Asian-American. These literatures are all central to our cultural heritage, and, as Houston Baker notes in his Preface, each of the three includes major works written in English and thus accessible to most readers, including members of other minorities, in the United States. All minority literatures could not be included in a volume this size. Afro-American literature is simply too massive. It is the nation's largest minority literature and needs a volume such as this to itself. Many other minority literatures, such as that of Vietnamese America, are slight or only incipient, and to include all would fragment even a large book. A good case could of course be made for some not here included, for example Puerto Rican. But some limitations had to be set. Even what is included had to be presented with certain constraints. The omnibus category of Asian-American literature, though useful and necessary, has only limited value, for it throws together such diverse traditions as Chinese, Japanese, Korean, and Filipino. The term "Native American" is also in fact an omnibus category, for the peoples whom the European settlers grouped together as "Indians" belonged to highly diversified cultures and spoke not only hundreds of different languages but also languages of many different families: one Native American language may be less related to another than English is related to Russian or Persian.

But though the end is never in sight, one has to start somewhere, and we can be grateful to the contributors and the editor for this sensitive and propitious beginning, hoping that it will encourage other beginnings on other minority fronts. This work is scholarly, though not difficult or abstruse. The authors describe, explain, and illustrate with examples to help the reader respond with empathy to cultural diversity.

Two studies here treat Chicano literature. Luis Leal and Pepe Barrón discuss chiefly its genres and themes and its relationship to social protest and revolution and to cultural identity, emphasizing its relevance to the totality of human experience in the United States. In a longer study of the evolution of Chicano literature, Raymund A. Paredes treats individual works and genres in greater historical detail. He concludes with one encouraging example that shows how cultural heritages are not entirely impenetrable to one another: the skillful and widely read Chicano writer Amado Muro was revealed after his death to be Chester Seltzer, an Anglo Ohio newspaperman who had settled in El Paso and married a Chicana, Amada Muro, to whose memory his own nom de plume and borrowed cultural identity are an abiding tribute.

Native American, or Indian, literature is the most complex of the traditions this book treats in the sense that it represents the greatest cultural diversity. The highly developed verbal art of the various Native American cultures was an oral art, diverse in the diverse cultures. Only belatedly are the oral creations of these many cultures being reduced to writing—and not fast enough, for much of the oral tradition is vanishing before it can be directly recorded and transcribed. (The situation is not new: such has been the fate of most early oral tradition in Europe, Asia, Africa, and pretty well across the globe.) Still, the old Native American cultures have acquired a transformed life. Younger Native American writers today are availing themselves of the old traditions in a variety of ways to produce a contemporary literature in English that is connected with the older oral tradition but generally quite different from what English-language readers have considered typically "Indian": a literature marked by deep irony, sometimes tragic and sometimes humorous, based on sensitive reflection and providing a sophisticated and deeply human sense of what it is to be a twentieth-century Native American in the United States.

Kenneth Lincoln treats in detail the oral traditions, the present-day literature, and the connection between the two. He discusses ancient and modern works in terms of their themes: Rooted Words, Minimal Presence, Sense Magic, and Poetry as Survival, among others. Ultimately, in organizing human experience, literature can serve other ends, too: for the Native American, as for all human beings, it can help ensure cultural survival. Lester A. Standiford reviews the complex history of Native Americans, the old oral traditions of the many peoples, their political history and the oppression they suffered at the hands of the colonists, their recognition of a "common set of socioeconomic problems" that today unite extant tribes of widely differing heritages in a new kind of Indian consciousness, and the mixture of ardent rhetoric and sheer poetry in the new voice developed by Native American writers through the late 1960s and 1970s.

In their essay on Asian-American literature, Jeffery Paul Chan, Frank Chin, Lawson Fusao Inada, and Shawn H. Wong discuss the double-identity problems. All persons growing up with a double identity, ethnic or cultural or linguistic, live in some state of tension. But the tension is often easier to resolve at the social, political, and ideological level than at the level of the creative literary imagination. The imagination cannot be programmed rationally or made to work by reasoning processes, although its output can to a degree be rationally managed and assessed.

Creativity has its roots in the unconscious and depends largely on the unconscious organization of experience. This organization cannot be forced; it is often slow in coming and painful. The authors here convey some idea of the agony and galling restlessness that result. Nothing fits, nothing expresses what the writer feels compelled to utter, neither the dominant culture nor the minority culture. Both cultures assert themselves and cannot be done away with. But it will not work to try to be Asian or to try to be simply American. A living fusion into something new is needed. The internal tensions of Asian-Americans have received far less general notice than those of other minority groups, such as blacks or Chicanos or Native Americans. For this reason, the tensions can be even more acute for Americans of Asian ancestry who face up to them.

The next study treats the work of one of the four authors of this essay on Asian-American literature and further defines the problems this last essay discusses. Dorothy Ritsuko McDonald leads the reader through the harrowing identity crises experienced by Frank Chin, a distinguished fifth-generation American of Chinese ancestry. Chin passionately and relentlessly faces intercultural tensions, particularly those felt by Chinese males haunted by the character type assigned to them in the American literary milieu: they were supposed to be "nice" men, unassertive, passive, quiet, obsequious, psychologically emasculated. Even the sinister Fu Manchu conformed externally to this type. The post-1925 literary character Charlie Chan, though clever, was essentially "nice," too. But to relieve the present tensions, there is no way back to an ancient Chinese culture, which, anyhow, had its own problems. A person's identity has to be found where he or she is, and Chin writes about people in the United States, and here for good. The conflicts are agonizing, but literature is about conflict, and Chin writes serious and compelling literature and drama.

In an imaginative tour of two prose works, Lawson Fusao Inada, another of the four authors of the essay on Asian-American literature, plunges his reader directly into the mind and heart of Japanese America, in its outgoing, irrepressibly positive and creative moods, and in the agonizing identity crises brought about by World War II, which could lead through almost unbearable personal suffering to deeply personal affirmation and love for others. This essay concludes the present volume.

The study of minority literatures is fascinating, but it is not easier to implement than the study of anything else. Some will insist that minority literatures in the United States are not worth the effort they call for, that their study further extends an already overextended curriculum. Class time indeed is limited. One cannot teach everything.

But some acquaintanceship with some minority literature or literatures is the right of all and would appear to be imperative for all teachers of American literature today if "American literature" is to mean more than merely the literature of the largest and most homogeneous cultural group in the United States. There is no way to avoid facing the question of what "American literature" means if one is going to use that term.

Moreover, even mainstream American literature often calls for familiarity with traditions that minority literatures open to the reader. Majorities cannot avoid defining themselves by relations, real and imaginary, with minorities. What is the reader to make of James Fenimore Cooper's Chingachgook or Mark Twain's Injun Joe or William Faulkner's Dilsey? One needs familiarity not only with the conventions these writers used but also with Native American cultures and black culture. Such familiarity can be acquired from the literatures of these cultures. Such knowledge makes it possible to assess the conventions themselves with minimal ethnic bias. For conventions do have to be assessed. To respond adequately to a work of literature it is important to know if it invites the reader to take seriously what may be in effect caricature or whether its symbolization works at a level deeper than caricature can attain.

The United States is fortunate in its diverse cultures. Literature both expresses and helps achieve cultural identity, and today, more than ever before, achieving one's own identity depends for all human beings on the incorporation of diversities into the psyche. As long as other cultures are always "they" and never "we" or "us" to a person from a majority or a minority group anywhere today, that person is psychologically, emotionally, aesthetically, and morally handicapped.

In the world of sensitive educated persons today, a publicly circulated text must speak with the awareness that everybody in all cultures is included in "we." "Homo sum; humani nihil a me alienum puto." Since Latin has been a minority language and literature for some time, perhaps this statement by the Roman dramatist Terence should be put into English. But if what it says is true, translating it should not be necessary. A paraphrase might suffice: "What is foreign is my own."

Chicano Literature: An Overview

Luis Leal and Pepe Barrón

I. The Birth of a Minority Literature

The American continent, the last region of the world to be discovered by Europeans, was settled mainly by Spanish-, Portuguese-, and English-speaking peoples. After its discovery, the New World became the promised land. Alfonso Reyes, the Mexican humanist, in his essay "Ultima Tule," tells us that since the sixteenth century America has been thought of as the land where a perfect republic could be established, where utopia could become a reality; he says that even today "the continent can be encompassed as a hope, and offers itself to Europe as a reservation for humanity."[1]

The Spaniards who conquered the New World were looking for more than gold; they were also in search of the promised land. From Tenochtitlán, the old Aztec capital, they set out to look for their utopia. Some headed south to the land of El Dorado; some went to Florida to seek the Fountain of Youth; and some pressed on to Aztlán (later to be called Texas), or Arizona, or New Mexico, or California. In Aztlán, this promised land, Chicanos would one day create their own literature, slightly different from that of central Mexico and quite different from that of the Anglo-Americans living on the periphery of their territory, which, according to legend, was the place of origin of the ancient Aztecs.

In 1836, part of that territory, Texas, became independent and later, in 1845, received its statehood. In 1848, with the signing of the Treaty of Guadalupe Hidalgo after the Mexican War, Mexico ceded the rest of the territory north of the Rio Grande to the United States. Some of the Spanish-speaking inhabitants decided to go south to Mexico, but most refused to move and automatically became American citizens. According to the treaty, however, they were to be allowed to keep their language, culture, and traditions. Thus, a new minority was created. Their number constantly increased as immigrants arrived from Mexico, attracted to Aztlán by the affluent economy of the United States.

The dream, however, was not to become a reality for most of the new immigrants or for the native settlers of the Southwest, for they soon discovered that the dominant English-speaking majority considered them outsiders and that America was not willing to share the good life with them. Caught between two cultures, segregated into barrios, ignorant of the ways of the law, and at a disadvantage because of language difficulties, they were soon relegated to the status of second-class citizens. In 1940 they were still the "forgotten people,"[2] and as recently as 1969, the "invisible minority." Philip D. Ortego in his review of the anthology *El Espejo—The Mirror* is moved to say, "Perhaps no history of a people has been more obscure, more apocryphal, and so utterly misapprehended by the majority of Anglo-Americans than the history of Mexican-Americans, for they continue to exist in the United States as an 'invisible minority.' "[3] If they are forgotten or invisible, it is not because of their number but because members of the dominant culture chose to ignore them. Chicanos, in fact, constitute the second largest minority group in the country, comprising more than five million, according to the 1970 U.S. Census,[4] but roughly estimated at up to twelve million today.

It is often implied that Chicanos are passive, unwilling to fight for a better place in the social scale of American life. The history of the Chicanos, however, shows that they have not been a passive, resigned people expecting all salvation to come from without.[5] As early as the 1800s they protested their treatment, and uprisings were recorded in the popular literature of the period. They also organized citizens' associations for mutual aid and protection and to secure civil rights due them under the law. Over the years, these organizations have become numerous and influential, reaching into all areas that affect the lives of Chicanos. But it was not until the 1960s that the Chicano movement was born and began to spread rapidly throughout the nation. The cultural aspect of the movement has been outstanding, resulting in a wealth of literature, much of which is bilingual (written in a mixture of Spanish and English), and the establishment of theater groups, newspapers, and literary reviews. It is a literature that aspires to give expression to the Chicanos' view of the society in which they live, and it describes how interrelations with the majority group affect Chicanos' attitudes toward themselves and toward life in general. It attempts to reveal the meaning of life for Chicanos living in a twentieth-century "utopia."

II. *Chicano Literature in the Context of American Literature*

Chicanos are Americans, and their literature should be a part of American literature, but until now it has been ignored by most historians of the national literature. Since a large part of Chicano literature is written in Spanish or is bilingual, however, its study has been taken over mainly by critics and professors of Latin American literature, primarily those acquainted with Mexican literature, for Chicano literature, like Janus, has two faces: one looks toward the long literary tradition of Mexico and the other toward the United States. Most is written for English or bilingual readers, especially Chicanos. Undoubtedly, the very nature of Chicano literature, in its use of a dual language, has posed a problem for critics. Nevertheless, specialists in both English and Latin American studies, such as Philip D. Ortego, Gerald Haslam, Joseph Sommers, Juan Bruce-Novoa, Herminio Ríos, Juan Rodríguez, Frank Pino, Luis Dávila, Charles M. Tatum, Guillermo Rojas, and Francisco Lomeli, have made excellent contributions to its criticism and analysis. The training of Chicano-literature specialists who are conversant not only with American literature (especially that of other minorities) but also with Mexican letters and Chicano culture will accelerate the formation of a tradition of Chicano literary criticism. In regard to this, Teresa McKenna has said, "The Chicano must not only address himself to the creation of a distinct literature emergent from his own reality, he must also contribute to the further richness of his art through the development of a body of criticism that approaches Chicano literature from a Chicano perspective."[6]

Why has Chicano literature been ignored? Principally because, historically, Chicanos have been considered a group apart. The rejection of the Chicano in the United States is well documented. One of the first studies to explore the plight of the Chicano in the United States was done by Carey McWilliams in 1949, when he published *North from Mexico*.[7] The rejection of the Chicano is also reflected in literature, as demonstrated by Cecil Robinson in his book, *With the Ears of Strangers: The Mexican in American Literature*, and in the anthology of short stories collected by Edward Simmen in *The Chicano: From Caricature to Self-Portrait*.[8]

If Chicano literature has not entered the mainstream of American literature, neither has it become part of Mexican literature, in which it has its roots and from which it derives its inspiration. One must be aware that Chicanos have not always been accepted in Mexico, or even by Mexicans visiting the United States, and that they themselves have often rejected both groups. This was true especially during the 1940s when the Pachucos, young Mexican-Americans of southern Texas and California, tried to assert their identity through a distinctive manner of dress and speech and by developing a close group consciousness. Octavio Paz has observed about the Pachuco, "The *pachuco* does not want to become Mexican again; at the same time he does not want to blend into the life of North America."⁹ This desire to establish a separate identity has resulted in the creation of a literature that reflects a unique culture and possesses characteristics that differentiate it from other literatures. One problem for the critic of Chicano literature is to identify and define these distinctive characteristics.

III. Characteristics of Chicano Literature

Chicano literature is new only in the sense that in the last six years writers have made a concerted effort to portray Chicano reality authentically. Its newness also lies in the recently abundant production of outstanding works, proof of the Chicanos' awareness that literary expression fulfills a historical void. But this does not imply that no talented writers existed in earlier times. The Chicano literary tradition is extensive, but we must study earlier writers to determine the point at which they stopped portraying a reality and a set of circumstances different from the Mexican's.

If there have been many writers, why have they remained in obscurity? What has happened to their works and why have they not been studied? There are several reasons. One is that colonial literature of the Southwest has never been given serious thought: it has been bypassed. American literature supposedly began with the settlement of Jamestown. Consideration is seldom given to a corresponding literature of Spanish settlers in the Southwest. Therefore, what was written in Spanish much earlier is disregarded. For that matter, any literature written by Americans in languages other than English has been ignored. Another case in point is that critics seldom seriously consider oral literature, such as that which abounds in the rich traditions of Hispanic peoples. Still another reason is that only literary modes and forms created in Europe are consistently studied. But the saddest truth is that ethnic prejudice exists in the study of literature. Gerald Haslam, in *Forgotten Pages of American Literature*, says: "The cruel fact [is] that the same Americans who have been denied social, economic and educational equality have been consistently ignored by literary scholars."¹⁰ The result has been an apparent void in history, a people who seem to have existed without self-expression or self-image. And this void has been filled by damaging stereotypes and by the narrow, extremist works of southwestern Anglo writers. A few chapters from Cecil Robinson's *With the Ears of Strangers* present a view of what we are talking about. Portraits that appear in Edward Simmen's *The Chicano: From Caricature to Self-Portrait* also reinforce our point.

It is thus logical for Chicano literature to be of a revolutionary or social-protest nature. But many times this literature goes far beyond mere rhetoric, for its writers are trying to represent *la raza* (the Spanish-speaking community) and its complex nature as vividly as possible. For this reason one finds that this literature attempts to encompass a vast area. Thus one encounters a picture not only of the Chicanos' socioeconomic circumstances but of their past history as well. At the same time the writers seek their own identities through their work. As they carry out this search, and as their roots take a firmer hold, they realize that they can create self-definition and identity only through action.

Action is much more effective when backed by knowledge of one's roots, however. Among the strongest elements in Chicano literature are the proud references to an Indian heritage. Sometimes these references are simple allusions, while in other cases they take the form of strong symbols. A good example is Rodolfo "Corky" Gonzales' long narrative poem, *I Am Joaquín*. One can see in this poem a vast number of Aztec images as the poet tries to interpret the character and composition of the Chicano. Alurista also makes use of the Indian culture for the most essential aspect of his work, *Floricanto en Aztlán*. Genaro González, a short story writer, uses the sun as the symbol of power and energy that leads to action. "Un hijo del sol" is indeed the affirmation of the Indian heritage, but it is not just an expression of pride in past history. The sun also symbolizes the fire that feeds the present struggle. Philip D. Ortego in "The Coming of Zamora" describes his protagonist as entirely Indian, physically, and uses him to provide a historical background. Another example is "Tata Casehua" by Miguel Méndez, in which we find the best characterization done by a Chicano writer. Tata Casehua is a Yaqui Indian who resists death itself as well as the extermination of *la raza*.

The Chicanos' total awareness of their past, as well as their identity, leads some writers to develop a theme common among Latin American writers, that of self-definition. But this exploration into the composition of the Chicano cannot find the maturity of, for example, an Octavio Paz or a Carlos Fuentes. Nevertheless, the preoccupation is there and at times becomes an existential anguish, although most works contain a strong current of struggle and optimism. In González' "Un hijo del sol," the protagonist, Adán, decides to go to Mexico in search of his roots. Through surrealist images, González presents Adán's attempt to conceive the essential bond that unites him to his past, but Adán concludes that he is nothing. So the protagonist decides to return and forge his own essence through action.

The note of optimism that is present in González is not found in Nick C. Vaca's "The Week of the Life of Manuel Hernández." Here the author uses an "animal" inside the protagonist's body to imply existential anguish. This bothersome cancer leads him to suicide. Some of Luis Omar Salinas' poetry is also pessimistic. In *Crazy Gypsy* one witnesses a metaphysical loneliness, conveyed sometimes through surrealism, at other times through personal images. Salinas is that bicultural man who feels alien as an "Aztec angel, criminal of a scholarly society/ a forlorn passenger on a train." The sad social condition of the Chicano also makes him feel "the horrible pain that keeps me silent."[11]

Nevertheless, as stated before, this pessimistic attitude is not predominant. More noticeable is the optimistic attitude, an affirmation of the Chicano nature and the constant struggle for existence. The best bilingual poetry, that of Alurista, communicates this message clearly. Here we see a chaotic Anglo world, mechanized and materialistic, in contrast to the poverty of the Chicanos' surroundings. But the essence of this work lies in the realistic portrayal of Chicano community and the philosophy the writer conveys: "I do not ask for freedom / I am freedom," he says, speaking of the freedom to mold one's own future through action. Alurista tells us that "mañana is now" and that by acting we can attain social freedom, since "our wounds of inaction have been stitched."

We find this same struggle over action in Tomás Rivera's prize-winning work, ". . . *y no se lo tragó la tierra.*" The protagonist fears that the earth will swallow him if he curses God; yet his anguish over his brother's poor physical condition forces him to do so. Then, to his surprise, he finds that he feels firmer ground beneath him. After that, "he felt himself capable of doing and undoing whatever he chose. He looked toward the ground and he kicked it and said to it, 'Not yet, you can't eat me yet. Someday. But I won't know.' "[12]

Miguel Méndez also expresses optimism in his poetic prose. In "Taller de Imágenes" ("Workshop for Images") hope comes with the birth of a child:

> The virgins, bathed in moonlight, dressed in nuptial white on their night for cultivation. The peasants are happy, they are singing; symbols of lemon flowers intoxicate them with their promise. Spring is on their lips and in their hair. A living desire inflames the blood, and a fertile hope ennobles the heart. The moist earth opens before the efforts of the planter who deposits the seed, then smooths the wound with the loving caresses of his hands. The seed is covered. In the eyes of the peasants appears the flame of the illusion that unites its warmth with the blaze of the germinator of all living things. The earth swells, it parts, and its prodigious heart offers the bud. Agony is also the signal of dawn, the sound of doves'

wings, happiness in exchanged glances. A miracle! Just like a plant, a child is born. [13]

Thus one can conclude that Chicano literature is, in essence, decidedly optimistic, even when it is set in what appears to be a hostile environment. Similarly, the Chicano self-image now emerging is a positive one, the antithesis of caricatures born of Anglo writers. Chicano writers are trying to paint a truer and more representative picture of themselves and their circumstances, of their present and past, while at the same time they are calling for conflict, action. But most important, Chicano writers are recording their own history, a history that never before has been written.

The forms and language of recent Chicano literature are still in an experimental stage. Most of the works are written in English, but some are bilingual. Perhaps the best bilingual work is done by Alurista, while Genaro González appears to have more facility in putting the metaphorical possibilities of English to good use. Méndez is a master of the Spanish language, and his powerful metaphors are unique. Finally, Tomás Rivera excels at using the simple and natural expressions of Texan-Chicano speech. Through this language he is able to portray some of the more important aspects of the life and culture not only of Texas Chicanos but of Chicanos in general, for the differences in the language spoken by them anywhere are slight, slighter perhaps than those existing in the languages of various Latin American countries. The Spanish of the Chicanos, of course, resembles the Spanish spoken in Mexico more than that of any other Spanish-speaking region. The spoken forms of Chicano Spanish and Mexican Spanish differ mainly in vocabulary and intonation. In the novel *Pocho* by José Antonio Villarreal, a girl from Cholula, Mexico, is introduced to Richard: "He said he had never known anyone from that far south, and she said she was sixteen years old. Once, she giggled as he spoke . . . Spanish, which was a California-Mexican-American Castilian.

" 'I am a Pocho,' he said, 'and we speak like this because here in California we make Castilian words out of English words.' "[14]

No less important than the use of modified English words is the vocabulary that has survived from the Mexican Spanish spoken in the Southwest before 1848. Many of these words, especially those referring to food, are common also in the English of that region. Their use in literature gives a distinctive touch to the style of Chicano writers, especially those writing in English, since the words do not have to be translated. The narrator in the novel *Bless Me, Ultima* by Rudolfo A.

Anaya says, "I sat across the table from Deborah and Theresa and ate my atole and the hot tortilla with butter."[15] This use of Mexican Spanish words as well as words not used even in Mexico may limit readers' understanding of the work outside the Southwest. Authors who use such diction often translate the words in the text, as does Villarreal, or they may add a glossary, as in the anthology *We are Chicanos*. But it is precisely this interlacing of Chicano words with either English or Spanish that gives the literature part of its originality.

IV. The Roots of Chicano Literature

A. Pre-Chicano Literature (to 1848)

The first examples of Chicano literature are writings of a historical or semihistorical nature and descriptions of the regions visited by explorers of the Southwest, where most Chicanos now live. Among these works we find the *relaciones* of Álvar Núñez Cabeza de Vaca, Fr. Marcos de Niza (*Relación del descubrimiento de las Siete Ciudades*), and Fr. Francisco Palou; the *diarios* of Juan Bautista de Anza, Miguel Costansó, Fr. Juan Crespi, Fr. Tomás de la Peña, Gaspar de Portalá, and Fr. Junípero Serra as well as a number of *historias*, *memorias*, *recuerdos*, *anales*, and *apuntes*. More significant, perhaps, is the *Historia de la Nueva México*, a rhymed history of the conquest of New Mexico in thirty-four cantos, by Gaspar Pérez de Villagrá.

The point could be made that these works belong to the history of Spanish literature. But Philip D. Ortego has pointed out that "In the New World, Spanish literature underwent a unique metamorphosis, integrating alien elements which were to herald a distinct kind of New World literature." As an example he mentions Alonso de Ercilla's *La Araucana* and calls it "the first modern epic in the New World dealing with an American theme."[16] Pérez de Villagrá's poem, if less skillfully written than Ercilla's, also deals with a distinctly American theme. Since *La Araucana* belongs to Chilean literature, why cannot the *Historia de la Nueva México* be a part of the literature of Aztlán? As Ray Padilla has said, "all works prior to 1848 can be treated as pre-Chicano Aztlanense materials."[17]

Popular literature, which was brought to the Southwest by earlier settlers from Mexico, constitutes one of the elements of pre-Chicano literature. The many romances, *corridos* ("ballads"), folktales, and religious plays popular during the colonial period have not entirely disappeared.

In 1600, for example, Juan de la Peña wrote a religious play, *Las cuatro apariciones de la Virgen de Guadalupe*, which was very popular in New Mexico.[18] Plays about the Virgen de Guadalupe are still popular today among Chicanos. Since nothing is known about de la Peña, we cannot determine if his play belongs to Mexico or New Mexico. We do know, however, that it was very popular in New Mexico and that it is not mentioned by historians of the Mexican theater. With another play, a *pastorela*, we are more fortunate. We know that it was written in California in 1820 by Francisco Ibáñez of Soledad Mission.[19]

The *corrido*, the typical poetic form of the Mexican people, is common in the Southwest and wherever Chicanos live. This form, apparently derived from the Spanish *romance*,[20] is still popular among Mexicans and Chicanos. Tomás Rivera, in his article "Into the Labyrinth: The Chicano in Literature," asks this question: "What have been the vehicles through which Chicano literature has been expressing itself?" In his answer he gives great importance to the *corrido* and says, "As in all literatures of all times the genesis manifests itself orally. It begins in the *corridos*, the ballads. . . . Américo Paredes, University of Texas professor of Anthropology and English, in his work, '*With His Pistol in His Hand*,' published in 1957, gives us what can be recognized as one of the first major works of Chicano literature. . . . The hero is revealed to us totally from the Mexican-American perspective. And this is of great importance for the Chicano being, as it is the *corrido*, a popular form, a form of the people, which is the primary vehicle through which a more spiritual totality is explained for this being."[21]

No less important than the *corrido* is the folktale, in which we often find reflected the psychology not only of the Mexican Indian but also of the American Indian. The folktale, as is well known, is a popular form that can easily employ cultural motifs to express the desires and aspirations of the people.[22] What Arthur L. Campa has to say about the folktale in New Mexico can be applied to the folktales of other states:

"Contar cuentos" is an old custom that unfortunately has been abandoned in most cities, although in the country and in remote villages the practice is kept up. From father to son these tales have come down to the present time, and in this transmission they have been somewhat altered. The source of the New Mexican folktale is easily recognized because of its universality. The oriental tale that forms such a great part of the European tale has been prevalent in New Mexico as well, and it is interesting to see the different versions of what was originally one story. The animal stories have been changed somewhat by substituting such animals as are familiar in the New World. The treasure and witch story is entirely of the New World, and each locality has its own repertoire of "cuentos de entierros y de brujas."[23]

Daily happenings were often recorded in the *corridos* and the memoirs, which give us an interesting insight into the life of the times. After Mexico achieved its independence from Spain in 1821, the northern provinces—the land now called Aztlán by the Chicanos—became part of the Republic of Mexico. This period, although short and unstable (it ended in 1848 with the Treaty of Guadalupe Hidalgo), was important to the development of Chicano literature, since it was then that the Hispanic-Mexican inhabitants of the region had to decide if they were to remain loyal to Mexico or fight for their independence. This spiritual struggle gives uniqueness to the literature produced during these years. The clashes between the local population and the authorities, usually sent from Mexico to govern the region, began almost immediately. For example, on 16 September 1830, during a celebration of the independence in the house of the governor of California, a violent fight broke out between some young Californios and "los de la otra banda." In another incident, a certain José Castro was imprisoned for posting derogatory remarks about the Mexicans. According to the memoirs of Governor Alvarado, Castro later beat up the Mexican Rodrigo del Pliego because he had insulted Californios by calling them ill-bred. (Blanco, p. 148).

Typical of the poetry of the period are the verses of Joaquín Buelna, who, in California between 1836 and 1840, wrote compositions dedicated to the native rancheros. History, memoirs, and diaries are represented by José Arnaz, Juan Bandini, and Juan Bautista Alvarado. A new interest in the cultures of the native Indians appears during this period. Gerónimo Boscana (1776–1831) wrote a historical account of the origin, customs, and traditions of the Indians of the Mission of San Juan Capistrano entitled *Chinigchinich*.[24] Popular literature continued to offer the same genres. There are several religious plays, among them a *Pastorela en dos actos* dated 1828 and signed "M.A. de la C." In New Mexico this popular play was performed regularly. An *auto pastoral*, of Mexican origin, was performed in Taos as early as 1840.[25]

B. Literature of Transition (1848–1910)

The period that began in 1848 and ended in 1910, the year of the Mexican Revolution, was the time during which Chicano literature laid the basis on which it was later to develop, a period in which

Mexicans living on land taken over by the United States had to decide whether to return to Mexico or stay and assume American citizenship. Most of them decided to stay but at the same time to remain faithful to their Mexican traditions and language. They became trapped in the Anglo-American milieu, however, forming, politically, a part of a society that, socially, rejected them. Finding themselves caught between two cultures, the Chicanos developed an ambivalent attitude that was to influence their thinking for some time. The literature of the period reflects this ambivalence, which is often expressed by the use of both Spanish and English. But some Chicanos were able to break through the rigid social barriers and become part of Anglo-American society. Such was the case with Miguel A. Otero, who was appointed governor of the Territory of New Mexico in 1897. He wrote an interesting book about life in the Old West, *My Life on the Frontier*, as well as a book about Billy the Kid.[26] Otero wrote in English. How such transitions from Spanish to English in Chicano literature took place is an area yet to be investigated. Naturally, though, in this period those writers using Spanish still predominate. As an example we shall mention the works of Francisco Palou, the biographer of Junípero Serra.[27]

Popular literature was perhaps the least affected by the political change. The people continued to produce *corridos*, *romances*, *pastorelas*, and *cuentos*. Nevertheless, even here, subject matter was expanded to include events not related to Chicanos, as can be seen in the *corrido* "Muerte del afamado Bilito," in which the death of Billy the Kid is related:

> El Bilito mentado
> por penas bien merecidas
> fue en Santa Fe encarcelado
> deudor de veinte en la vida
> de Santa Fe a la Mesilla.
>
> Billy, that renowned Kid,
> for causes well deserved
> in Santa Fe he was detained
> as the debtor of twenty lives
> from Santa Fe to la Mesilla.
> (Lucero, p. 142, authors' trans.)

Another *corrido*, "La voz de mi conciencia," is significant because it introduces the theme of social protest. The *corridista* says:

> Treinti trés días de carcel
> injustamente he sufrido

por un falso testimonio
de un crimen no cometido.
. . . .

Cuando el juez nos sentenció
fue cosa de reír—
al culpable casi libre
y al inocente a sufrir.

Twenty-three days in jail
we have unjustly endured
the accusation of a crime
of a crime never committed.
. . . .

When the judge passed sentence
he made us laugh—
the guilty one he set free
and made the innocent ones suffer.
(Lucero, p. 137., authors' trans.)

C. The Emergence of a Group Consciousness (1910–1943)

Immigration from Mexico to the United States from 1848 to 1910 was negligible. After 1910, however, and especially during the critical years of the Mexican Revolution (1913–1915), which coincided with the outbreak of World War I and the consequent expansion of American industry and agriculture, large numbers of immigrants crossed the border. Not all of them were running from a revolution, as some have inferred; many came to work in the green fields of Texas, New Mexico, and California and in the factories of Illinois, Indiana, and Michigan, where they were much needed. Most of these immigrants never returned to their native land (except during the depression years of the thirties when they were no longer needed here), and their sons and daughters became American citizens by birth, although still attached to the traditional way of life of their parents. The new immigrants brought new blood into the Mexican-American community and reinforced its Mexican heritage. The same thing occurred in intellectual circles with the interchange of ideas among writers such as José Vasconcelos, Martín Luis Guzmán, Mariano Azuela, Ricardo Flores Magón, and others who lived in the United States.

This period in Chicano history, which comes to an end with World War II, was characterized by the appearance of a group consciousness that manifested itself in the formation of societies whose purpose was to provide mutual help and protection. Some of these associations, such as the League of United Latin American Citizens (LULAC), which was founded in 1929, and the G. I. Forum, established in 1948, became politically oriented and spearheaded the struggle for civil rights. Their periodicals and the many Spanish-language newspapers that became popular during the period included poetry, short stories, and scholarly articles.[28] The pages of *LULAC News*, *Alianza*, and others are good sources for the literary production of this period. Ortego, in his study of Chicano poetry, has brought to light the names of some poets who wrote for these periodicals. He also discusses the poetry of Vicente Bernal, author of an early book of poems, *Las primicias* (1916), and Angélico Chávez, a representative of the mystic tradition in three of his works: *New Mexico Triptych* (1940), *Eleven Lady-Lyrics and other Poems* (1945), and *The Single Rose* (1948).[29]

As a consequence of the revolution, Mariano Azuela published his famous novel, *Los de abajo*, in the newspaper *El Paso del Norte*, of El Paso, Texas, in November 1915. Later Teodoro Torres, who lived nine years in the United States and was editor of *La Prensa* of San Antonio, Texas, published the novel *La patria perdida* (1935), the first part of which takes place in the United States and deals with life among Mexican-Americans. Another Mexican, Alberto Rembao, who lived in New York and edited the review *La Nueva Democracia*, also published novels, although with Mexican themes and settings. In general, the novel and short story of this period still need to be studied. Research will no doubt uncover many novels written by Mexican-Americans both in English and in Spanish.

The *corrido* continued as a popular form of expression with social protest and politics entering more prominently into its content. In 1936 a *corrido* was written about some Gallup coal miners who had been subdued with gunfire by the sheriff and his men during a strike. Senator Bronson Cutting's defense of the lawmen elicited a protest poem that ended with the following lines:

> Ud. se come sus coles
> Con su pan y mantequilla
> Y yo me como mis frijoles
> Con un pedazo de tortilla.
>
> You eat your cabbage
> With bread and butter
> I eat my beans
> With a piece of tortilla.[30]

Also during this period, serious scholarship and literary criticism appear with the works of Carlos Castañeda (*History of Texas, 1673–1779,* 1935), Juan B. Rael (*A Study of Phonology and Morphology of New Mexican Spanish Based on a Collection of 410 Folktales,* 1937), George I. Sánchez ("Pachucos in the Making," 1943), Arthur L. Campa ("The New Mexican Spanish Folktheatre," 1941), and Aurelio M. Espinosa ("Spanish Folktales from California," 1940).

D. A Literature of Confrontation (1943–1981)

June 1943 marked the beginning of a new period in Chicano history. The so-called Zoot Suit Riots that took place in Los Angeles that month began an open confrontation that was to intensify as thousands of Chicano veterans returned from World War II. This was not, however, an all-inclusive movement. It was not until 1966—as a result of student protests, the black civil rights movement, and the efforts of labor and campesino leaders like César Chávez and Corky Gonzales—that "la causa" became a powerful national movement affecting all Chicanos in all regions of the country and not only those living in the Southwest.[31] As a result of this new social awareness a new type of literature emerged, animated by a rebellious spirit often inspired by revolutionary leaders of Mexico such as Villa and Zapata. Characteristic of this writing is the Chicanos' search for identity, probing for their roots in the Indian past of Mexico. This theme is found in the poetry of Luis Omar Salinas, Angela de Hoyos, Miguel Ponce, Alurista, Miguel Méndez, Aristeo Brito, Sergio Elizondo, and Corky Gonzales, who expresses this sentiment in his poem, *I Am Joaquín* (1967):

> I am Cuauhtémoc,
> Proud and noble leader of men
> . . . .
>
> I am the Maya Prince,
> I am Nezahualcóyotl,
> Great leader of the Chichimecas
> . . . .
>
> I am the Eagle and Serpent of
> the Aztec civilization.[32]

Other writers, such as Ricardo Sánchez, José Montoya, Abelardo Delgado, and Raúl Salinas, derive inspiration for their poetry and prose from their barrio experiences. Sometimes their language is that of the barrio; almost always they use Spanish and English in startling juxtaposition. Often this poetry makes use of popular forms, and among these the most common is the *corrido*, the most enduring of popular genres. The *corrido* is especially suited to protest, since it can be sung to the accompaniment of a guitar. The *huelguistas* have availed themselves of the interest of the campesinos in the *corridos* to acquaint them with the events affecting their social condition as well as to help them identify with their leaders. This is the primary function of "The *Corrido* of César Chávez," which in part says:

> The seventeenth of March,
> First Thursday morning of Lent,
> César walked from Delano,
> Taking with him his faith.
>
> When we arrive in Fresno,
> All the people shout:
> Long live César Chávez,
> And all who follow him.[33]

At the other extreme of the popular current are those who fall under the influence of American and Latin American writers. Their poetry, dealing with universal themes, is represented by Tino Villanueva (*Hay otra voz*, 1972), Bernice Zamora (*Restless Serpents*, 1976), Gary Soto (*The Elements of San Joaquín*, 1977), and Juan Bruce-Novoa (*Perverse Innocence*, 1977), among others.

The most effective form for the literature of social protest has been the novel. Although the Chicano novel has not attained the quality that the black novel has achieved in the fiction of Ralph Ellison and others, it must be kept in mind that the Chicano novel does not have a long tradition unless we consider it within the tradition of the Mexican novel. This could be done with novels written in Spanish such as Miguel Méndez' *Peregrinos de Aztlán* (1974)[34] and Aristeo Brito's *El diablo en Texas* (1976), works akin to such Mexican novels as Azuela's *Los de abajo*, Revueltas' *El luto humano*, and Rulfo's *Pedro Páramo*. Novels written in English, however, such as *Tattoo the Wicked Cross* (1967) by Floyd Salas, *City of Night* (1963) by John Rechy, and *Victuum* (1974) by Isabella Ríos, have more in common with the Anglo-American novel than with the Mexican novel, an observation already advanced by Gerald Haslam: "Floyd Salas' *Tattoo the Wicked Cross* (1967) is more clearly related to the so-called new novels, evidencing the powerful influence of Ernest Hemingway, James Joyce, William Faulkner, and Alain Robbe-Grillet, than to any specific Latin-American author" (*Forgotten Pages*, p. 176). This type of novel, however, does not predominate. It is more common to find, among the novels of social protest written in English, traditional structures similar to those of the social novels of Mexico. This trend begins in 1959 with José Antonio Villarreal's *Pocho* and continues in Raymond Barrio's *The Plum Plum Pickers* (1969) and Richard Vásquez' *Chicano* (1970).[35] Not all recent novels, however, fall within this pattern. Ernesto Galarza uses the autobiographical form to depict life in the city in *Barrio Bay* (1971), as does Oscar "Zeta" Acosta in *The Autobiography of a Brown Buffalo* (1972). Rudolfo A. Anaya in *Bless Me, Ultima* (1972), perhaps the most successful Chicano novel, re-creates life in the countryside of New Mexico, where the people have kept their traditional way of life. Like the poets, some novelists give preference to universal themes. Two such novelists are Ron Arias, whose *The Road to Tamazunchale* (1975) depicts an old man's preoccupation with death, and Alejandro Morales who, in his first novel *Caras viejas y vino nuevo* (1975), deals with the problems of the adolescent.

Short story writers have been successful in creating, both in English and in Spanish, artistic works that are at the same time excellent portrayals of Chicano life and customs. The most successful, in Spanish, have been Tomás Rivera with ". . . y no se lo tragó la tierra" (1971); Sabine R. Ulibarrí with *Tierra amarilla* (1971); and Rolando Hinojosa-S. with *Por esas cosas que pasan* (1972); and in English, Enrique "Hank" López with "Back to Bachimba" (1967); Philip D. Ortego with "The Coming of Zamora" (1968); and Nick C. Vaca with "The Week of the Life of Manuel Hernández" (1969).

Of the literary genres, drama has had the greatest immediate impact on the education of the Chicano. As a result of the traditional interest in the popular theater, it has not been difficult to attract audiences to plays dealing with social and educational issues. In 1965, as a direct result of the *Huelga* at Delano, California, Luis Valdez organized the now famous El Teatro Campesino,[36] which served to inspire other groups to stage Chicano plays dealing with daily situations and crises, such as strikes. The proliferation of popular theaters[37] led to the formation of TENAZ (Teatro Nacional de Aztlán), which had its first meeting in Fresno, California, in 1971.[38] The purpose of this organization is threefold: to establish communication between theatrical groups, to exchange materials, and to organize summer workshops related to theatrical problems. More than twenty-five groups attended the Annual Festival of Chicano Theatre in 1972. Most of the plays presented by these groups carry a political message. That is the style of most Chicano dramatists, among whom the most successful has been Luis Valdez, the author of plays designed to arouse the social consciousness of the audience. His dramas include *Los vendidos* (1967), *The Militants*

(1969), and *Soldado Raso* (1971), as well as symbolic plays tracing the roots of Chicano psyche, such as *Bernabé* and *The Dark Root of a Scream*.[39] In 1969 El Teatro Campesino filmed with great success Corky Gonzales' epic poem *I Am Joaquín*. The example of Valdez has inspired many other theater directors, such as Jorge A. Huerta, organizer of the successful Teatro de la Esperanza in Santa Barbara. Both dramatists use a traditional form, the *acto*, a short sketch dealing with an everyday situation. Valdez also uses the *mito*, an original form sharing elements of the ritual and dealing with the Indian heritage of the Chicano, as expressed in simple parables and from the perspective of the Indian. The technique used by these Chicano dramatists is derived from the popular manifestations of dramatic tradition, such as the commedia dell'arte, puppet shows, vaudeville comedy, carnival sideshows (known in Mexico as *carpas*), circus pantomimes, and religious *pastorelas*.

Representative of the *acto* is Luis Valdez' one-act play "No saco nada de la escuela" ("I don't learn anything at school"), in which he satirizes the educational system that rejects the Chicano, as we see in the following scene:

ABRAHAM: You Mexicans ought to be out in the fields.
ESPERANZA: (*To Abraham*) You tell him, sugar.
FRANCISCO: That's all you think I can do, huh? Well I'm gonna go to college on the E.O.P. program!
ESPERANZA: Look. I made it through college without any assistance. I don't see why you can't. .
FRANCISCO: (*Mimics her*) I made it through college . . .
(*Professor enters stage center, Monty and Florence enter stage right.*)
PROFESSOR: Ladies and gentlemen, can we prepare for our college seminar? (*spots Francisco*) Aren't you the custodian?
FRANCISCO: Yes, but, a . . . Monty wants to talk to you.
MONTY: Oh, sir, we thought we might be able to get him in under MOCO, you know, Mexican Opportunity Commission Organization?
PROFESSOR: Now look, Monty, we got you in here and unless you want to be out get back into your place. (*To Francisco*) No, I'm sorry, there's no room. No room! (*pushing him out*)
FRANCISCO: I want to go to college!
PROFESSOR: These students, they don't understand (*to audience*). They don't realize that there is no room in our college, no room at all. In this college there is not room for one more student—not one more *minority* student.[40]

The language of the Chicano theater, like that of other genres, is bilingual, a mixture of Spanish and English. Often the actors utilize signs with the name of the stock character they represent in order to make it easier for the audience to identify them. Frequently, writers use another literary form, the *corrido*, not only to communicate the message more easily but also to give unity to the thematic structure of the play. These *corridos*, familiar to the audience, are very effective. The innovative nature of Chicano theater was well expressed by Luis Valdez when he wrote, "Chicano theater must be revolutionary in technique as well as content. It must be popular, subject to no other critics except the pueblo itself, but it must also educate the pueblo towards an appreciation of social change, on and off the stage." (Valdez and Steiner, p. 356).

Another trend in the development of Chicano theater is that represented by the works of Estela Portillo, whose play *The Day of the Swallows*[41] is a tragedy after the manner of Lorca and Casona. The characters are Chicanos, but that is incidental to the universal nature of the subject matter, as well as to the fact that the conflict is not social but personal. Josefa, Alysea, Tomás, Eduardo, and Don Esquinas are Chicanos preoccupied not with their standing in the community in relation to the Anglo majority but with their own personal problems. The protagonist Josefa, a combination of Doña Perfecta and Doña Bárbara, is a universal character whose tragedy is the result of human foibles, although she happens to be immersed in the Chicano experience. This play opens new possibilities to the Chicano theater of the future, when drama doubtless will constitute an important aspect of Chicano literature.

V. A Different Approach to the Teaching of Chicano Literature

Literature (or distinct writing styles) is the aesthetically entertaining use of language. As such, it knows no cultural or ethnic boundaries. Seemingly, a culturally pluralistic society is best served by a culturally pluralistic approach to the selection of the literature we teach. Whether our critical approach to the teaching of literature is primarily a pragmatic one—concern for the social, human, moral, and personal development of the student—or basically an aesthetic one—a desire to stress the skills needed for understanding and appreciating the structure of literature—we can benefit from a study of Chicano literature. Teachers who wish to offer their students more than a token representation of ethnic literature have an adequate supply from which to choose.

The Culturally Democratic Learning Environments model is a new approach to education that takes as its starting point a newly emerging philosophy in education known as cultural democracy. The advocates of this new philosophy propose that it is the institutions, not the students, that must change. They want the institutions to take into account each student's cultural background, language, learning ability, and personality. In other words, the educational institution must be altered to provide a culturally democratic learning environment that is consonant with the past learning experiences of the students it serves. Therefore, the first priority involves innovation in the curriculum.

Such educators propose that curricula at all levels include the study of Chicano literature. Equally important is the modification of courses already established to include the contributions of Chicanos to the development of American culture. Teachers of American literature would do well to include some of the contributions of Spanish-speaking minorities. And indeed, historians are already beginning to revise the definition of American literature and to take into consideration the contributions of minorities, without which the field would be incomplete.

An acquaintance with Chicano literature presupposes a knowledge of Spanish, without which the works cannot be entirely understood, since many writers—including some of the most important—write entirely in Spanish. Often, especially in poetry, the work is written in a mixture of Spanish and English, the result of which is striking and demands a bilingual reader or at least one well acquainted with both languages. A good illustration of this is the poem "La jefita" ("My dear old mother") by José Montoya (*El Espejo*, p. 188), where the integration of the two languages is the main characteristic of the composition:

> When I remember the campos
>   Y las noches and the sounds
> Of those nights en carpas o
> Vagones I remember my jefita's
>   Palote
>   Clik-clok; clik-clak-clok
>   Y su tosecita
> (I swear, she never slept!) (*El Espejo*, p. 188)

Also important in understanding Chicano literature is an acquaintance with the culture of Mexico, its history, art, and folklore, especially the Indian contributions, for the imagery of many Chicano writers is derived from Mexico's past. Often, as we have seen with the work of Corky Gonzales, the poet identifies with the gods and heroes of Mexico's Indian past. The same identification is found in Aristeo Brito's poem "A Moctezuma":

> Porque yo ya no soy yo
> Soy el mismo Moctezuma, Huitzilopochtli, Quetzalcoatl.

In his poem "Insomnio," with its desert imagery, he invokes the Toltec
rain god Tláloc:

> ¡Tláloc!
> ¡Llueve por piedad!
> ¡Llueve![42]

The third area of knowledge necessary to understand Chicano literature
fully is the history of the Chicanos and their culture, especially their
struggle to obtain social justice and a better standard of living. The
literature of social protest is often considered a truly representative
Chicano art form, although Chicano literature, as we have seen, encompasses not only social but also personal literary expression. The
literature of social protest is identified with two groups, field workers
and barrio inhabitants. The first glorifies the struggle of the campesinos
in their fight for a better life, and the second reflects the abject conditions
of life in the barrio. Miguel Ponce, in his poem "Lament," derives his
imagery from city life in a state of decay:

> From the slag of the rotten city
> I pass into the throat of the objecting house.
> Into a stair's crevice, a mouse huddles in fear;
> A shape contorting in dread terror of the bulk.
> A child descending those stairs,
> Pierces the sphere of my sight.
> With rusty claws of tired regret,
> I lift the mouse writhing, by his tail.
> Take him out to the heap, and bust him
> Like a putrid plum.
> Below, the city reels,
> As claws of despair loosen and fall. (*El Espejo*, p. 168)

Alurista, perhaps the best known and most prolific Chicano poet, often
writes about the confrontation between the Chicano and the law in the
barrio. This is the theme of his poem "tarde sobria":

> mañana el jale
> pero "orita" el tiempo es mío
>   patrol car—he stop me
> no time to walk, too young
> the man
>   he doesn't know my raza is old
> on the streets he frisks me

on the job he kills al jefe
en la tienda no atiende a mi mamá
the man
    he says he wanna marry my carnala
hell no!
    ella es mujer, no juguete
the man
    he likes to play
he got a lot o' toys
and he don't know
    que las tardes que me alumbran
y las nubes que me visten
            pertenecen a mi raza
            a mi barrio (*El Espejo*, p. 173)

In looking back, then, we may say that Chicano literature cannot be regarded as just a by-product of the recent struggle for civil rights. By this we do not mean to belittle the efforts of the Chicano movement or to underestimate the new sense of direction that it has provided, for the very term "Chicano," whatever connotations it may eventually carry,[43] has surely spurred the production of literature. If we look at Chicano literature from a historical perspective, however, we may be better able to understand its nature. From Mexican literature it has derived its forms, both erudite and popular, as well as its spirit of rebellion. Although Chicano literature may emphasize social protest and the search for identity and although its content depends on the writers' experiences in the Chicano milieu, we have found that metaphorical prose and poetry, experimental forms and techniques, and regional and universal themes abound in this body of literature. And, just as the Chicano movement has ignited a burst of literary fervor, so this literature, in turn, has become a vital part of the movement. And no doubt, with further research, the voids in the history of the Chicano will disappear and what emerges will be a valid and exciting part of American history and literature.

Notes

[1] Alfonso Reyes, "Ultima Tule," in his *Obras completas*, XI (México: Fondo de Cultura Económica, 1960), 58, 60.

[2] George I. Sánchez, *Forgotten People, A Study of New Mexicans* (Albuquerque: Univ. of New Mexico Press, 1940).

[3] Philip D. Ortego, "Mexican Literature," *The Nation*, 15 Sept. 1969, p. 258.

⁴ *Persons of Spanish Origin in the United States: March 1972 and 1971.* Series P.-20, No. 250 (Washington, D.C.: Bureau of the Census, April, 1973).

⁵ Octavio Ignacio Romano-V., "The Anthropology and Sociology of the Mexican-American: The Distortion of Mexican-American History," *El Grito*, 2 (Fall 1968), 13–26.

⁶ Teresa McKenna, "Three Novels: An Analysis," *Aztlán*, 1 (Fall 1970). 47.

⁷ Carey McWilliams, *North from Mexico* (Philadelphia: Lippincott, 1949). For a recent study summarizing the problem see John Womack, Jr., "The Chicanos," *New York Review of Books*, 31 Aug. 1972.

⁸ Cecil Robinson, *With the Ears of Strangers: The Mexican in American Literature* (Tucson: Univ. of Arizona Press, 1963); Edward Simmen, ed., *The Chicano: From Caricature to Self-Portrait* (New York: Mentor, 1971).

⁹ Octavio Paz, *The Labyrinth of Solitude*, trans. Lysander Kemp (New York: Grove Press, 1961), p. 14.

¹⁰ Gerald Haslam, *Forgotten Pages of American Literature* (Boston: Houghton Mifflin, 1970), p. 9; hereafter cited in text.

¹¹ Luis Omar Salinas, *Crazy Gypsy* (Fresno, Calif.: Orígenes, 1970).

¹² Tomás Rivera, ". . . y no se lo tragó la tierra," trans. Herminio Ríos (Berkeley: Quinto Sol, 1971), p. 79.

¹³ Miguel Méndez M., "Workshop for Images," trans. Octavio I. Romano-V., *El Espejo— The Mirror*, ed. Octavio Romano and Herminio Ríos (Berkeley: Quinto Sol, 1969), p. 74.

¹⁴ José Antonio Villarreal, *Pocho* (Garden City, N.Y.: Doubleday, 1970), p. 165. "Pocho" was the name given in Mexico to Mexican-Americans before the name "Chicano" became popular.

¹⁵ Rudolfo A. Anaya, *Bless Me, Ultima* (Berkeley: Quinto Sol, 1972), p. 6.

¹⁶ Philip D. Ortego, "Chicano Poetry: Roots and Writers," *New Voices in Literature: The Mexican American.* Symposium, Pan American University, Edinburg, Tex., 7–8 Oct. 1971, p. 3.

¹⁷ Ray Padilla, "Apuntes para la documentación de la cultura chicana," *El Grito*, 5, No. 2 (1971–72), 19. Other *cronistas* are Pedro de Nágera Castañeda and Alonso de Benavides.

¹⁸ See Aurora Lucero-White Lea, *Literary Folklore of the Hispanic Southwest* (San Antonio: Naylor, 1953), pp. 16–21, 86–106. Further references to this work are cited in the text. Another popular play in New Mexico and Colorado was *Los Comanches*, which commemorated the defeat of the Indians by the Spanish in Colorado. The play was edited by Aurelio M. Espinosa in 1907. See also A. L. Campa, *"Los Comanches*, A New Mexico Folk Drama," *University of New Mexico Bulletin*, 7 (April 1942).

¹⁹ See Antonio Blanco S., *La lengua española en la historia de California* (Madrid: Ediciones Cultura Hispánica, 1971), pp. 653–729.

²⁰ See Vicente T. Mendoza, *El romance español y el corrido mexicano* (México: Universidad Nacional Audónoma, 1939). For a different view see Caledonio Serrano Martínez, *El corrido mexicano no deriva del romance español* (México: Centro Cultural Guerrerense, 1963).

²¹ Tomás Rivera, "Into the Labyrinth: The Chicano in Literature," *New Voices in Literature: The Mexican American*, p. 20. Américo Paredes, *"With His Pistol in His Hand," A Border Ballad and Its Hero* (1958; rpt. Austin: Univ. of Texas Press, 1971), deals with the life of a southern Texas folk hero, Gregorio Cortez.

²² See Lucero, Part III; José M. Espinosa, *Spanish Folk Tales from New Mexico* (New York: American Folklore Society, 1937); Juan B. Rael, *Cuentos españoles de Colorado y de Nuevo México*, 2 vols. (Stanford, Calif.: Stanford Univ. Press, 1957).

²³ Arthur L. Campa. *A Bibliography of Spanish Folk-Lore in New Mexico* (Albuquerque: Univ. of New Mexico Press, 1930), p. 27.

²⁴ Gerónimo Boscana, *Chinigchinich*, trans. Alfred Robinson, in his *Life in California* (1846: rpt. Oakland, Calif.: Biobooks, 1947), pp. 227–341.

²⁵ See Juan B. Rael, *The Source and Diffusion of the Mexican Shepherds' Plays* (Guadalajara, Mexico: Librería La Joyita, 1965); Arthur L. Campa, "Spanish Religious Folktheatre

in the Spanish Southwest," *University of New Mexico Bulletin*, Language Series, V, 1-2 (1934).

[26] Miguel Antonio Otero, *The Real Billy the Kid* (New York: Wilson, 1936). See also *My Nine Years as Governor of the Territory of New Mexico, 1897–1906* (Albuquerque: Univ. of New Mexico Press, 1940).

[27] Francisco Palou, *Noticias históricas de la Antigua y Nueva California* (1875), trans. by Bolton as *Historical Memoirs of New California* (Berkeley, 1926); *Relación histórica de la vida y apostólicas tareas del venerable padre Fray Junípero Serra* (Madrid: Aguilar, 1958).

[28] For a listing of these newspapers see Herminio Ríos and Guadalupe Castillo, "Toward a True Chicano Bibliography: Mexican-American Newspapers: 1848–1942," *El Grito*, 3, No. 4 (1970), 17–24, and 5, No. 4 (1972), 40–47. See also Guillermo Rojas, "Chicano/Raza Newspaper and Periodical Serials Listing," *Hispania*, 58 (1975), 851–63.

[29] Other works by Angélico Chávez are *Clothed with the Sun* (Santa Fe: Writers' Editions, 1939); *La Conquistadora. The Autobiography of an Ancient Statue* (Paterson, N.J.: St. Anthony Guild Press, 1954); *The Virgin and the Port Lligat* (Fresno, Calif.: Academy Literary Guild, 1956); *The Lady from Toledo* (Fresno, Calif.: Academy Literary Guild, 1960); *Selected Poems* (Sante Fe, N.M.: Press of the Territorian, 1970).

[30] See Mabel Major and T. M. Pearce, *Southwest Heritage, A Literary History with Bibliographies*, 3rd ed. (Albuquerque: Univ. of New Mexico Press, 1972), p. 38.

[31] For a more detailed account of the emergence of the Chicano movement see Alfredo Cuéllar, Introd., *From the Barrio, a Chicano Anthology* by Luis Omar Salinas and Lillian Faderman (San Francisco: Canfield, 1973).

[32] Rodolfo Gonzales, *I Am Joaquín/Yo soy Joaquín. An Epic Poem* (New York: Bantam, 1972), p. 16.

[33] Stan Steiner, *La Raza: The Mexican Americans* (New York: Harper, 1970), p. 315.

[34] See Juan Rodríguez' review of this novel in *Revista Chicano-Riqueña*, 2 (Verano 1974), 51–55.

[35] For an analysis of *Tattoo, Plum Plum*, and *Chicano* see McKenna, 47–56. See also Guillermo Rojas, "La prosa chicana: res epígonos de la novela mexicana de la Revolución," in *Cuadernos Americanos*, México (1975), pp. 198–209.

[36] For information on this theatrical group see Luis Valdez, "El Teatro Campesino, Its Beginnings," and James Santibáñez, "El Teatro Campesino Today and El Teatro Urbano," in *The Chicanos: Mexican American Voices* (New York: Penguin, 1971), pp. 115–19, 141–48.

[37] For a list of the most important theatrical groups see Francisco Jiménez, "Dramatic Principles of the Teatro Campesino," *Bilingual Review*, 2 1/2 (Jan.-Aug. 1975), 109–10.

[38] See Jorge A. Huerta, "Concerning Teatro Chicano," *Latin American Theatre Review*, 6 (Spring 1973), 13–20.

[39] For Scene iii of *Bernabé* with notes by the playwright see Luis Valdez and Stan Steiner, *Aztlán, An Anthology of Mexican American Literature* (New York: Knopf, 1972), pp. 361–76; for *The Dark Root of a Scream* see Luis Omar Salinas and Lillian Faderman, *From the Barrio, A Chicano Anthology* (New York; Canfield, 1973), pp. 79–98.

[40] Luis Valdez y El Teatro Campesino, *Actos* (San Juan Bautista, Calif.: Cucaracha, 1971), pp. 86–87.

[41] *The Day of the Swallows* appears in *El Espejo*, and in Philip D. Ortego, ed., *We Are Chicanos, An Anthology of Mexican-American Literature* (New York: Washington Square Press, 1973), pp. 224–71.

[42] Both poems appear in *Cuentos i poemas de Aristeo Brito* (Washington, D.C.: Congreso Nacional de Asuntos Colegiales, 1974), pp. 48, 52. (This publication constitutes Vol. 1, no. 4 of *Fomento Literario*). Our translations: "Because I am no longer I, I am Moctezuma, Huitzilopochtli, Quetzalcoatl himself," and "Tláloc, rain! Have pity, rain!"

[43] For discussions on the concept of the Chicano, see Jesús Chavarría, "A Précis and a

Tentative Bibliography of Chicano History," *Aztlán*, 1 (Spring 1970), 133–41, and Fernando Peñalosa, "Towards an Operational Definition of the Mexican American," *Aztlán*, 1 (Spring 1970), 1–12.

The Evolution of Chicano Literature[1]

Raymund A. Paredes

Adiós, Guanajuato hermoso,
mi Estado donde nací,
me voy para Estados Unidos
lejos, muy lejos de tí.
—Mexican *corrido*

I

The cultural forces that eventually gave rise to Chicano literature date from the late sixteenth century, when the Spanish conquistadores moved northward from the Mexican interior and began the colonization of what is now the southwestern United States. These forces were, at least in the early colonial period, predominantly Spanish. Although the native peoples had developed sophisticated cultures, including impressive traditions of folklore and literature,[2] the Spaniards quickly imposed their own institutions, particularly those of language and religion, throughout this vast territory. It should be pointed out that the conquest occurred during Spain's greatest literary age, the era of Cervantes, Lope de Vega, and Góngora. Spanish drama flourished especially during this period, stimulated by the custom of the *teatro de los corrales*, according to which theater groups would rope off available public space in towns and settlements, set up a small stage, and perform not only established dramas but ephemeral works created for special occasions. Another point that bears mention is that many Spanish officers were intelligent and cultured men eager to leave the imprint of their country's highest traditions in the New World. As for the foot soldiers and commoners, they too influenced the course of Spanish-American culture. Steeped in folklore, they deposited their legends, tales, and songs along the paths of conquest.[3]

It is thus not surprising that in 1598, Juan de Oñate and a contingent of over five hundred colonists entered New Mexico and promptly established a tradition of Spanish folk drama. In celebration of Oñate's feat, Captain Marcos Farfán composed a play that described the Spaniards' *entrada* into New Mexico and their reception by gracious Indians eager to hear the word of God.[4] Farfán's drama, now unfortunately lost, was doubtless crude, but its performance within a fortnight of Oñate's arrival on the Rio Grande suggests something of the vigor of literary activity among a people struggling to conquer a continent. We know that the colonists performed at least one other play in New Mexico during 1598: the traditional Spanish work, "The Moors and the Christians."[5]

Folk drama flourished in New Mexico, and to a lesser extent throughout the Spanish-speaking Southwest, until the late nineteenth century. Many of the earliest works were *autos* (religious pieces), often composed by priests and used by them for instructional purposes among the Indians. Spanish-American folk drama ranged from simple and unpolished pieces to sophisticated works such as the celebrated "Shepherds" play, which manifested the influence of Spain's greatest dramatists.[6] In addition to "The Moors and the Christians," other Spanish dramas became well known in the Southwest, but these frequently underwent changes to conform to an American environment. One early drama from New Mexico, for example, featured the abduction of the Christ Child by Comanches.[7] Other plays, like that by Farfán, were strictly southwestern creations. But the largest number of dramas presented in the Spanish Southwest originated in the Mexican heartland and diffused northward through oral tradition.[8]

Other types of literary folklore prospered in the region. Legends treating a variety of subjects such as witchcraft, miracles, and lost treasure are of special significance.[9] One of the oldest and most popular legends in the Spanish-speaking Southwest is the story of *la llorona* ("the weeping woman"), who was first noticed in Mexico City in 1550, dressed in a white shroudlike garment, wailing in the streets.[10] The source of her despair varies from one version of the legend to another. *La llorona* sometimes appears as a pathetic figure who, jilted by her lover, murders her bastard children and then, driven mad by the monstrousness of her action, runs wildly through the streets calling after her victims. In other accounts, she is a ghostly villain who, having been executed, returns to avenge herself on men and small children. A true synthesis of Spanish and Indian traditions,[11] *la llorona* has become an important cultural symbol and the prototype of numerous female figures in Mexican and Chicano fiction.[12]

The custom of folksong also contributed greatly to the establishment of a literary tradition among the Mexicans of the Southwest. Here again, the types of folksong that took root in the region—the *romance, copla,* and *décima,* for example—were Spanish forms modified by Indian and mestizo influences. The process of cultural blending took place with extraordinary speed: only thirty years after the conquest of 1521, Mexican Indians were composing *romance*-like ballads. [13]

The traditional forms of Spanish balladry flourished in Greater Mexico[14] until they were superseded in mid–nineteenth century by a Mexican type, the *corrido*. [15] The name derives from the verb *correr*—to run—and the *corrido* does just that; it is a fast-paced narrative ballad, usually with a theme of struggle, adventure, or catastrophe. It often appears in stanzas of four eight-syllable lines, but exceptions are common, for the story, not the form, is its key element (Hansen, p. 204). Nowhere did the *corrido* flourish more than in the lower borderlands of Texas. The animosity between Anglos and Mexicans, which coalesced in the Texas Revolution of 1836 and persisted well into the present century, created the perfect conditions for the emergence of a *corrido* tradition. [16] Most of these ballads were composed anonymously in rural areas and made their way to city printing shops on both sides of the border. A few apparently first appeared as broadsides and were then transformed through oral transmission (A. Paredes, "Mexican *Corrido*," p. 101). Frequently, only the lyrics of the *corridos* were printed or transmitted, in which case the ballads survived as a kind of folk poetry. [17]

The literary folklore of the Chicano, four hundred years in the making, is extensive and comprises not only drama, legends, and songs but also such elements as tales and proverbs. [18] This body of work, primarily in Spanish, serves as the repository of much Chicano history and culture. Folklore thus ties the Chicanos to their Mexican origins and serves as the core of their literary sensibility. As we shall see, a number of Chicano writers have employed folkloric materials as the building blocks of fiction, believing that the most distinctive and enduring cultural values are found not in genteel society but in the traditions of the common people. Legends and *corridos* have been especially fruitful sources of fictional themes. Legends are perhaps the most "literary" of folk narratives, since they are often infused with a sense of realism and evince such qualities as plot, characterization, dialogue, and figurative language. The *corrido* has these features and is, in a sense, a legend set to music. [19] The *corrido*'s great attraction to the fictionalist lies in the proven appeal of its stories; no other type of folklore treats more vividly events that have stirred the imagination of the Mexican people.

This is not to say that the early settlers of the Mexican Southwest did not create literature of the conventional variety. Travel narratives, such as those of Cabeza de Vaca and Castañeda, appeared in the early colonial period. In 1610 Gaspar Pérez de Villagrá, a classical scholar from Salamanca and a companion of Oñate, published his *Historia de la*

Nueva México in thirty-four Vergilian cantos. During the next century, Francisco Palou, a Franciscan priest, composed his four-volume *Noticias de la Nueva California*. Other residents of the Southwest wrote a good deal, not belles lettres generally, but diaries, descriptive narratives, and light verse.[20] Because of a long-standing negligence, our understanding of the literary culture of the Mexican Southwest is still fragmentary and awaits a thorough investigation of appropriate archives and the numerous Spanish-language newspapers and literary journals of the region. No doubt a large body of literature remains undiscovered.

II

The great divide in Chicano history is the year 1848 when the Treaty of Guadalupe Hidalgo ended twenty-one months of warfare between Mexico and the United States. According to the treaty, Mexico ceded half its national territory to the United States: the present states of California, Nevada, Arizona, Utah, New Mexico, and half of Colorado. The Mexican residents of these areas had the choice of migrating southward across the new boundary or accepting American citizenship. Only two thousand people left their homes, while some eighty thousand remained, thus becoming, in the most literal sense of the term, Mexican-Americans. Although a distinctive Mexican-American literary sensibility was not to emerge for several generations, the signing of the Treaty of Guadalupe Hidalgo, more than any other event, required southwestern Mexicans to reassess their relationships to the old country and to the United States.

Given Anglo- and Mexican-American history, no one could have expected affairs between the two peoples to be harmonious. The bitterness that persistently marred their relations had its origins in the English-Spanish hostilities of the sixteenth century. The Anglo-Americans believed that Mexicans were lazy, priest-ridden, treacherous, and cruel, while Mexicans regarded Anglos as arrogant, ruthless, and avaricious.[21] To arouse their suspicions further, southwestern Mexicans had watched the unfolding of an American scheme of penetration and appropriation in their territory since 1807, the year of the Zebulon Pike expedition. As the number of Americans in the region increased dramatically, particularly after the opening of the Texas settlements and the Santa Fe Trail in 1821, Mexican concern turned to alarm. The inevitable conflicts between the two groups soon became a major theme in the Mexican literature of the Southwest.

The southwestern Mexicans disliked Anglos in general, but they regarded Texans as the worst of the breed. After their successful revolution of 1836, Texans sought to extend their domination over other Mexican territories and subsequently launched the Santa Fe Expedition of 1841, an inept attempt by some three hundred volunteers to "liberate" New Mexico. The invaders set out from Austin and immediately fell into disarray, lost their bearings and supplies, and finally staggered into New Mexico, tired, hungry, and dispirited, with hardly a thought of conquest. The Mexican forces in the area, having got wind of the intrigue, quickly pounced on the Texans. The episode was the stuff of low comedy, a point not wasted on a nameless New Mexico playwright who within five years of the expedition composed the play "Los Tejanos." The surviving manuscript is incomplete but instructive nonetheless. [22]

The play opens in the Texans' camp with a General McLeod attempting to gather intelligence for an assault on Santa Fe. An Indian prisoner leads the Texans to the hideout of Jorge Ramírez, a well-connected New Mexican who pretends to be a traitor. Ramírez offers to direct McLeod to Santa Fe, and the Texan accepts eagerly, never noticing the Mexican's obvious duplicity. Later, as the astonished McLeod is led away by his Mexican captors, Ramírez snarls at him: "Die, you dog! Now you are going to pay for all the evil you had planned. . . . This will teach you not to trust the New Mexicans. Whenever you hear them bark at foreigners they always bite them. There is no doubt about it" (Espinosa and Espinosa, p. 308).

We have in this play the outlines of a pattern that would appear in several variations in later Chicano works. Anglos and Mexicans (or Chicanos) are locked in conflict. The Anglos, usually bullies like McLeod, disdain their opponents and so take the contests lightly. The Mexicans, however, plan carefully, play on their foes' prejudices and beat their foes, often through trickery. Such a sequence of events, of course, is not restricted to Chicano literature but occurs in virtually all minority writing. The members of an ethnic or racial minority, deprived of material goods and sophisticated technology, rely on their wits to survive in an oppressive society. Their key advantage over their adversaries is greater understanding. The tricksters know their enemy intimately, while the oppressors, thinking in stereotypes, know little of theirs. [23] A figure like Jorge Ramírez, created just as the Anglo-Americans were commencing their appropriation of the Southwest, was intended to assure Mexicans of their ability to survive the changing order.

Nowhere was the enmity between Mexicans and Anglo-Americans more intense than in the border regions of southern Texas. Guadalupe Hidalgo had guaranteed Mexican-Americans full rights as citizens, but, in fact, they were frequently stripped of their property and subjected to severe discrimination. The Mexican-Americans expressed their resentment of this treatment in the large number of *corridos* that sprang from the region. The ballad makers found one of their earliest heroes in Juan Nepomuceno Cortina, a member of an old Rio Grande family who endeared himself to the border Mexicans in 1859 when he shot the Anglo marshal of Brownsville for pistol-whipping a vaquero. This incident stirred in Cortina memories of other Anglo outrages, and he consequently launched a campaign of reprisal.

All this was fine with the border Mexicans, who admired any man who fought for his rights. Thus *corridos* about Cortina were apparently composed promptly after his Brownsville skirmish, and others appeared as he continued his war against the gringos. Here are verses from two separate ballads:

> Ese general Cortinas
> es libre y muy soberano,
> han subido sus honores
> porque salvó a un mexicano.

> Los americanos hacían huelga,
> borracheras en las cantinas,
> de gusto que había muerto
> ese general Cortinas.

> The famed General Cortina
> is quite sovereign and free,
> the honor due him is greater,
> for he saved a Mexican life.

> The Americans made merry,
> they got drunk in the saloons,
> out of joy over the death
> of the famed General Cortina.[24]

The folklore provides ample evidence that the newly created Mexican-Americans believed they would survive the Anglo challenge, whether by guile as with Jorge Ramírez or through greater courage and physical superiority as with Cortina. But the unanswered question was: at what cost, measured not only in human life but in cultural terms? A *décima* from New Mexico, composed in the face of growing encroachment by Anglo-Americans, contains this lament:

> Nuevo México infeliz
> ¿Qué es lo que nos ha pasado?

Unhappy New Mexico
What is it that has happened to us?
(Campa, p. 163)

Here, then, are the components of a nascent Chicano sensibility: ethnic pride and a strong belief in the group's durability coupled with a vague but fearful realization that survival requires cultural compromise, some as yet indeterminate loss of Mexican-ness.

Just as the seventeenth-century narratives of Indian captivity may be said to constitute the earliest examples of Anglo-American writing, so the *corridos* of border conflict and other types of folk song may be regarded as an incipient form of Chicano literature. The forms and the language of these songs are conventionally Mexican, but the themes, the intensity of sentiment, and the level of cultural awareness associated with these themes represent a departure from Mexican models. A striking feature of the folklore from central Mexico in the generation after Guadalupe Hidalgo is the relatively little attention given to Anglo-Americans, the Mexicans presumably being preoccupied with such matters as the rebuilding of a defeated nation, the social upheavals associated with the *Reforma*, and the French occupation.[25] These issues were familiar to the Mexican-Americans of "Mexico de Afuera" (Mexico Outside), but their primary concerns lay elsewhere.

The oldest *corrido* from southern Texas to survive in complete form expresses some of these concerns. Texas, like other confederate states, suffered an economic depression after the Civil War, and Mexican Americans, like their Anglo compatriots, had to scramble for work. One source of income was the cattle drive. The *Corrido de Kiansis* treats this experience in bittersweet fashion, articulating first the sadness and fear the vaqueros felt about traveling far from home to face unknown dangers: "Ah, what a long trail it was! / I was not sure I would survive." Next, the ballad expresses exasperation with the arrogant Anglos who had forgotten that working cattle was a trade at which they were neophytes and the Mexicans veterans. Finally comes the conflict, which in this *corrido* takes shape as a competition between the Mexican-American and Anglo cowboys:

Quinientos novillos eran,
todos grandes y livianos,
y entre treinta americanos
no los podían embalar.

Llegan cinco mexicanos,
todos bien enchivarrados,

y en menos de un cuarto de hora
los tenían encerrados.

Esos cinco mexicanos
al momento los echaron,
y los treinta americanos
se quedaron azorados.

Five hundred steers there were,
all big and quick;
thirty American cowboys
could not keep them bunched together.

Then five Mexicans arrive,
all of them wearing good chaps;
and in less than a quarter-hour,
they had the steers penned up.

Those five Mexicans
penned up the steers in a moment,
and the thirty Americans
were left staring in amazement.

                    (A. Paredes, *Cancionero*, p.55)

Bad feelings in the southern Texas borderlands reached their peak after the turn of the century, and the *corridos* document these animosities fully. The best-known ballad of the period is "Gregorio Cortez," which is still heard in Chicano communities throughout the United States. Cortez was a Mexican-born vaquero who in 1901 killed Sheriff Brack Morris of Karnes County. Morris had tried to arrest Cortez and his brother Romaldo for horse stealing, a crime of which both men were innocent. Gregorio protested the arrest and Morris fired, wounding Romaldo in the mouth. Gregorio then shot the Anglo gunman dead. Realizing that his chances for a fair trial were slight, Cortez fled, walking and riding more than five hundred miles with hundreds of sheriffs, Texas Rangers, and Mexican-hating civilians in pursuit. Cortez made it to the border city of Laredo before he was captured.

Corridos are frequently reliable sources of history, but the Cortez ballads are more valuable for what they tell us about the psychology of border Mexicans. They not only express an intense resentment of Anglos but also denounce Anglo views of Mexican character. In Anglo-Texas mythology, the Mexican is a poor marksman (a knife, preferably thrust into an enemy's back, being the weapon of preference) and is stupid and cowardly: in sum, hardly a match for an Anglo-Saxon.[26] The Texas Mexicans knew these attitudes well and were deeply hurt by them. In the *corridos*, it is Cortez who is the crack shot and so expert a horseman that trying to overtake him is "like following a star." At one point in his flight, Cortez is surrounded by over three hundred rangers, whose faces are "whiter than poppies":

> Cuando les brincó el corral,
> según lo que aquí se dice,
> se agarraron a balazos
> y les mató otro cherife.

> Decía Gregorio Cortez
> con su pistola en la mano
> —No corran, rinches cobardes,
> con un solo mexicano.

> When he jumped out of their corral,
> according to what is said here,
> They got into a gunfight,
> and he killed them another sheriff.

> Then said Gregorio Cortez,
> with his pistol in his hand,
> "Don't run, you cowardly *rinches* [Rangers],
> from a single Mexican.[27]

The Gregorio Cortez of the ballads—certainly a more interesting character than the historical figure—represents an attempt by Mexican-Americans to reclaim the most admired qualities of vaquero culture—horsemanship, marksmanship, courage, and endurance—which Anglo-Americans had appropriated. The *corrido* Cortez is, quite simply, a John Wayne in brownface.

Despite the cultural drift that Mexican-Americans in Texas were experiencing around the turn of the century, they still considered themselves Mexicans and were so designated by Anglos. They regarded the Rio Grande less as a political boundary separating two countries than as a water-giving artery in an arid land, a river that drew Mexicans on either side to its banks and held them in a common culture. In the days before the United States Border Patrol, travel across the river was an easy matter; Mexicans born on the southern bank could move to the other side and experience little change. But all the while, as we can see in the *corridos* after 1900, the pressures of Anglo-American culture were intensifying, and the cries of Mexican allegiance occasionally turned shrill, with a ballad maker here and there trying too hard to make a point:

Nací en la frontera
de acá de este lado,
de acá de este lado
puro mexicano,
por más que la gente
me juzque texano
yo les aseguro
que soy mexicano
de acá de este lado.

I was born on the border
though here on this side,
though here on this side
I'm a pure Mexican,
even though people
may think I'm Texan
I now assure you
that I'm all Mexican
from here on this side.[28]

The *corrido* ends, significantly, with a repetition of the same stanza. Throughout this period, Mexican-Americans were changing more than they knew or, rather, than they admitted; they clung to their culture in the face of forces that were inevitably altering it.

Many of these alterations were perceptible by the 1920s. Certainly the Spanish of the Mexican-Americans had been modified by—some said infested with—*pochismos* ("Americanisms"). Even worse, some Mexican-Americans preferred English altogether. This did not sit well with the tunesmith who composed "Los mexicanos que hablan inglés" ("The Mexicans Who Speak English") with something less than sympathetic humor (A. Paredes, *Cancionero*, pp. 163–64). As many Mexicans saw it, abandoning Spanish was akin to pulling one's finger out of the dike: the whole culture was bound to crumble eventually. One frequent complaint among Mexican males in the United States concerned the domineering character of American women. This *canción* from New Mexico obliquely suggests that *pochis* (the term refers to Americanized Mexicans but usually appears as *pochos*) are likely to have absorbed more of American culture than merely the language:

Me casé con una pochi
Para aprender inglés
y a los tres días de casado
Yo ya le decía *yes*.

I married a *pochi*
so that I could learn English
And after three days of marriage,
I was already telling her "yes." (Campa, p. 214)

Some degree of acculturation was accepted as inevitable by most Mexican-Americans, but the ballads describe a character universally held in contempt: the Mexican who completely rejected his or her heritage. Here is a ballad from Los Angeles in the 1920s entitled "El renegado" ("The Renegade"):

Andas por hay luciendo
gran automóvil
me llamas desgraciado,
y muerto de hambre
y es que ya no te acuerdas
cuando en mi rancho
andabas casi en cueros
y sin huaraches.
Así pasa a muchos
que aquí conozco
cuando aprenden un poco
de americano
y se visten catrines
y van al baile.
Y el que niega su raza
ni madre tiene,
pues no hay nada en el mundo
tan asqueroso
como la ruin figura del renegado.
Y aunque lejos de ti,
Patria querida,
me han echado
continuas revoluciones,
no reniega jamás
un buen mexicano
de la Patria querida
de sus amores.

You go along showing off
In a big automobile.
You call me a pauper
And dead with hunger,
And what you don't remember is
That on my farm

You went around almost naked
And without sandals.
This happens to many
That I know here
When they learn a little
American
And dress up like dudes,
And go to the dance.
But he who denies his race
Is the most miserable creature.
There is nothing in the world
So vile as he,
The mean figure of the renegade.
And although far from you,
Dear Fatherland,
Continual revolutions
Have cast me out—
A good Mexican
Never disowns
The dear fatherland
Of his affections. [29]

This ballad serves as an interesting complement to the "corrido del norte." While the *tejano* ardently proclaims allegiance to Mexico despite his American origins, the Mexican-born composer of "El renegado" recognizes the easy temptations of American life, particularly its materialism and status consciousness. The bitter denunciations of the "renegade" also help to explain the adamant patriotism of the "corrido del norte."

But "El renegado" is also interesting in its own right, expressing the pain of dislocation felt by many Mexicans forced to leave their homeland during the revolutionary period. Thousands of campesinos came north because the fighting had all but destroyed the country's agriculture. Other immigrants were political refugees. Many Mexicans, from every social class, left Mexico because they found the prevailing atmosphere of random violence intolerable. But in no sense did the immigration movement represent a widespread rejection of Mexican culture. These people saw themselves as exiles, and many dreamed of returning home. In the meantime, they held as best they could to their traditions and deplored those who did not.

The *corrido* tradition has declined somewhat in Greater Mexico since 1930, the victim of commercialism, overexposure, and cultural changes (A. Paredes, "Mexican *Corrido*," p. 102). While *corridos* and other types of ballads are composed and played today, they often lack the epic appeal of earlier versions.[30] Still, *corridos*, even more than other genres of folklore, played a critical role in the establishment of a Chicano literary tradition when conventional literary works were relatively scarce. The *corridos* have provided the Chicano writer not only with themes and stories but also with a narrative and cultural stance, a way of transcending the prevailing gloom of American minority experience. Better than any other art form, *corridos* celebrate and vindicate the Greater Mexico experience. The most effective depiction of the *corrido* as a force in Chicano literary culture appears in a recent play by Luís Valdez entitled, appropriately enough, "El corrido." The work deals with the experiences of a Mexican campesino who comes to the United States as a migrant worker. He leads a hardscrabble existence, encountering prejudice, the frustration of failed expectations, and the alienation of his Americanized children. The dialogue is beautifully supplemented not by a narrator but by a singer of *corridos*, which are referred to as "canciones de los pobres" ("songs of the poor"). One of the fine moments in the play takes place in the back of a truck as it carries migrant workers out to the fields early one cold morning. A young man is casually strumming a guitar when an older fellow slides next to him and asks for a *corrido*. The youngster, somewhat embarrassed, explains that he is not sure he knows any. Retorts the *viejo*: "You're a Chicano, aren't you?" The boy plays.

III

For several generations after Guadalupe Hidalgo, the literary record of Mexican-Americans—what we have of it—shows a considerably slower movement toward a distinctly Chicano perspective than does the folklore. The *corridos*, for example, as early as the 1860s focused on cultural conflict with the Anglos as the fundamental fact of the Mexican-American experience; much of the conventional literature, however, is nostalgic and oddly detached from contemporary issues, as if the present reality were too painful to confront. Moreover, when writers did choose to treat current issues, their tone was not proud and defiant but usually tentative and subdued, even submissive.

Although the southwestern territories were never as culturally isolated—either before or after the coming of the Anglo—as scholars have generally claimed, opportunities for formal education were scarce until well into the twentieth century. Before 1848, schooling, except in its most rudimentary form, was limited primarily to the privileged classes.

After the region was absorbed by the United States, education for Mexican-Americans did not greatly improve, because of discrimination and differences over curricula and control of schools. But for those Mexican-Americans who had the tool of literacy, writing was a highly popular activity. Mexican-Americans kept diaries, journals,[31] and "books of personal verses" to which several members of a family might contribute.[32] For those writers interested in a larger audience, there were Spanish-language newspapers throughout the Southwest that published creative works; in New Mexico alone, the period from 1880 to 1900 saw the establishment of sixty-one such newspapers.[33]

Of the published material, verse was by far the most popular form of literary expression. Mexican-American poets, clearly under the influence of prevailing Mexican literary conventions, demonstrated a taste for lyrical verse, especially in the generation after 1848 when romanticism was a powerful cultural movement in Mexico. A young editor named Francisco Ramírez published love poetry in *El Clamor Público*, a Los Angeles newspaper from the period 1855–59. A few of his verses have been reprinted, but these are of little interest, burdened as they are by evocations of "angels of love" and "enchanting nymphs." Another poet from *El Clamor Público*, José Elías González, wrote these lines:

> Tu cabellera es de oro;
> Tu talle esbelto, ligero;
> Eres mi bien, mi tesoro,
> El ídolo que venero.

> Your long hair is golden,
> your figure well-shaped, lithe;
> You are my love, my treasure,
> the idol I venerate.[34]

The work of other Mexican-American poets of the period also suffers from sentimentalism and from an unwillingness to restrain romantic impulses. Undoubtedly, such verse was popular in its day, but now seems precious and effete.

In New Mexico, where the literary record is less fragmentary than in other regions, several factors combined to create a distinctive Mexican-American perspective. Of all the southwestern states, New Mexico was the first colonized by the Spaniards, and its citizens took pride in the richness of their Spanish traditions. Of the three major centers of Mexican culture in the Southwest, New Mexico was the last to be affected dramatically by Anglo penetration. Texas began receiving large numbers of Anglos in 1822 and California in the 1840s, but New Mexico—with the exception of Santa Fe, which prospered as a trading center—was relatively undisturbed by Anglo influences until the arrival of the railroad in 1880. Consequently, the literature of New Mexico bears few signs of cultural conflict until the late nineteenth century. Even then, the prevailing tone was more accommodating than combative. Significantly, the *corrido* tradition, which flourished in the culturally tense borderlands of southern Texas, is undistinguished in New Mexico, dealing not with the exploits of vaqueros who defy Anglo oppression but with more prosaic topics such as romance and family tragedy.[35]

The custom of anonymous versifying, dating back to the earliest days of the Spanish colonization, remained vigorous in New Mexico long after the advent of the Anglo. Spanish-language newspapers were apparently inundated with this kind of poetry to the point where, in 1884, the exasperated editor of *La Aurora* in Santa Fe published an item entitled "Remedios para la Versomania" ("Remedies for Verse Mania") (Meyer, "Anonymous Poetry," p. 267). This poetry, in many cases virtually indistinguishable from folk verse, generally followed traditional Spanish forms such as the *canción* and the *décima*. Not surprisingly, much of this verse was of low literary quality, flawed by excessive romanticism and a lack of originality. One poem, obviously derivative of the Spaniard Bécquer, is a religious piece entitled "A la Virgen." It rhapsodizes about the poet's deliverance of his "affection, heart, and faith" to the Virgin "with all the trust of an innocent child."[36] Not all the anonymous verse was trivial, however. In New Mexico, as in Texas and California, Mexican Americans lamented the erosion of their heritage and the intrusion of Anglo technology. One talented poet, who signed his work "X.X.X.," dealt with such issues as the quality of the territorial educational system and the impact of the Spanish-American War on New Mexicans (Meyer, "Anonymous Poetry," pp. 270–74). The device of anonymity worked effectively for the New Mexican poets. It offered some protection from reprisal when they treated controversial subjects and, more important, gave their work a universal quality, as if each poem were a nameless cry from the collective consciousness.

Nothing exercised the poets and virtually all New Mexican writers like the subject of Anglo prejudice. Writers particularly resented prevailing Anglo views that Mexican-Americans were backward and alien, believing that these attitudes had postponed the admission of New Mexico to the Union for half a century.[37] The poet X.X.X. complained that the United States had treated New Mexico like a "ragged beggar," yet still hoped that statehood would come. When the Spanish-American War began

in 1898, the New Mexican writers quickly proclaimed their allegiance
to the United States and their willingness to take up arms against the
"mother country." One New Mexican essayist expressed the view that,
cultural differences notwithstanding, all "citizens and those who reside
in this country, whatever their nationality, race or blood ties may be,
must remember that they are living under this government and enjoying
its beneficent protection."[38] Certainly there was plenty of room for
debate about the quality and sincerity of the United States' "beneficent
protection" of New Mexico, but still the writers rallied their people
around the American flag.[39]

As a group, the Mexican-American writers of New Mexico sought
some sort of cultural compromise for their people. They encouraged the
retention of Hispanic traditions and the Spanish language, but they also
supported statehood, New Mexican participation in American wars, and
the acquisition of English for practical purposes.[40] In effect, these writers
advocated the creation of a culture that was neither Hispanic-Mexican
nor Anglo-American but a synthesis of the two. Later Chicano writers
would also advocate movement toward this goal.

Such a cultural synthesis was not easily attainable, however, as
Mariano Vallejo, a California writer, made clear. A member of one of
the most prominent families in the region, Vallejo had early supported
statehood for California, maintaining that Mexico had neglected its
northernmost territory and that the United States was the "happiest
and most free nation in the world."[41] His feelings began to change,
however, after he was swindled by *yanquis* in various business deals.
When H. H. Bancroft encouraged him to write a history of California,
Vallejo plunged into the project, eager to tell the Mexican side. He
submitted his manuscript in five volumes to Bancroft in 1875.

"What a difference," wrote Vallejo in 1877, "between the present
time and those that preceded the usurpation by the Americans. If the
Californians could all gather together to breathe a lament, it would
reach Heaven as a moving sigh which would cause fear and consternation
to the Universe. What misery!" (Emparan, pp. 139–40). And so went
the theme of Vallejo's massive history. The Anglos, propelled by greed,
swarmed into California, trampling everything in their paths. Vallejo
wrote of Anglo "malefactors" to whom human life had no value. Ultimately, he regarded the Americanization of California as the despoilment
of the "true Eden":

> When gold was discovered, the flag of stars already waved over Alta
> California. No longer were we ruled by the Mexican laws, under whose
> shadow some had advanced while others fell back, but under which no

one had perished of hunger, and only two individuals had been by law deprived of their lives, a very common event during the early years of the North American domination in California.

The language now spoken in our country, the laws which govern us, the faces which we encounter daily, are those of the masters of the land, and, of course, antagonistic to our interests and rights, but what does that matter to the conqueror? He wishes his own well-being and not ours!—a thing that I consider only natural in individuals, but which I condemn in a government which has promised to respect and make respected our rights, and to treat us as its own sons. But what does it avail us to complain? The thing has happened and there is no remedy.

. . . I ask, what has the state government done for the Californians since the victory over Mexico? Have they kept the promises with which they deluded us? I do not ask for miracles; I am not and never have been exacting; I do not demand gold, a pleasing gift only to abject peoples. But I ask and I have a right to ask for an answer.[42]

Vallejo's history was an intensely personal work, written to show that the Californians "were not indigents or a band of beasts," as they were so frequently depicted by Anglo-Americans. But he held little hope that the Mexican culture of California could withstand the collision with that of the United States. Instead, he foresaw a day when his people might "disappear, ignored of the whole world."[43]

Vallejo was not writing for the whole world, but he did want to bring the "true history" of California to Anglo readers.[44] In this endeavor he was exceptional, for in the nineteenth century, Mexican-American authors generally wrote for their own people. It was only after the first decade of the twentieth century that a few Mexican-Americans began to publish stories and poetry in large-circulation American magazines. This difference in audience dramatically affected the character of the literature itself.

María Cristina Mena published a series of Mexican stories and sketches in *The Century* and *American* magazines during the early 1900s. Mena was a talented storyteller whose sensibility unfortunately tended toward sentimentalism and preciousness. She aimed to portray Mexican culture in a positive light but with great decorum; as a consequence, her stories seem trivial and condescending. Mena took pride in the aboriginal past of Mexico, and she had real sympathy for the downtrodden Indians, but she could not, for the life of her, resist describing how they "washed their little brown faces . . . and assumed expressions of astonishing intelligence and zeal."[45] Occasionally, she struck a blow at the pretensions of Mexico's ruling class, but to little effect; Mena's genteelness simply was incapable of warming the reader's blood.

Her story-telling gifts are best displayed in "The Vine-Leaf."[46] The main character is Dr. Malsufrido ("impatient of suffering"), a Mexico City physician more interested in the sins of his wealthy patients than their ailments. He recalls his first patient, a veiled woman who had come to have a birthmark—in the shape of a vine leaf—removed from her lower back. The surgery went perfectly, but throughout the operation, the patient remained veiled. Malsufrido immediately fell in love with this mystery woman but never probed her identity. Five years later, he discovers by accident that the woman is a murderer, but when he encounters her again, this time face to face, he cannot think of bringing her to justice. The woman, now a *marquesa*, is as beautiful as the doctor had imagined, and so, loving her still after all this time, he accedes to her secrecy. And there Mena's story ends, a charming and well-told piece, but nothing more.

In trying to depict and explicate Mexican culture to an American audience, Mena was undone by a strategy that would enervate the work of other Mexican-American writers. She tried to depict her characters within the boundaries of conventional American attitudes toward Mexico. She knew what Americans like to read about Mexico, so she gave it to them: quaint and humble *inditos*, passionate senoritas with eyes that "were wonderful, even in a land of wonderful eyes," dashing caballeros "with music in their fingers"—all these characters in a country Mena described as "the land of resignation." Mena's portrayals are ultimately obsequious, and if one can appreciate the weight of popular attitudes on Mena's consciousness, one can also say that a braver, more perceptive writer would have confronted the life of her culture more forcefully.

Burton?   Virtually all Mexican-American authors before 1900 wrote only in Spanish, thus severely restricting their potential readership. Mena, of course, published in English, although she tried, as later writers would, to capture in English the sound and feeling of Spanish.[47] Her work signaled the possibility that a new generation of Mexican-American writers would reach a larger audience. In the mid-1930s, for example, Robert Torres published stories about the Mexican Revolution in *Esquire*.[48] A powerful writer in the Hemingway style, he focused on the pointless brutality of war. Roberto Félix Salazar also published in *Esquire*, but his stories are less interesting and less skillfully rendered than those of Torres; significantly, they have no ethnic content whatsoever.[49] Salazar was certainly concerned with ethnic affairs, but his most effective statement on the Mexican-American condition appeared not in a general-interest magazine but in the *LULAC News*, published by the League of United Latin American Citizens. The piece is entitled "The Other Pioneers"; this is the first stanza:

Now I must write
Of those of mine who rode these plains
Long years before the Saxon and the Irish came.
Of those who plowed the land and built the towns
And gave the towns soft-woven Spanish names.
Of those who moved across the Río Grande
Toward the hiss of Texas snake and Indian yell.
Of men who from the earth made thick-walled homes
And from the earth raised churches to their god.
And of the wives who bore them sons
And smiled with knowing joy.[50]

Now this is a mild expression of cultural affirmation and is characteristic of early Mexican-American work published in English. In learning the English language, Mexican-American writers invariably relinquished some part of their culture; their subdued tone when discussing their heritage suggests a certain cultural ambivalence or perhaps a lack of understanding of the extent of their cultural loss.

In confronting the prevailing Anglo stereotypes of their people, these writers tended not to demolish them but to assent to the least negative of such images. Mena's Mexicans, for example, are not swarthy, treacherous greasers but charming—if artificial—creatures, much in the popular tradition of Bret Harte, Helen Hunt Jackson, and Gertrude Atherton.[51] Undoubtedly, a good part, if not most, of this sort of characterization can be attributed to popular taste and editorial control; it has only been in recent years, after all, that Americans have recognized honest expressions of minority consciousness.

Historically, the very term "Mexican" has had so harshly pejorative a connotation in the United States that a number of Mexican-American writers shrank from it and, ultimately, from their true heritage, creating in its place a mythical past of unsullied Europeanism.[52] The New Mexicans particularly venerated and exaggerated the Spanish component of their heritage. For example, the prominent folklorist, Aurelio M. Espinosa, determined that the oral traditions of New Mexico were essentially Spanish and had survived virtually untouched by other influences, whether Indian, mestizo, or Negro.[53] It was only a short step to conclude that all existing New Mexican culture was essentially Spanish: as one writer put it, "an echo of Spain across the seas."[54]

The Mexican-American literature in English that emerged from New Mexico during the 1930s evokes a past that, while largely imaginary, is presented with rigid conviction. Much of the fiction is closely related to the oral traditions that Espinosa and his followers collected so assiduously. The writers described a culture seemingly locked in time and barricaded against outside forces. Here the New Mexican Hispanos passed their lives in dignity and civility, confronting the harsh environment with a religiosity and resolve reminiscent of the conquistadores themselves. But although the people struggled, they moved as if to a waltz and lived in villages with names like Río Dormido (Sleeping River). A story by Juan A. A. Sedillo begins this way:

> It took months of negotiation to come to an understanding with the old man. He was in no hurry. What he had the most of was time. He lived up in Río en Medio, where his people had been for hundreds of years. He tilled the same land they had tilled. His house was small and wretched, but quaint. The little creek ran through his land. His orchard was gnarled and beautiful.[55]

Other New Mexican writers also stressed the continuity of the culture. But like the old man's cottage, that culture had fallen into a decadence that was perhaps quaint but surely irreversible.

There is something profoundly disturbing about this body of work. It seems a literature created out of fear and intimidation, a defensive response to racial prejudice—particularly the Anglo distaste for miscegenation—and ethnocentrism. The New Mexican writers retreated from the contemporary world into nostalgia, and it is a striking quality of their work that there are so few Anglos in it, as if each one were a gross impertinence. The problem is that the New Mexicans' literary past is so pathetically unreal. Nina Otero Warren, a chief advocate of New Mexico Hispanicism, defended the oppressive system of peonage by explaining that the peons "were not slaves, but working people who preferred submission to the *patrón* rather than an independent chance alone" (Warren, p. 10). She went on to observe that Hispanos "lived close to the soil and to nature. They cherished the traditions they had inherited from Spain and adapted to their new life. Theirs was a part of the feudal age, when master and men, although separate in class, were bound together by mutual interests and a close community of human sympathy. Much of this life remains today" (Warren, p. 51). If we may say that some of the southern Anglo writers suffered from a plantation mentality, then we may also say that New Mexican writers like Warren suffered from a hacienda syndrome.[56]

In sum, the body of early Mexican-American literature that has survived, both in Spanish and in English, is less interesting than the folklore and certainly less representative of the collective spirit. The vigor, the tone of defiance so typical of the *corridos*, is lacking in the written materials. What we find instead, generally, is a rather ingenuous hopefulness, a submissiveness, and a contrived and derivative romanticism. Much of the early literature, especially that written in English, is so much persiflage. The reason for this dichotomy is likely that, until about 1940, most Mexican-American writers came from relatively privileged backgrounds, from families of position and property that had a considerable stake in cultural and political accommodation. The oral traditions in this period, however, were essentially a proletarian form of expression, articulating the sentiments of those who had little capital and few material goods to lose. These people sought to preserve their culture and were ready to defend it, as the expression went, "con la pistola en la mano." All in all, an interesting rebuke to the stereotype of the humble Mexican as a docile, meek individual.

IV

Mexican-American literary history reached a landmark in 1945 with the publication of Josephina Niggli's *Mexican Village*, an unduly neglected work consisting of ten related stories that constitute a literary chronicle of Hidalgo, a town in the northern state of Nuevo Leon. The major character in the book is Bob Webster, an American-born product of a liaison between a Mexican woman and an Anglo who rejects his son when his Mexican blood manifests itself rather too clearly. Deeply hurt, Bob runs off to Europe, fighting with the Irish patriots and later with the French during World War I. But his loneliness is relentless, and in desperation he travels to Hidalgo, the village of the Mexican grandmother who had raised him, to satisfy a "nostalgia of the blood." To the villagers, he seems an incongruity: his dark skin and fluent Spanish clash with the foreignness of his name. Yet, for the first time in his life, Webster comes to feel a sense of belonging in Hidalgo, the stories of his grandmother running through his mind and tying him to the people and the land. He forms friendships unlike any he had known before, friendships "that grew not so much from a meeting of minds as from a relationship of blood."[57] At the end of *Mexican Village*, Bob has been fully assimilated into the community, even to the point of taking his mother's name. He has reclaimed his cultural heritage, and thus his self-esteem, as Roberto Ortega Menéndez. Through Webster, Niggli suggests that few Mexican-Americans (or few people, for that matter) are truly detached from their origins. Their cultural memories— often received as folklore, as in Bob's story—reside in the back of their minds, ready to emerge. In Hidalgo, a town Webster had never visited save through his grandmother's stories, he feels as if he had come home.

But, although Webster comes to understand that his essential self is Mexican, he knows too that, having been raised in the United States and inevitably touched by its culture, he cannot be wholly Mexican. His American qualities, as Niggli sees them, manifest themselves in several ways. Webster is impatient and restless and, even in his most profound moments of tranquillity in Mexico, he is troubled by an almost inexpressible feeling that his life must somehow be better still. Occasionally, he disdains the Indians of Hidalgo for their superstition, their provincialism, their fondness for subterfuge. Some of Webster's American traits are admirable, however, none more so than his irreverence for custom and ritual. Perhaps the most striking feature of the villagers is their blind allegiance to tradition, and they suffer for it. Webster, unlike the townspeople, carries on with an individualism and an assumption of free choice that the villagers can only envy. In creating Webster, Niggli was pointing to the Mexican-American as a distinctive type, as someone apart from both the *mexicano* and the *yanqui*, who could build an identity on the foundation of two cultures. The process was not a painless one, but in negotiating the distance between self-hate and self-esteem and in rediscovering his Mexican past, Webster presages the contemporary Chicano spirit.

In treating Mexican culture, Niggli intended not only to describe it but to create a fictional ambience that itself imparts a sense of the culture to the reader. No device served this end more effectively than the extensive use of folkloric materials. For example, Niggli introduces each story of *Mexican Village* with a proverb related to its theme; the characters themselves also have a fondness for *dichos*. Here are some examples:

> When you talk, be friends. When you act, be enemies.
> A man fool enough to marry cannot expect to own the world.
> Though we are all of the same clay, a jug is not a vase.

In addition, Mexican folk songs reverberate throughout the book, and Niggli recounts legends of noble bandits and buried treasure typical of the oral traditions of northern Mexico. One major character is Tía Magdalena, a *bruja* ("witch") who can dispense a remedy or a curse for any occasion, depending on her inclination. Several of the fictional situations in *Mexican Village* are variations of well-known folktales. One episode features a daring young man who sneaks into a rival town to romance its prettiest girl, a modification of a Mexican tale in which the devil assumes a disguise, appears on earth, and dances with an innocent young woman.

Like María Cristina Mena, Niggli simulated the flavor of Spanish by reproducing in English its syntactical and idiomatic qualities. Although *Mexican Village* was composed in English, it intentionally reads like a translation. Sometimes Niggli uses literal translations such as "the family Castillo" to achieve the effect of Spanish; she also renders into English distinctively Mexican expressions: arrogant boys are called "young roosters"; Tía Magdalena speaks affectionately of "Grandfather Devil"; another character, trying to emphasize his honesty, swears by "the five wounds of God." With such devices, Niggli creates a folkloric language highly evocative of that of the villagers themselves.

Niggli's work is significant also because, unlike earlier Mexican-American writers in English, she refused to accept conventional American views of her people. To be sure, some of her characters come close to stereotypes: the swaggering macho, the haughty Spaniard, the long-suffering Mexican woman. But Niggli also presents strong men who are nonetheless sensitive and vulnerable, *gachupines* who treat the Indians decently, and women like the unforgettable Tía who truckle before no man. Niggli manipulates her large cast of characters with rare skill; in the end, the reader sees that the fictional citizens of Hidalgo represent the complexity and diversity of Mexico itself.

Mexican Village stands as a major transitional work in the development of Chicano fiction. In its sensitive rendering of rural life, its emotionalism, and its affectionate portrayal of exotic experiences and personalities, the book culminated the romantic tradition in Mexican-American writing. But *Mexican Village* also pointed forward to an emerging school of realism, confronting such issues as racism, the oppression of women, and the failure of the Mexican Revolution. Before Niggli, no writer of fiction in the United States, with the possible exception of Katherine Anne Porter, had so vividly depicted the fundamental tensions in Mexican life: the sometimes volatile interaction of Spanish and Indian cultures, the profound sense of history and tradition pulling against the fascination with that which is modern and voguish.[58] But Niggli's greatest achievement was to delineate an important aspect of Mexican-American experience and to create a distinctive ambience for its presentation.

V

World War II profoundly affected the Mexican people of the United States. In the first place, the war greatly increased their numbers. Shortages in the domestic labor force brought on by military demands were alleviated by the importation of thousands of Mexican workers, many of whom settled permanently in the United States. The war also triggered a shift in occupational and residential patterns. Mexican-Americans left agricultural work in small communities for factory and service jobs in large cities, particularly Los Angeles and San Antonio. The participation of Mexican-Americans in the military services provided many with their first intimate contact with Anglo-American culture. Military experience undoubtedly heightened the expectations of many Mexican-Americans. Having risked their lives for the United States, they demanded more of its institutions in return. In sum, World War II pulled Mexican-Americans closer to—although clearly not into—the American mainstream. By the late 1940s, Mexican-Americans had established a cultural identity distinct from that of their brethren south of the Rio Grande. Whereas an earlier generation had fought in Chihuahua and composed *corridos* about Pancho Villa, the present generation fought in the Philippines and composed *corridos* commemorating Douglas MacArthur (see Hansen, pp. 314–15).

In 1947 Mario Suárez began to publish a series of stories in the *Arizona Quarterly*. The stories are about the people of El Hoyo ("the Hole"), a barrio in Tucson, and Suárez describes the residents not as Mexicans or Mexican-Americans but as Chicanos. Suárez explains that "Chicano" is simply the short way of saying *mexicano*, but it is clear the term suggests something more. His Chicanos are an embattled minority, in some ways reminiscent of Steinbeck's *paisanos* of *Tortilla Flat* but drawn less in caricature and with greater understanding and compassion. They are an assortment of individuals who combine Mexican and American characteristics with marvelous effects. Suárez himself best describes the varieties of Chicano individualism:

> Perhaps El Hoyo, its inhabitants, and its essence can best be explained by telling you a little bit about a dish called *capirotada*. Its origin is uncertain. But it is made of old, new, stale, and hard bread. It is sprinkled with water and then it is cooked with raisins, olives, onions, tomatoes, peanuts, cheese, and general leftovers of that which is good and bad. It is seasoned with salt, sugar, pepper, and sometimes chili or tomato sauce. It is fired with tequila or sherry wine. It is served hot, cold, or just "on the weather" as they say in El Hoyo. The Garcias like it one way, the Quevedos another. While in general appearance it does not differ much from one home to another it tastes different everywhere. Nevertheless it is still *capirotada*. And so it is with El Hoyo's *chicanos*. While many seem to the undiscerning eye to be alike it is only because collectively they are referred to as *chicanos*. But like *capirotada*, fixed in a thousand ways and served on a thousand tables, which can only be evaluated by individual taste, the *chicanos* must be so distinguished.[59]

Although El Hoyo is physically a part of Tucson, culturally it is a world unto itself where different principles obtain. One of its leading citizens is Señor Garza, a barber who operates his business according to the unshakable conviction that "a man should not work too hard." Suárez explains that Garza's "day begins according to the humor of his wife. When Garza drives up late, conditions are perhaps good. When Garza drives up early, all is perhaps not well. Garza's Barber Shop has been known, accordingly, to stay closed for a week. It has also been known to open before the sun comes up and to remain open for three consecutive days."[60] When business gets too heavy, Garza closes his shop and escapes to Mexico. He is not lazy but simply does not assign a high importance to the making of money. As Suárez writes: "Garza, a philosopher. Owner of Garza's Barber Shop. But the shop will never own Garza."

Suárez understood that the merging of Mexican and American cultures was a delicate process, particularly in a fast-paced urban environment with its bewildering array of institutions. In "Kid Zopilote," Suárez depicts the transformation of Pepe García, a young man from El Hoyo who, during a summer in Los Angeles, is exposed to the zoot-suit craze and comes away much impressed. The Mexican zoot-suiters, or pachucos, had affected an elaborate life-style based on a bizarre combination of Mexican and American traits. They spoke a patois of English and Spanish, creating terms such as "returniar," "watchiando," and "styleacho." Pepe is especially impressed by the camaraderie of the pachucos and so becomes one himself, much to the horror of his tradition-minded mother. Under the influence of his new friends, Pepe takes to smoking and selling marijuana and is eventually arrested. In the jailhouse, the police destroy his zoot suit and shear his magnificent pompadour. When Pepe is released, his humiliation is so great that he stays at home and practices his guitar. He becomes a quite proficient musician, but when his hair grows long and "meets in the back of the head in the shape of a duck's tail,"[61] he puts down his guitar and returns to the street. As Pepe's uncle observes, a *zopilote* ("buzzard") can never be a peacock.

Suárez' most poignant treatment of the acculturation process appears in "Maestría." This story features Gonzalo Pereda, a "master" of the art of raising fighting cocks. One day a friend in Chihuahua presents him with a young rooster, and Gonzalo nurtures the bird, called "Killer," with special affection. After a few victories in the pit, Killer is badly beaten. Gonzalo nurses the bird back to health but, ironically, sees Killer choke to death on a piece of liver. Writes Suárez:

> Like Killer's plight, it might be added, is the plight of many things the
> *maestros* cherish. Each year they hear their sons talk English with a rapidly

disappearing accent, that accent which one early accustomed only to Spanish never fails to have. Each year the *maestros* notice that their sons' Spanish loses fluency. But perhaps it is natural. The *maestros* themselves seem to forget about bulls and bullfighters, about guitars and other things so much a part of the world that years ago circumstance forced them to leave behind. They hear instead more about the difference between one baseball swing and another. Yes, perhaps it is only natural.[62]

Suárez was the first truly Chicano writer. He was comfortable with the term itself, as many are not still, recognizing its symbolic importance and understanding its slight suggestion of self-deprecation. In Suárez' fiction, the Chicano is a truncated variety of Mexican in a cultural sense, but no less a dignified and individualized human being. Suárez portrayed sympathetically the maestros and their yearning for the old days, but did not himself linger long in nostalgia. He was compassionate toward those pachucos like Pepe García who were badly confused by the process of cultural transformation and so lapsed into grotesque exhibitionism.[63] But Suárez' favorite Chicanos were characters like the barber Garza who retained their fundamental Mexican-ness and yet thrived in American culture. These Chicanos were not marginal men and women but cultural hybrids who prided themselves on their ability to function successfully in two worlds.

An interesting contrast to Suárez' work is *Pocho*, a novel by José Antonio Villarreal published in 1959. The work has the usual first-novel defects: a certain lack of control, an awkwardness of style. But *Pocho* is flawed in other ways, these owing to its being the first Chicano novel (*Mexican Village*, not properly a novel in any case, belongs to an earlier Mexican-American period). Villarreal wrote essentially for an Anglo-American audience and understood, given the prevailing ignorance of Chicano life in the United States, that he was working in something of a cultural vacuum. He had no antecedents, as it were, no one on whose work to enlarge, and so he tried to tell the whole of the *pocho* experience himself. Inevitably, his novel is thin in places, hurried in others. Occasionally, it bogs down in excessive explication.

The opening chapter of *Pocho* follows the movements of Juan Rubio, a colonel during the Mexican Revolution who, after killing a rich "Spaniard," is forced to leave the country and accept a life as a migrant farm worker in California. Here his son Richard is born. The Rubio family eventually moves to Santa Clara during the depression; at this point, the novel becomes Richard's story.

Richard is a bright, curious child, but he quickly discovers that opportunities for "Mexicans" are not great. He is humiliated by a teacher for his accent, and he finds the Catholic church a suffocating force, whose priests are concerned with little more than suppressing the assumed hypersexuality of their Mexican parishioners. Richard's parents do not encourage him in his quest for knowledge: his mother's education is limited, and she is, in any event, too much in the church's thrall. Juan, the father, is preoccupied with the disintegration of his family's cultural values and with his own hopes of returning to Mexico. Richard is thus left to go his way alone, and the journey is a painful one. The basic conflict in the book is between Richard's powerful sense of individuality and the burden of ethnicity imposed by himself, his family, and the community. The issue is complicated by the rapidity of the cultural change that engulfs and finally destroys the Rubio family: Juan runs off with a young woman while his wife, Consuelo, remains at home, vindictive and full of self-pity. The oldest daughter, Luz, becomes thoroughly Americanized and verges on outright rebellion. As for Richard, he finally realizes that his foremost responsibility is to seek his own identity; as a result, he joins the Navy, "knowing that for him there would never be a coming back."[64]

Villarreal's subject is important and sensitive, but his treatment is flawed by oversimplification. He attacks, for example, the Catholic church and the oppression of women in Mexican culture, but he draws his targets in such a way that they are all too easy to hit. The reader discovers, for example, that the church does nothing of redeeming value and that Mexican women are hardly more than mindless automatons, created to fulfill men's pleasure and to raise children. Villarreal simply lacked the insight to deal effectively with his materials. In treating Consuelo's pathetic effort at liberation, Villarreal observes: "Although he loved his mother, Richard realized that a family could not survive when the woman desired to command, and he knew that his mother was like a starving child who had become gluttonous when confronted with food. She had lived so long in the tradition of her country that she could not help herself now, and abused the privilege of equality afforded the women of her new country." In the same scene, Villarreal offers this limp analysis as Richard surveys the wreckage of his family life: "What was done was beyond repair. To be just, no one could be blamed, for the transition from the culture of the old world to that of the new should never have been attempted in one generation."[65]

Although Richard is well developed and credible, some of the other characters in *Pocho* are merely caricatures. From the moment Juan appears in the novel, we know we are in the presence of a true macho. He strolls through Ciudad Juárez, thinking back to his days with Pancho Villa and "carelessly wonders how many men he had killed there." Later in the same day, Rubio kills another man, calmly shooting his victim as he lies writhing on the floor of a cantina. Consuelo, before her meager attempt at self-realization, is the epitome of woeful Mexican motherhood. And, finally, Villarreal presents us with the Marxist who becomes "very middle-class" when he finds Richard in bed with his comely wife.

Today, *Pocho* stands as a curiosity, notable for its evocation of an ingenuous expectation: that a young man of obvious Mexican ancestry coming of age in California during the late 1930s would be regarded strictly on individual merit without concern for his ethnicity. Richard clings to this hope to the end of the novel, but he is, after all, still a boy. Villarreal seems to share Richard's illusion against the weight of Chicano experience in this country, and it is this lack of acute vision that most severely undermines his accomplishment as a novelist.

VI

Until recently, the growth of Chicano literature has been hampered by the general unwillingness of American publishers to issue such works, on the assumption that they—particularly those pieces in Spanish— had too limited an appeal to be profitable. In 1967, however, Quinto Sol Publications was established in Berkeley, California, to provide an outlet for Chicano writers. The success of Quinto Sol led to the opening of other Chicano publishing houses. The result has been a burst of Chicano literary activity.

The writers of the Quinto Sol school manifested a literary sensibility that contrasts sharply with that of earlier writers such as Niggli, Suárez, and Villarreal. The irony and the tone of controlled disappointment were replaced by more intense emotions, sometimes by an almost violent sense of outrage. The careful explication, born of a desire to acquaint Anglo readers with the Mexican culture of the United States, is generally absent from the works of the Quinto Sol authors. They wrote primarily for an audience that shared their experiences; they felt no need, therefore, to justify their culture.

Although authors like Suárez and Villarreal had written sensitively on Chicano subjects, their styles and techniques were in no important ways different from those of Anglo-American writers. Indeed, Suárez' work, especially in its fascination with human eccentricity and its casual lyricism, reminds one of John Steinbeck in *Tortilla Flat*. But the Quinto Sol writers often rejected Anglo-American literary models and instead did what writers of Mexican heritage in the Southwest had done traditionally: they turned southward and did their literary apprenticeships in the works of authors such as Rulfo, Borges, and García Márquez. These new Chicano writers not only reaffirmed their ties to the cultures of contemporary Mexico and Latin America but also rediscovered, as Mexican artists had earlier in the century, their aboriginal heritage.[66] They invoked Aztec philosophy and metaphors and were particularly attracted to the concept of Aztlán, the ancestral home of the Aztecs, which lay somewhere in the vicinity of the American Southwest. Some scholars have quibbled that the concept of Aztlán is historically fraudulent, but they miss the point: its importance is symbolic, in that it provides Chicanos with a deeper and more intimate sense of cultural continuity.

Finally, the Quinto Sol writers developed a variety of linguistic techniques with which to portray their cultural distinctiveness. In the past, Mexican-American writers had written in conventional Spanish or English, while a few writers like Mena and Niggli (and Villarreal to a lesser degree) tried to re-create the flavor of Spanish in English, occasionally employing the original Spanish for special effect. But these new authors aimed to reproduce Chicano speech exactly. They used not only conventional Spanish and English but various regional dialects of both languages and combinations of all of these.[67] They also used distinctive Chicano neologisms such as *wachar* ("to watch"), *lonche* ("lunch"), and *troca* ("truck"). The results have been gratifying, particularly in poetry. Here is "Aquellos Vatos" by Tino Villanueva:

> Simón,
> we knew him as la Zorra—uncouth but
> squared away;
> messed around unpaved streets. No different
> from el Caballo de Littlefield, or from
> la Chiva de McAllen who never let himself down;
> always had a movida chueca somewhere up town.
> Then there was la Polla de San Anto—lived
> across the creek, y tenía un ranfle sentao
> pa'tras, ¿me entiendes?
> And el Pato de Nuquis, el que se la madereaba;
> and la Rata was already growing a mouse-tache at
> early ten.
> El Conejo estaba todo locote, y era más largo
>   que no sé qué; had rucas all over the place, man:
> not even Don Juan carried a rabbit's foot.
> El Bear se salía del cuadro; he was forever
>   polishing his Cat's Paw double-sole derechonas,
> and heterosexual la Perra used to snicker and
> warn in Spanish—"You keep bending down like that
> Bear, and you'll wind up in dallas.

Chale,
I don't recall el Tiger . . . they tell me he was
a chavalón que se curaba con las gabas.
I do remember el Gorrión, un carnal a todo dar—
never said much, but his tattoos were sure a
conversation piece.
¿A la Burra?, ¡qué gacho le filorearon la madre
en el chancleo!, and el Canario went to the pinta
for it. Not to Sing Sing but the State Farm is
just as bad. La palomilla hasn't been the same since.

They're probably married by now,
those cats,
and their kids try to comprehend culture and
identity by reading "See Spot, See Spot run,"
and by going to the zoo on a Greyhound bus with
Miss Foxx.[68]

As a bilingual poet, Villanueva greatly enhances the aesthetic potentialities
of his work by selecting words, phrases, sounds from the two languages
to achieve precisely his desired effects.[69] Other poets use bilingualism
not only to achieve an aesthetic result but also to denote a cultural
situation. In "M'ijo No Mira Nada" ("My Son Doesn't See Anything")
by Tomás Rivera, a father talks to his son in Spanish, but the son
answers, with one exception, in English:

—Mira, m'ijo, qué rascacielo.
  "Does it reach the sky and heaven?"
—Mira, m'ijo, qué carrazo.
  "Can it get to the end of the world?"
—Mira, m'ijo, ese soldado.
  "¿Por que pelea?"
—Mira, m'ijo, qué bonita fuente.
  "Yes, but I want to go to the restroom."
—Mira, m'ijo, qué tiendota de J. C. Penney,
  alli trabajarás un día.
  "Do you know the people there, daddy?"
—No,
  vámanos a casa,
  tù no miras nada.[70]

Clearly, the boy not only understands Spanish but can speak it; he
simply chooses not to, much to his father's distress. The different
languages that father and son use, as well as the differences in perception

about the world around them, indicate the cultural gulf that separates them.[71]

Quinto Sol Publications, particularly in the first five years of its existence, was a tremendously invigorating force in Chicano literature. It challenged Chicanos to proclaim their cultural uniqueness, encouraged experimentation and innovation, and awarded cash prizes to the authors of distinguished works. On the most fundamental level, the firm's very existence gave aspiring Chicano writers a sense of self-respect and an assurance that their subject matter was worthy.

No writer better exemplified the new sensibility than Tomás Rivera, who won the first Quinto Sol literary award in 1970 for his work " . . . *y no se lo tragó la tierra*" ("*And the Earth Did Not Part*"). This collection of fictional sketches—which together may be regarded as constituting, in D. H. Lawrence's phrase, a "fragmentary novel"—focuses on the Chicano migrant workers of southern Texas during the 1950s. Whereas José Antonio Villarreal described a Chicano family that was all but crushed by assimilationist pressures, Rivera's work proclaims a people's vitality despite almost unspeakable hardships. The book opens on a note reminiscent of various Latin American writers, particularly Borges and García Márquez, in that Rivera obscures distinctions between reality and fantasy:

> That year was lost to him. Sometimes he tried to remember, but then when things appeared to become somewhat clear his thoughts would elude him. It usually began with a dream in which suddenly he thought he was awake, and then he would realize he was actually asleep. That was why he could not be sure whether or not what he had recalled was actually what had happened.[72]

Imagined or not, the events described (primarily by an anonymous narrator) have the ring of painful truth. In the opening sketch, a young farm worker is shot through the head by his foreman; later, we see children searching for food in a garbage dump; still later, two children burn to death in a migrant worker's shack. Rivera describes these episodes in a spare, detached manner, very much after the style of Juan Rulfo in *El llano en llamas* (*The Burning Plain*).

Structurally, " . . . *y no se lo tragó la tierra*" consists of twelve loosely connected sketches (representing the months of the narrator's "lost year")—each introduced by a very brief vignette—an introduction, and a closing. Together, the sketches offer a broad study of the Chicano migrant subculture as a kind of literary collage. The device of anonymity enhances the representational and collective qualities of the work; for the most part, Rivera is describing not distinctive individuals but human beings bound in a common experience.

"*. . . y no se lo tragó la tierra*" is a profoundly humanistic work. In one sketch, the nameless young protagonist of the book goes out at midnight to summon the devil, first by cajoling him and then, in desperation, by hurling invectives. The devil never appears, of course. In the following story, the boy is so embittered by a series of family tragedies that he proceeds to curse God, a sacrilege that would result, or so his mother had told him, in his being swallowed up by the earth. But, surprisingly, the earth feels firmer than it had before, and the boy suddenly "felt himself capable of doing and undoing whatever he chose" (p. 56). In Rivera's fictional world, there is no God and no Satan; there is only human will.

Rivera is no apologist for his fictional Chicanos or for their culture. In his remarkable sketch "La mano en la bolsa" ("His Hand in His Pocket"), Rivera presents don Laíto and doña Boni, two grotesques of unsurpassed vulgarity and cruelty; in a later piece he introduces a Chicano con man who collects money for portraits but never delivers them. Like other Chicano writers, Rivera vigorously attacks the Catholic church for its exploitation of the poor and its preoccupation with the human potentiality not for good but for evil. Still, Rivera's main interest lies in characters like the nameless boy who finally discovers that knowledge and wisdom can be salvaged from any experience:

> Suddenly he felt very happy because . . . he realized that he hadn't lost anything. He had discovered something. To discover and to rediscover and synthesize. To relate this entity with that entity, and that entity with still another, and finally relating everything with everything else. That was what he had to do, that was all. And he became even happier. Later, when he arrived at home, he went to the tree that was in the yard. He climbed it. On the horizon he saw a palm tree and he imagined that someone was on top looking at him. He even raised his arm and waved it back and forth so that the other person could see that he knew that he was there. (p. 128)

Rolando Hinojosa-S., who has won not only the Quinto Sol Prize (1972) but also the Premio Casa de las Américas (1976), is another Chicano writer whose literary sensibility and technique derive largely from Latin American traditions. His work is similar to Rivera's in that he, too, writes about southern Texas in a combination of conventional and *pocho* Spanish and because his preferred literary form is the sketch. Hinojosa's sketches are brief, sometimes no more than one or two paragraphs. In this regard, as Herminio Ríos has pointed out, he seems a kindred spirit of Julio Torri, who in popularizing the *estampa* in Mexico, argued that the greatest defect in literature is excessive explication. In an opening note to his *Estampas del valle y otras obras (Sketches of the Valley and Other Works)*, Hinojosa writes: "The people who appear and disappear in these sketches, as well as the events that occur in them, may or may not be real. The writer writes and tries to do what he can. Explaining all this is the function of others."[73]

Again like Rivera, Hinojosa presents a literary collage of Chicano culture in southern Texas but to somewhat different effect. The nameless young protagonist of Rivera's work spends his "lost year" learning the fundamental lesson that the gift of life, under whatever circumstances, is to be profoundly cherished, while Hinojosa's work rises out of this assumption. At the beginning of *Generaciones y semblanzas (Generations and Biographies)*, the anonymous narrator offers this view:

> These are no legendary heroes here. These people go to the toilet, they sneeze and blow their noses, they raise families, know how to die with one eye on guard, and they yield with difficulty like most green wood and thus do not crack easily. Those seeking heroes of the caliber of El Cid, say, can very well go to Hell and stay there.
>
> It's true that there are several ways of being heroic. It's no laughing matter to work from day to day, putting up with any damn fool who shows up along the way. One thing should be clear however: to endure is not to ignore things or to deceive oneself. Bearing one's burden doesn't mean that one is a blind fool unaware of what's really going on.
>
> People suspect that living by itself is heroic enough. The rest of it, bearing whatever life brings, is heroic as well.[74]

Hinojosa differs from Rivera in other ways as well. While Rivera's tone is serious and generally melancholy and his sense of outrage simmers just beneath the surface of his narrative, Hinojosa's fictions are humorous and ironic; he regards the whole gamut of human behavior from heroism to foolishness to depravity with a judicious and humane tolerance. Furthermore, Hinojosa sweeps over a much broader range of Chicano experience than Rivera, speaking through the voices of numerous characters, some named and others anonymous. Hinojosa's works vibrate with the sounds of the barrio: family gossip, conversation about Anglos, children chanting Mexican rhymes. As one of his narrators describes the activity of the writer, Hinojosa, "without anyone's leave, goes out into the street and takes a little bit from here and there" (*Estampas*, p. 121).

The statement is charming in its modesty, but in fact Hinojosa, in *Estampas* and *Generaciones*, has created a remarkably coherent chronicle of Belken County, his fictional locale in the Rio Grande Valley of southern Texas. He traces Belken's origins to the eighteenth century, when the Spaniard Escandón first established a colony in the vicinity. Several of Belken's families, notably the Buenrostros, arrived in the area with Escandón. Hinojosa follows the Buenrostros through several generations, each of which finds its members participating in notable historical events such as the Mexican Revolution and the Korean War. With his wide array of characters and experiences, Hinojosa evokes the richness and vitality of southern Texas Chicano culture.

A recurring concern in Hinojosa's work is the presence of fatalism among his people, a quality widely believed to be intrinsic to Mexican and Chicano culture and often denigrated by Anglo observers. Hinojosa finds that fatalism is indeed a characteristic of Chicano life but not in any sense a defect. The lives of his Chicanos are difficult, marked by relentless economic and political oppression, yet the people accept these conditions, knowing that in this world we are not always the keepers of our destiny. While Rivera's themes—the triumph of human will over hardship, the human struggle to throw off cultural and psychological fetters—are existentialist, Hinojosa seems more the stoic, writing about human dignity in the face of adversity. This is to say not that Hinojosa's Chicanos refuse to struggle against capricious fate but that they recognize their human limitations. In the sketch entitled "Thus It Was Fulfilled," the anonymous narrator, on the occasion of a friend's premature death, observes: "There are people born that way, branded and singled out as if someone were saying: you're going to be that way, you this way, and you this other way; in short, as always, man proposes and God disposes" (*Estampas*, p. 123). Hinojosa's Chicanos aim not to conquer but to endure. And in the act of endurance there is accomplishment and satisfaction and quiet courage.

Together, Rivera and Hinojosa exemplify many of the best tendencies in contemporary Chicano literature written in Spanish.[75] Both employ in their works the distinctive Chicano variety of Spanish, a significant undertaking given the traditional view that Chicano Spanish is a linguistic barbarism. But Rivera and Hinojosa demonstrate that the language of Chicanos is a fully developed idiom, capable of representing the full extent of human emotion and action. Furthermore, in embracing current Latin American literary principles and techniques, they have reinforced the cultural ties between Chicanos and other Latins, while simultaneously rejecting the archaic romanticism of earlier Chicano writers in Spanish. But the major achievement of Rivera and Hinojosa is to reaffirm the primacy of the common people as the guardians and purveyors of Chicano cultural values. In communicating this idea to their readers, both writers infuse their stories with folkloric qualities. Their use of ordinary and proverbial language (especially in Hinojosa), their focus on commonplace experiences, their technique of using alternating and anonymous narrators, and their deliberate de-emphasis of authorial participation give their works a spontaneous, proletarian quality, but one that springs from a proletariat with a distinctive ethnic consciousness. One of Hinojosa's sketches, appropriately entitled "Voices from the Barrio," ends with this observation: "The *barrios* can be called el Rebaje, el de las Conchas, el Cantarranas, el Rincón del Diablo, el Pueblo Mexicano—really, names don't matter much. What does count, as always, are the people" (*Estampas*, p. 73).

VII

It is a rather self-evident principle of Chicano writing that authors who compose in English generally follow Anglo-American literary styles and conventions, while those who write in Spanish are more influenced by Latin American authors. A Chicano novelist of the first group who nevertheless retains his ethnic distinctiveness is Rudolfo A. Anaya, another winner of the Quinto Sol prize. His first and most satisfying work, *Bless Me, Ultima* (1972), reminiscent in some ways of Joyce's *Portrait of the Artist as a Young Man*, is a moving study of a boy, Antonio Márez, coming of age during the 1940s in a remote village in central New Mexico. The action of the novel centers on Antonio's attempt to forge his own identity in an environment of conflicting cultures and expectations as represented by the two branches of his family: his father's people, who are ranchers and horsemen—a restless, powerful clan who cherish the rugged life on the high plains of New Mexico—and his mother's family, the Lunas, who are farmers—sedentary, tradition-bound, rigidly Catholic. Antonio is the last of four sons; the others have not turned out well, having gone off to war and returned jaded and contemptuous of their heritage. To guard against a repetition of this calamity, Antonio's parents entrust his care to Ultima, a *curandera* ("healer") of immense wisdom and compassion. Antonio discovers that Ultima's greatness derives from her accumulation of cultural knowledge, her understanding of her people's experience, their values and customs. While other characters in the novel seem confused and disheartened, Ultima retains an unshakable sense of identity and purpose. Her gift to Antonio is the lesson of honoring one's culture without being trammeled by it, of using one's cultural identity as the foundation for the development of an individual spirit. "Build strength from life," Ultima counsels Antonio and, indeed, his life under her tutelage becomes a storehouse of cultural riches. At the end of the novel, Antonio rejects the confining traditionalism of the Lunas in favor of the Márez' doctrine of personal freedom.

Like other Chicano writers, Anaya creates a distinctive cultural ambience primarily through the use of folklore. (The language of *Bless Me, Ultima*, except for an occasional word or phrase, is conventional English.) The narrator, Antonio, refers frequently to *cuentos* of witchcraft and to legends of *la llorona* and the Virgin of Guadalupe that he hears throughout his childhood. He describes in great detail Ultima's healing powers, which derive from traditional Mexican folk medicine. Occasionally, Anaya modifies conventional folk traditions or creates a kind of pseudo-folklore for his fictional purposes. For example, the owl is usually a symbol of evil in Mexican folklore, the *nagual* ("companion") of witches. But in Anaya's work, the owl is the guardian spirit of Ultima. The effect is to dramatize Ultima's powers and the air of mystery surrounding her, for although she exercises her magic primarily for the good of the community, she is quite capable of pronouncing curses on her enemies. Anaya also creates the "legend" of the Golden Carp, a symbol of benevolent pantheism reminiscent of the Aztec god Quetzalcoatl. Anaya virtually immerses Antonio in oral tradition, by way of suggesting that for the Chicano, folklore is the foundation of a cultural identity. Antonio learns as much. "Ultima told me the stories and legends of my ancestors," he explains. "From her I learned the glory and the tragedy of the history of my people, and I came to understand how that history stirred in my blood."[76]

Bless Me, Ultima is a deeply moving work of genuine excellence, certainly one of the finest Chicano works published to date. Not the least of Anaya's accomplishments is his rejection of the contrived Hispanicism that so enervated the works of earlier New Mexican writers. Anaya portrays the mestizo component of New Mexican culture as a positive quality; it is precisely Ultima's ability to draw from the traditions of both Spanish and Indian cultures that provides her with extraordinary powers.

Throughout his work, Anaya celebrates the liberating potentiality of imagination in a drab and mechanistic world.[77] This has also been a favorite theme of Gary Soto, perhaps the most talented of young Chicano poets. In his two published volumes, *The Elements of San Joaquin* (1977) and *The Tale of Sunlight* (1978), Soto presents an extraordinarily compelling view of contemporary Chicano/Mexican life as he transports his readers southward from Fresno and the San Joaquin Valley farms to Taxco in central Mexico, the town where, as Soto's narrator puts it, "we all begin."[78]

The Elements is divided into three sections, the first of which treats the squalor of urban life. Violence, loneliness, degradation are the constants of these poems: a dope dealer is murdered by the police; a character named Leonard labors in a grimy factory scrubbing "the circles/ From toilets/No one flushed."[79] Religion provides no relief from misery. In "Telephoning God," the drunken narrator "rings God and gets Wichita." Despite the harshness of these poems, their tone is generally restrained and even detached, as if the poet were himself inured to suffering.

In the second and title section of the volume, Soto skillfully depicts the natural beauty of the farming areas outside Fresno, but here again the setting is an arena of human misery. In the poem "Field," we hear the voice of a farm worker: "Already I am becoming the valley, / A soil that sprouts nothing / For any of us." Farm workers toil in anonymity, the general public oblivious to their painful drudgery. Nature, so often revered in American literature, is no beneficent presence here; rather, nature seems indifferent to human beings and, at times, hostile. Fog, for example, obscures not only people's activities but their very existence. And when the fog lifts, there is the dust, one of Soto's recurrent symbols. In a prosaic sense, it vivifies the dirtiness of contemporary life, but it also suggests the eventual disintegration of living matter. Natural forces conspire to assure this outcome: "The wind strokes / The skulls and spines of cattle / To white dust, to nothing. . . ."[80] The human being, just another of earth's creatures, can expect no better treatment.

The last section of *The Elements* comprises reminiscences of family, childhood experiences, and the poet's old neighborhood in Fresno. As a group, these poems are the most poignant and engaging in the collection. "In December" traces the poet's exploration of a deserted house and presents this striking image:

> In the kitchen a draft
> Moved like a housewife,
> Reaching into cupboards
> To find nothing
> But vinegar
> And an unstrung necklace
> Of dead flies.

As the poet proceeds along the streets of Fresno, he mourns the dispersal of his family and the destruction of the neighborhood to make room for warehouses and freeways. Occasionally, a pleasant memory emerges: the early mornings shared silently with a brother, a childish game between the poet and his mother. Most fondly of all, the poet recalls his grandmother, a proud and defiant woman who somehow nurtured her children in spite of all obstacles. But, inevitably, the poet's memories turn sad as he recalls the tragic and early deaths of his father and uncle. In "Braly Street," the poet records his profound grief:

> When I come
> To where our house was,
> I come to weeds
> And a sewer line tied off
> Like an umbilical cord;
> To the chinaberry
> Not pulled down
> And to its rings
> My father and uncle
> Would equal, if alive.

The Tale of Sunlight takes up where *The Elements of San Joaquin* leaves off, with the poet surveying his childhood recollections of Fresno. But the harsh and spare realism of the earlier volume gives way to fantasy and the previously unfocused sense of cultural loss emerges full-blown. The first stanza of the first poem in *The Tale* establishes the shift in mood:

> The moment he stepped out
> Of the spark
> Struck from a rock,
> Our old yard opened
> Like a curtain
> And what appeared was what I lost
> Years back.[81]

Presumably the unnamed figure here is Molina, alter ego to the young poet; Molina shares the poet's suffering, anger, and awe before life's mysteries, but most of all he stimulates the poet's imagination and ethnic and cultural consciousness. Relentlessly curious, Molina tries to transcend his poverty by creating alternative realities and visions. In "The Map," on a day when "the sun's whiteness closes around us / Like a noose," Molina rearranges American geography and his own personal history. Another time, he combats his hunger at two in the morning by drawing bowls of soup. Molina's actions seem pathetic at times, but the reader can admire his courage and his refusal to lapse into self-pity.

Notwithstanding his prominence in the first group of poems, Molina is only one of many characters in Soto's barrio who, bound in a camaraderie of shared oppression, struggle against long odds and survive. Soto writes about their experiences compassionately and even wistfully, lamenting his narrator's cultural drift away from them. In "The Cellar," the poet listens to the sounds "he would never know again" and writes:

> And because I stood
> In this place for hours,
> I imagined I could climb
> From this promise of old air
> And enter a street
> Stunned gray with evening
> Where, if someone
> Moved, I could turn,
> And seeing him through the years,
> Call him brother, call him Molina.

The poet leaves Fresno on a southward journey to his ancestral homeland, finally settling near Taxco. Here he encounters Manuel Zaragoza, a tavern keeper who has not recovered from the death of his wife during pregnancy. Grief follows him "perched like a bird on his shoulder," and so he passes his nights at his cantina, drinking and folding his hands in the shapes of animals against the dim light. Like Molina, Zaragoza perceives no good reason for his misfortune. He walks the streets of his village "perplexed like a priest" and watches burros "sniffing their own dung." But his pain, the reader is happy to learn, is not permanent, for Manuel escapes eventually into a world of marvelous fantasies, some of which he offers as actual occurrences. He dreams of owning a circus, complete with nude dancers and a talking rooster. In the title poem, he describes his most bizarre fantasy, featuring a beam of sunlight, without any source, that brightens his tavern. Eventually the beam settles on a wall and vaporizes any object that touches it; Zaragoza, by now thoroughly liberated from the banalities of conventional existence, offers a stub of a finger as confirmation of the beam's magical powers.

In "The Space," the volume's final poem, we find Manuel reclining in a hammock outside his village, enjoying a world he has largely made over:

I say it is enough
To be where the smells
Of creatures
Braid like rope
And to know if
The grasses [sic] rustle
Is only
A lizard passing.
It is enough, brother,
Listening to a bird coo
A leash of parables,
Keeping an eye
On the moon,
The space
Between cork trees
Where the sun first appears.

In his travels from a Fresno barrio to the countryside around Taxco, Soto has found a common denominator not only of suffering but of willful endurance. Through the characters of Molina and Zaragoza, Soto affirms the triumph of imagination over squalor and adversity.

Soto's poetry represents a culmination in contemporary Chicano literature, embodying many of its best qualities. Soto moves easily across national boundaries to mark the lines of continuity between Chicanos and Mexicans and to portray man's essential dignity. Like Rivera, he writes compassionately, but without sentimentality, of the Chicano poor, many of whom labor far removed from public concern and who learn that their vindication must come from within themselves. Soto's characters are brilliantly individual, yet they recognize their need to participate as members of cultural communities. From *The Elements of San Joaquin* to *The Tale of Sunlight*, Soto seems himself to have grown in ethnic consciousness, and as a Chicano poet he creates many images of great charm and insight. Yet he carries his ethnicity unobtrusively, and it is this combination of talents that places him in the first rank of young American poets.

VII

In an age when the literature of the United States is marked by a profound pessimism and a retreat from the national culture, Chicano writing is notable for its celebration of ethnic values and traditions.

Like most other contemporary authors, Chicano writers see modern industrial culture as a destructive and dehumanizing force, but, while others detect no sanctuary against it, writers like Niggli, Suárez, and Anaya find relief in their Mexican-Chicano heritage.

Tomás Rivera has called the current burst of Chicano literary activity a "festival of the living," but a number of scholars and critics argue that the phenomenon is more accurately described as the parting gesture of a dying culture. The argument goes that Chicano culture will undergo the same fate as all ethnic and immigrant cultures in the United States: it will be flattened by American assimilationist pressures, leaving only a few Spanish words and phrases, an obligatory orgy of drunkenness on the *cinco de mayo*, and a recipe or two for enchiladas. There is little doubt that immigrant cultures have not thrived in the United States, but Chicanos represent a special case. Most live relatively close to the Mexican border so that cultural transfusion occurs regularly. And then there is the intensive immigration, both legal and illegal, from Mexico to the United States, which shows no sign of abating. Finally, there is the basic principle mentioned earlier in this essay: that for many Chicanos, the political boundary between the United States and Mexico has no real significance, that it is an impertinence arbitrarily separating people of a common cultural heritage. The point is simply that Chicanos in no sense live in isolation; culturally and physically, they receive constant reinforcement from Mexico. In a remarkable essay about the durability of Mexican culture in the United States, John Rechy wrote: "Because only geographically the Río Grande . . . divides the United States from Mexico. Only geographically. The Mexican people of El Paso, more than half the population—and practically all of Smeltertown, Canutillo, Ysleta—are all and always completely Mexican, and will be. They speak only Spanish to each other and when they say the Capital they mean Mexico DF."[82]

The real threat to Chicano literature is not the pressure of cultural assimilation but the attrition brought on by exploitation and imitation. The exploitation I speak of is of two varieties; the first is economic. We live in a time when ethnicity is fashionable and ethnic literature salable. The upshot has been that in the rush to satisfy this interest, publishers sometimes issue works that are crude and inept and undeserving of publication.[83] This practice does not just distract; it also discourages writers from taking the time to cultivate their art. The second type of exploitation is practiced by those who use literature strictly for political purposes. Political literature, of course, is a tradition among Latin Americans and Chicanos, but the danger lies in the abandonment of aesthetic principles for purely political considerations. It is one thing to be a poet who writes about politics and quite another to be a political activist who simply uses poetry as a polemical device.

The dangers associated with imitation in Chicano literature are the result of the widespread praise—often condescending or offered out of a limited knowledge of the subject—lavished on only a few writers such as Anaya and Rivera. Unestablished writers sometimes hope to duplicate the achievement by imitating successful authors. Lately, for example, there has been a spate of works treating the magic and mysticism of Chicano folk culture after the fashion of Anaya, none with much success. At the same time, critics sometimes stifle creativity by rigidly defining what a Chicano work must be or by expecting young authors to match the achievement of established writers.

This leads us to a final question: What exactly is Chicano literature? I offer here not so much a definition as a characterization: Chicano literature is that body of work produced by United States citizens and residents of Mexican descent for whom a sense of ethnicity is a critical part of their literary sensibilities and for whom the portrayal of their ethnic experience is a major concern. Obviously, any attempt to categorize literature presents serious difficulties. For example, the work of Oscar Zeta Acosta is problematical here because Acosta wants so desperately to retrieve his ethnic heritage. But the reader is struck by the superficiality of his quest and the flimsiness of the foundation on which he hopes to build his ethnic identity. In the end, Acosta's books seem indistinguishable from numerous other works that lament the destruction of ethnicity in America.[84] Another problem related to labeling literary works is simply that authors frequently shift interests from one work to another. John Rechy's essay "El Paso del Norte" certainly should be considered Chicano literature, but his novel *City of Night*, which is virtually devoid of ethnic content, probably should not. Finally, because the Chicano experience is essentially cultural rather than racial, a question arises: Can a sense of Chicano ethnicity be acquired by a person who is not of Mexican heritage? The case of Amado Muro is instructive here. During the 1950s and 1960s, Muro wrote a series of sensitive and expertly wrought stories about Chicano life, some of which have been collected in anthologies of Chicano writing. After the writer's death, it came out that Muro was really Chester Seltzer, an Anglo newspaperman from Ohio who had married a Chicana named Amada Muro and settled in El Paso. He immersed himself in Chicano culture and finally wrote about it with great understanding.[85] Obviously, anyone characterizing Chicano literature has to allow for the rare exception like Seltzer who can bridge a wide cultural gulf and overcome traditional Anglo-American ethnocentrism. I do so happily.

Notes

1 This essay is a revised and expanded version of an earlier piece of the same title that appeared in *MELUS*, 5 (1978), 71–110.

2 The literature on the pre-Columbian cultures of Mexico is voluminous. Some of the best accounts in English are Miguel León-Portilla, *Aztec Thought and Culture* (Norman: Univ. of Oklahoma Press, 1963); León-Portilla, *Pre-Columbian Literature of Mexico* (Norman: Univ. of Oklahoma Press, 1969); and Laurette Séjourné, *Burning Water: Thought and Religion in Ancient Mexico* (London: Thames and Hudson, 1957).

3 It was, in fact, a foot soldier, Bernal Díaz del Castillo, who wrote one of the best accounts of the Spanish conquest, a work that included numerous references to Spanish folklore. See his *The Discovery and Conquest of Mexico* (New York: Farrar, 1956).

4 Gaspar Pérez de Villagrá, *History of New Mexico*, trans. Gilberto Espinosa (Los Angeles: Quivira Society, 1933), p. 129.

5 John E. Englekirk, "Notes on the Repertoire of the New Mexico Spanish Folk Theater," *Southern Folklore Quarterly*, 4 (1940), 227.

6 M. R. Cole, in *Los Pastores* (Boston: American Folklore Society, 1907), p. xx, traces some lines in a late ninteenth-century version of the "Shepherds" play to Calderón and Góngora.

7 Hostility toward the Indian was a major theme in both Spanish-American and Anglo-American literature. See Gilberto Espinosa, "Los Comanches," *New Mexico Quarterly*, 1 (1931), 133–46, as another example of New Mexican drama; this piece possibly dates from the late eighteenth century.

8 The question of the origins of the folk culture of the Spanish-speaking peoples of the Southwest has been hotly disputed. One camp argues that much of this culture, especially that in New Mexico, was transmitted directly from Spain and has retained its Spanish characteristics. A second group argues that southwestern culture is essentially Mexican, a contention that implies far greater Indian and mestizo influences. The problem is that traditions among the Spanish-speaking people in the Southwest, having been transmitted orally to a great extent, are difficult to trace. It is clear, however, that proponents of the Mexican position have the stronger case. For a good discussion of the controversy as related to drama see John E. Englekirk, "The Source and Dating of New Mexican Spanish Folk Plays," *Western Folklore*, 16 (1957), 232–55. For a broader consideration of the issue, see Paul Radin, "The Nature and Problems of Mexican Indian Mythology," *Journal of American Folklore*, 57 (1944), 26–36; and George M. Foster, "Some Characteristics of Mexican Indian Folklore," *Journal of American Folklore*, 58 (1945), 225–35.

9 See William Bascom, "The Forms of Folklore: Prose Narratives," *Journal of American Folklore*, 78 (1965), 3–20, for a treatment of differences among folk narratives.

10 Bacil F. Kirtley, " 'La Llorona' and Related Themes," *Western Folklore*, 19 (1960), 156.

11 See Robert A. Barakat, "Aztec Motifs in 'La Llorona,' " *Southern Folklore Quarterly*, 29 (1965), 288–96.

12 The other great figure of sixteenth-century Mexican legendry is the Virgin of Guadalupe, the patron saint of Mexico and another example of early Spanish-Indian cultural synthesis. If *la llorona* is a symbol of suffering, guilt, and fear, the Virgin represents the highest qualities of love and consolation and is herself an important force in Mexican and Chicano letters. For a provocative discussion of these two feminine

symbols in Mexican life, see Octavio Paz, *The Labyrinth of Solitude*, trans. Lysander Kemp (New York: Grove, 1961), pp. 65–88.

[13] See Américo Paredes, "The Mexican *Corrido*: Its Rise and Fall," in *Madstones and Twisters*, ed. Mody Boatright (Dallas: Southern Methodist Univ. Press, 1958) pp. 91–105, hereafter cited in text.

[14] This term was coined by Américo Paredes to refer to the presently defined nation of Mexico plus the adjacent areas of the United States where Mexican culture is still strong.

[15] There are a number of important folk-song collections from the Spanish-speaking Southwest. Among the best are Aurelio M. Espinosa, "Romancero nuevomejicano," *Revue Hispanique*, 33 (April 1915), 446–560; 40 (June 1917), 215–27; 41 (Dec. 1917), 678–80; Espinosa, "Los romances tradicionales en California," in *Homenaje ofrecido a Menéndez Pidal* (Madrid: Casa Editorial Hernando, 1925), I, 299–313; Terrence L. Hansen, "Corridos in Southern California," *Western Folklore*, 18 (1959), 203–32, 295–315; Arthur L. Campa, *Spanish Folk-Poetry in New Mexico* (Albuquerque: Univ. of New Mexico Press, 1946); and Américo Paredes, *A Texas-Mexican Cancionero* (Urbana: Univ. of Illinois Press, 1976). Further references to these works appear in the text.

[16] Américo Paredes, *"With His Pistol in His Hand"* (Austin: Univ. of Texas Press, 1958), pp. 132–50.

[17] For a discussion of the differences between folk poetry and "sophisticated" poetry, see Américo Paredes, "Some Aspects of Folk Poetry," *Texas Studies in Literature and Language*, 6 (1964), 213–25.

[18] A useful guide to the folklore of Chicanos is Michael Heisley, *An Annotated Bibliography of Chicano Folklore from the Southwestern United States* (Los Angeles: UCLA Center for the Study of Comparative Folklore and Mythology, 1977). A good sampling of Chicano folklore may be found in Richard Dorson, *Buying the Wind* (Chicago: Univ. of Chicago Press, 1964), pp. 415–95.

[19] I am indebted to Stanley Robe for his helpful comments on the relationship between the legend and the *corrido*.

[20] For further discussion of this early writing, see Philip D. Ortego, "Backgrounds of Mexican American Literature," Diss. Univ. of New. Mexico 1971. For some examples of this early narrative prose, see David Weber, *Northern Mexico on the Eve of the United States Invasion* (New York: Arno, 1976).

[21] See Raymund A. Paredes, "The Origins of Anti-Mexican Sentiment in the United States," in *New Directions in Chicano Scholarship*, ed. Ricardo Romo and Raymund Paredes (San Diego: Univ. of California, 1978), pp. 139–65. For a discussion of general Mexican attitudes toward the United States during this period, see Gene Brack, *Mexico Views Manifest Destiny*, 1821–1846 (Albuquerque: Univ. of New Mexico Press, 1975).

[22] Aurelio M. Espinosa and J. Manuel Espinosa, "The Texans," *New Mexico Quarterly Review*, 13 (1943), 299–308.

[23] In folklore, the trickster frequently assumes the form of an animal. See, for example, the discussion of Br'er Rabbit as a trickster in black American culture in Houston A. Baker, Jr., *Long Black Song* (Charlottesville: Univ. of Virginia Press, 1972), pp. 11–27.

[24] Verses and translations from Américo Paredes, *Cancionero*, p. 48. Translations are provided simply for the convenience of readers. No attempt has been made to retain lyrical flavor of original Spanish.

[25] See Américo Paredes, "The Anglo-American in Mexican Folklore," in *New Voices in American Studies*, ed. Ray B. Browne, Donald M. Winkel, and Allen Hayman (Lafayette, Ind.: Purdue Univ. Press, 1965), pp. 113–28. See also Merle E. Simmons, *The Mexican Corrido as a Source for the Interpretive Study of Modern Mexico, 1870–1950* (Bloomington: Univ. of Indiana Press, 1957), esp. pp. 419–60.

[26] The popular writer Joseph Holt Ingraham succinctly depicted the prevailing Texan disdain for Mexicans in his potboiler of 1846, *The Texas Rangers*. At one point in

the story, seventy rangers encounter three hundred Mexicans; the ranger captain, relishing the odds, throws his men into the fray with predictable results. The scene ends with the Mexicans careening toward the nearest sanctuary and the captain explaining the mathematical implications of the affair to his troops. "Now, my boys," he laughs, "never after this say one and one make two, but five and one make two. One Texan and five Mexicans. This is Rangers' arithmetic."

[27] Paredes, *Cancionero*, pp. 65–66. Paredes treats the Cortez ballad fully in *"With His Pistol in His Hand."*

[28] "El corrido del norte" in Hansen, p. 312.

[29] "El Renegado" in Manuel Gamio, *Mexican Immigration to the United States* (Chicago: Univ. of Chicago Press, 1930), pp. 93–94. See also Paul S. Taylor, "Songs of the Mexican Migration" in *Puro Mexicano*, ed. J. Frank Dobie (Dallas: Southern Methodist Univ. Press, 1935), pp. 221–45.

[30] See, for example, Rumel Fuentes, "Corridos de Rumel," *El Grito*, 6, No. 3 (1973), 4–40.

[31] Some diaries and journals turn up in strange places. Andrew García, a Texan who finally settled among the Nez Percé in Montana, began to record his memoirs about 1878 and eventually accumulated several thousand pages of manuscript. These were discovered in 1948, packed in dynamite boxes. See García, *Tough Trip through Paradise* (Boston: Houghton, 1967).

[32] For a study of one Mexican-American's book of personal verses, see T. M. Pearce, "What Is a Folk Poet?" *Western Folklore*, 12 (1953), 242–48.

[33] Doris L. Meyer, "Anonymous Poetry in Spanish-Language New Mexico Newspapers (1880–1900)," *Bilingual Review*, 2 (1975), 259–75. For a bibliogrqaphy of these newspapers, see Herminio Ríos and Lupe Castillo, "Toward a True Chicano Bibliography: Mexican-American Newspapers: 1848–1942," *El Grito*, 3, No. 4 (1970), 17–24, and *El Grito*, 5, No. 4 (1972), 40–47.

[34] José Elías González, "A C . . . V . . . ," *El Grito*, 5, No. 1 (1971), 26.

[35] See, for example, the *corridos* collected in Aurora Lucero-White Lea, *Literary Folklore of the Hispanic Southwest* (San Antonio: Naylor, 1953), pp. 134–50.

[36] Meyer, p. 268. Educated New Mexicans of the period were familiar with recent developments in Spanish-language literature. Newspapers, for example, published the works of contemporary Mexican poets like Manuel Gutiérrez Nájera and Justo Sierra. See Doris L. Meyer, "The Poetry of José Escobar: Mexican Emigré in New Mexico," *Hispania*, 61 (1978), 24–34. I am indebted to Meyer for providing me with several unpublished manuscripts dealing with the development of Mexican-American literature in New Mexico. My comments on the subject rely heavily on her work.

[37] Doris L. Meyer, "Early Mexican-American Responses to Negative Stereotyping," *New Mexico Historical Review*, 53 (1978), 75–91.

[38] Meyer, "Stereotyping," p. 8, trans. Meyer.

[39] For further comment on this issue, see Miguel A. Otero, *My Nine Years as Governor of the Territory of New Mexico, 1897–1906* (Albuquerque: Univ. of New Mexico Press, 1940), pp. 35–39.

[40] See Doris L. Meyer, "The Language Issue in New Mexico, 1880–1900: Mexican-American Resistance against Cultural Erosion," *Bilingual Review*, 4 (1977), 99–106.

[41] Madie Brown Emparan, *The Vallejos of California* (San Francisco: Univ. of San Francisco Press, 1968), p. 43; hereafter cited in text.

[42] Mariano G. Vallejo, "At Six Dollars an Ounce," in *California: A Literary Chronicle*, ed. W. Storrs Lee (New York: Funk and Wagnalls, 1968), p. 183.

[43] Quoted in Leonard Pitt, *The Decline of the Californios* (Berkeley: Univ. of California Press, 1968), p. 280. This work provides a discussion and bibliography of other historical works by Mexican-Americans in California.

[44] Vallejo's manuscript, except for an occasional excerpt, has gone unpublished. Bancroft regarded Vallejo as a valuable source but also as a writer who often mistook his

imagination for his memory. See Vallejo's reaction to Bancroft's charges in Emparan, p. 171.

[45] María Cristina Mena, "Marriage by Miracle," *Century*, March 1916, p. 727.

[46] Mena, "The Vine-Leaf," *Century*, Dec. 1914, pp. 289–92.

[47] By the 1920s Mexican-American authors were writing in both Spanish and English. See Doris L. Meyer, "Felipe Maximiliano Chacon: A Forgotten Mexican-American Author," in *New Directions in Chicano Scholarship*, 111–26.

[48] See Robert H. Torres, "Mutiny in Jalisco," *Esquire*, March 1935, pp. 37, 167–69; "The Brothers Jiminez," *Esquire*, June 1936, pp. 90–92.

[49] See Roberto Félix Salazar, "She Had Good Legs," *Esquire*, Oct. 1937, pp. 106, 182, 184; "Nobody Laughed in Yldes," *Esquire*, March 1938, pp. 84–85, 147.

[50] Salazar, "The Other Pioneers," in *We Are Chicanos*, ed. Philip D. Ortego (New York: Washington Square, 1973), pp. 150–51.

[51] It is noteworthy that, in depicting the Mexican revolutionaries, Torres is careful not to lend credence to the *bandido* caricature. His revolutionaries, violent and crude as they are, exist not as specifically defined Mexicans but merely as men utterly debased by the experience of war.

[52] The dynamics of this phenomenon are effectively portrayed by Willa Cather in *The Song of the Lark*. The novel features a Mexican named Juan Tellamantez who is so esteemed by the Anglo residents of Moonstone, Colorado, that they decorously avoid reference to his correct ethnicity; instead, they call him "Spanish Johnny." Notice, too, the name of a Mexican-American political organization started in 1928: League of United Latin American Citizens.

[53] See Aurelio M. Espinosa, "New Mexican Spanish Folklore," *Journal of American Folklore*, 27 (1914), 211.

[54] Nina Otero Warren, *Old Spain in Our Southwest* (1936; rpt. Chicago: Rio Grande, 1962), p. 64, hereafter cited in text.

[55] Juan A. A. Sedillo, "Gentleman of Río en Medio," *New Mexico Quarterly*, 9 (1939), 181.

[56] For other examples of New Mexican writing of this type, which are engaging and skillful despite the narrow sensibility, see the works of Angélico Chávez, particularly *New Mexico Triptych* (Paterson, N.J.: St. Anthony Guild, 1940); see also Sabine Ulibarrí, *Tierra Amarilla* (Albuquerque: Univ. of New Mexico Press, 1971).

[57] Josephina Niggli, *Mexican Village* (Chapel Hill: Univ. of North Carolina Press, 1945), p. 60.

[58] At one point in the book, the railroad train makes a special stop in Hidalgo, an event that occasions a large celebration. The local orchestra is engaged, and it does well enough until its members disagree over the next selection. Suddenly, the orchestra splits into two sections, both presumably still on the same platform, one group "playing a sad ballad of an illegitimate child to whom no one would speak because of his misfortune, and the other half concentrating on 'My Blue Heaven.' " Such, as Niggli sees it, is the paradox of Mexico.

[59] Mario Suárez, "El Hoyo," *Arizona Quarterly*, 3 (1947), 114–15.

[60] Suárez, "Señor Garza," *Arizona Quarterly*, 3 (1947), 116.

[61] Suárez, "Kid Zopilote," *Arizona Quarterly*, 3 (1947), 137.

[62] Suárez, "Maestría," *Arizona Quarterly*, 4 (1948) 373.

[63] For a fascinating discussion of the pachuco's relationship to the Mexican see Paz, *Labyrinth*, pp. 2–28.

[64] José Antonio Villarreal, *Pocho* (1959; rpt. Garden City, N.Y.: Doubleday-Anchor, 1970), p. 187.

[65] Villarreal, *Pocho*, p. 187.

[66] The term "Quinto Sol" itself refers to the Age of the Fifth Sun, which, according to Aztec belief, was to be the era of greatest achievement and prosperity.

[67] A good general study of Chicano language is Eduardo Hernández Chávez et al., *El lengua de los chicanos* (Arlington, Va.: Center for Applied Linguistics, 1975).

[68] Tino Villanueva, "Aquellos Vatos," in *El Espejo—The Mirror*, ed. Octavio Romano and Herminio Ríos (Berkeley: Quinto Sol, 1972), p. 265.

[69] An excellent study of this type of poetry is Guadalupe Valdés Fallis, "Code-Switching in Bi-Lingual Chicano Poetry," *Hispania*, 59 (1976), 877–86.

[70] Tomás Rivera, "M'ijo No Mira Nada," in *El Espejo*, p. 244.

[71] For a good general survey of Chicano poetry, see Joel Hancock, "The Emergence of Chicano Poetry," *Arizona Quarterly*, 29 (1973), 57–73; and Tomás Ybarra-Frausto, "The Chicano Movement and the Emergence of a Chicano Poetic Consciousness," *New Directions in Chicano Scholarship*, pp. 81–110.

[72] Tomás Rivera, ". . . y no se lo tragó la tierra," trans. Herminio Ríos C. (1971; rpt. Berkeley: Editorial Justa, 1977), p. 2; hereafter cited in text.

[73] Rolando Hinojosa-S., *Estampas del Valle y Otras Obras*, trans. Gustavo Valadez and José Reyna (1973; rpt. Berkeley: Editorial Justa, 1977), p. 39; hereafter cited in text.

[74] Hinojosa-S., *Generaciones y semblanzas* (Berkeley: Editorial Justa, 1977), p. 2.

[75] Another Chicano writer in Spanish of considerable skill is Miguel Méndez; see his *Peregrinos de Aztlán* (Tucson: Peregrinos, 1974).

[76] Rudolfo A. Anaya, *Bless me, Ultima* (Berkeley: Quinto Sol, 1972), p. 115.

[77] In addition to *Bless Me, Ultima*, Anaya has published two other novels: *Heart of Aztlán* (1976) and *Tortuga* (1979). Unfortunately, Anaya's fondness for mysticism, so nicely controlled in his first novel, becomes contrived and excessive in his later works.

[78] The following comments on Soto draw heavily from my two reviews of Soto's volumes, published in *Minority Voices*, 1 (1977), 106–08, and 2 (1978), 67–68.

[79] Gary Soto, "San Fernando Road," in *The Elements of San Joaquin* (Pittsburgh: Univ. of Pittsburgh Press, 1977), p. 3.

[80] Soto, "Wind," in *Elements*, p. 16.

[81] Soto, "El Niño," in *The Tale of Sunlight* (Pittsburgh: Univ. of Pittsburgh Press, 1978), p. 3.

[82] John Rechy, "El Paso del Norte," *Evergreen Review*, 2 (1958), 127. "DF" stands for *Distrito Federal* ("federal district"), a designation equivalent to District of Columbia.

[83] The most notable novel of this kind, complete with snappy title for instant identification, is Richard Vásquez, *Chicano* (Garden City, N.Y.: Doubleday, 1970).

[84] See Oscar Zeta Acosta, *The Autobiography of a Brown Buffalo* (San Francisco: Straight Arrow, 1972) and *The Revolt of the Cockroach People* (San Francisco: Straight Arrow, 1973).

[85] See *The Collected Stories of Amado Muro* (Austin: Thorpe Springs, 1979).

Native American Literatures: "old like hills, like stars"

Kenneth Lincoln

Foreword

"Listen"

Native Americans: the stress falls on a hemispheric complex of original peoples, histories, languages, cultures, ecologies, radically diverse and native to America for no less than forty thousand years.[1] Perhaps Native Americans go even further back, "older than men can ever be—old like hills, like stars," as Black Elk, the Lakota holy man, dreams of his tribal ancestors.[2] Native American origin myths speak of the peoples emerging out of this land. And the literatures of these many cultures are deeply rooted in America. "I do not know how many there are of these songs of mine," the Netsilik Eskimo, Orpingalik, told Knud Rasmussen. "Only I know that they are many, and that all in me is song. I sing as I draw breath."[3]

Out of at least five hundred original cultures in North America (perhaps four to eight million peoples speaking 500 distinct languages), by Vine Deloria's count 315 "tribes" remain in the United States alone.[4] They comprise roughly 700,000 full-bloods, or "bloods," in the reservation idiom; mixed-bloods, those with parents from different tribes; and "breeds," those who have one non-Indian parent. There are probably another half-million part-Indian people who live as whites.[5] The working definition of "Indian," though criteria vary from region to region, is a person with at least one quarter Indian blood and tribal membership.

Each tribe—whether an Alaskan Tlingit fishing village of forty extended kin or the Navajo "nation" of 140,000 in Arizona, Utah, and New Mexico—can be traditionally defined through a native language, an inherited place, and a set of traditions (speech, folklore, ceremony, and religion), a heritage passed from generation to generation in songs, legends, jokes, morality plays, healing rituals, event histories, social protocol, spiritual rites of passage, and vision journies to the sacred world. These cultural traditions evolved before the Old World "discovered" the New World, and many have been adapted to changing circumstances and remain strong today. The literature here "surprises by its contemplative perception of the visual world, its delicacy, its magic, and its terseness," as Jorge Luis Borges has said of "American Literature," taught from George Cronyn's early anthology *The Path on the Rainbow* (1918).[6]

The essay here begins with extant fragments of translated texts that have been recorded over the past century, for the most part—selected details that suggest the larger history and terrain of hundreds of tribal peoples. The discussion then leads into adaptations and translations by contemporary Indian writers. The method is more collective and impressionistic at the outset than documentary, responding in kind to the tones and states of mind implicit in Native American literatures. Though diverse, these many cultures are bonded in their sense of original tenure in America. Collectively they share native concerns and ways of thinking that transcend their differences. A beginning premise here posits that literature remains integrated with and inextricable from its embracing culture.

Given their diversities, Native American peoples share a long presence in the land. They traditionally idealize ancestral bonds, spiritual observances, oral cultural traditions, tribal life-styles involving shared goods and responsibilities, and they acknowledge an ecological inter-dependence—the principle of "sacred reciprocation," in the words of the anthropologist Barre Toelken.[7] Personal concerns are communal matters. Black Elk opens his life story, a remembered history that is part of the tribal literature of the Oglala Sioux: "It is a story of all life that is holy and is good to tell, and of us two-leggeds sharing in it with the four-leggeds and the wings of the air and all green things; for these are children of one mother and their father is one Spirit" (*BES*, p. 1). Literatures, in this sense, do not separate from the daily contexts of people's lives; the spoken, sung, and danced language binds the people as the living text of tribal life.

Ideally, then, Native American studies is a holistic subject that addresses indigenous tribes in their environments, grounded in their traditions, enacting their histories. Its methods are interdisciplinary and exploratory; its research asks questions in order to learn, rather than to assert.[8] Claude Lévi-Strauss in *Tristes Tropiques* recalls that as a beginning student he declined philosophy and law as self-referential, skirted geology as too widely defined in nonhuman terms, and bypassed psychology as too individually oriented; as an anthropologist who was open to im-provisation, he sought to fuse geological time, psychological humanism, and the epistemological concerns of philosophy with the disciplines of legal reasoning.[9] Lévi-Strauss' structural anthropology offers one international approach to native cultural studies, balanced by the more immediate field work of scholars in direct contact with tribal peoples.

The many native peoples with ancient tenure in America remain as varied as the land itself, rich in forests, prairies, rivers, valleys, seacoasts, mountains, and deserts; they were traditionally farmers, fishermen, food gatherers, and hunters, all inseparable from the land. Their cultures and histories differ as widely as do the terrain and climate, the flora and fauna, but all Native American tribes look back to indigenous time on this "turtle island," as some origin myths relate, unified in an ancient ancestral heritage. The Hopi village of Old Oraibi, on the third mesa in northern Arizona, has stood for at least 850 years. Canyon de Chelly, on the Navajo reservation near the Four Corners area, has been occupied for 2,500 years. In contrast, the landscape east of the Mississippi carries slim evidence of the once powerful tribes who lived in the forests now all but gone. Among others were the Powhatans who saved Jamestown colony with gifts of corn in the first severe winter of 1607, when the colonists, unprepared for the climate, were starving; the Five Civilized Tribes in the Southeast; the Ohio River and the Great Lakes tribes; and the Iroquois Confederacy, five and then six tribal alliances who negotiated "at the forest's edge" as equal powers with the Confederation of United States in the eighteenth century. Thomas Jefferson, who, like Benjamin Franklin, was an expert in Indian language and culture, is said to have translated "Iroquois" as "We the people". Some eastern tribes did survive displacement and revitalize their cultures over several centuries; Anthony Wallace gives as an example the twenty thousand Iroquois now living on reservations in New York State, Quebec, and Ontario.[10]

Beginning in the 1830s many Indian cultures were "removed" to the "Great American Desert" west of the Mississippi—a diaspora under presidential decree and military escort. Andrew Jackson told the eastern tribes, through agents:

> Say to them as friends and brothers to listen to their father, and their friend. Where they now are, they and my white children are too near to each other to live in harmony and peace. . . . Beyond the great River Mississippi . . . their father has provided a country large enough for them all, and he advises them to move to it. There their white brothers will not trouble them, and they will have no claim to the land, and they can live upon it, they and all their children, as long as grass grows and waters run.[11]

Already settled there, the Plains Indians resisted, protesting encroachment from eastern tribes shoved west and fighting the invasion of land-grabbing, gold-searching, buffalo-slaughtering, treaty-violating white immigrants who brought with them the railroad, guns, plows, fences, plagues, alcohol, and the Bible. When "the very animals of the forest" began fleeing "the hairy man from the east," Luther Standing Bear notes, "then it was for us that the Wild West began." The Indian Wars lasted from the 1860s to the Wounded Knee Massacre in 1890. From 1881 to 1883 the government employed marksmen to slaughter the remaining two and a half million buffalo (there had been fifteen million in 1700) that were the tribes' main life support.[12] The seasonal migrations of the tribes, following the game, were disrupted forever. Soldiers herded the survivors onto "reserves" of wasteland, issued "citizen's dress" (coat and trousers), and ordered them to "civilize." The secretary of the interior commented in 1872 on the policy of killing the buffalo to starve Indians onto reservations: "A few years of cessation from the chase will tend to unfit them for their former mode of life, and they will be the more readily led into new directions, toward industrial pursuits and peaceful habits."[13] The transition did not take place so easily or so soon; over a hundred years later many Indian peoples are still caught between cultures, living the worst conditions of both.

The many treaties and speeches spanning three centuries of contact represent the first recorded Indian literatures and give evidence of the precision and eloquence of Indian oratory. Constance Rourke sees these documents as the first American "chronicle plays,"[14] and Lawrence Wroth observes that the Indians "spoke as free men to free men, or often indeed as kings speaking to kings."[15] For over two hundred years even military defeat could not dislodge the Indians' spirit or their belief that America was their rightful place. After fleeing seventeen hundred miles during the bitter winter of 1877, Chief Joseph grieved with dignity as he surrendered the Nez Percé:

> My people, some of them, have run away to the hills and have no blankets, no food. No one knows where they are—perhaps they are freezing to death. I want to have time to look for my children and see how many of them I can find. Maybe I shall find them among the dead. Hear me, my chiefs, I am tired. My heart is sad and sick. From where the sun now stands I will fight no more forever.[16]

There is still honor in this sense of defeat. And in 1883 Sitting Bull, the Lakota warrior extradited from Canada, spoke to reservation bureaucrats:

> I am here by the will of the Great Spirit, and by His will I am a chief. My heart is red and sweet, and I know it is sweet, because whatever passes

near me puts out its tongue to me; and yet you men have come here to talk with us, and you say you do not know who I am. I want to tell you that if the Great Spirit has chosen anyone to be the chief of this country, it is myself. [17]

The Indian Bureau was first established in 1824 as part of the War Department. Despite their cultural and geographical diversities, Native Americans are aligned on one point: they are the only ethnic group in this nation that the United States has warred against and made treaties with—389 broken treaties. Vine Deloria discusses these claims in *Of Utmost Good Faith*, the opening words of a Continental Congress treaty signed by George Washington, the Northwest Ordinance of 1787:

> The utmost good faith shall always be observed toward the Indians, their lands and property shall never be taken from them without their consent; and in their property, rights, and liberty, they shall never be invaded or disturbed, unless in just and lawful wars authorized by Congress; but laws founded in justice and humanity shall from time to time be made, for preventing wrongs being done to them, and for preserving peace and friendship with them. [18]

Black Elk remembers of the 1870s that "they were chasing us now because we remembered and they forgot" (*BES*, p. 138).

While fighting to preserve their own cultural integrity and life-styles, Indians survived national policies of removal, starvation, warfare, and genocide. F. Scott Fitzgerald eulogized the national myth of a virgin land, "the green breast of the new world" in *The Great Gatsby*. Historian Francis Jennings revised that myth in *The Invasion of America*: "The American land was more like a widow than a virgin. Europeans did not find a wilderness here; rather, however involuntarily, they made one. . . . The so-called settlement of America was a *re*settlement, a reoccupation of a land made waste by the diseases and demoralization introduced by the newcomers." [19] It is an old and shameful story—a history largely fabled in the popular mind, seldom taught honestly in American schools, of murder and cultural suppression and displacement from native lands. It is most commonly dramatized in the 1830s Long March "removal" of the Five Civilized Tribes when over a third of the people died during forced relocation to Oklahoma. Asked his age by a census taker in 1910, the old Creek, Itshas Harjo, gave a purely elegiac answer:

> I have passed through many days and traveled a long way,
> the shadows have fallen all about me and I

can see but dimly.
But my mind is clear and my memory has not failed me.
I cannot count the years I have lived.
All that I know about my age is that I was old enough to draw the bow
and kill squirrels at the time of the second emigration of the
Creeks and Cherokees from the old country under
the leadership of Chief Cooweescoowee.
I was born near Eufaula, Alabama, and left there
when about fifteen years of age and the trip
took about a year,
for the peaches were green when we left Alabama
and the wild onions plentiful here when we arrived. [20]

In spite of such natural gift for poetry, Indians and their traditions were dismissed as barbaric, heathen, pagan. The commissioner of Indian Affairs stated in 1889:

> The Indians must conform to "the white man's ways," peaceably if they will, forcibly if they must. They must adjust themselves to their environment, and conform their mode of living substantially to our civilization. This civilization may not be the best possible, but it is the best the Indians can get. They can not escape it, and must either conform to it or be crushed by it. [21]

Even the skilled ethnologist James Mooney could write paternalistically in 1898, "The savage is intellectually a child, and from the point of view of the civilized man his history is shaped by trivial things."[22] Children "kidnapped" into government boarding schools, as Indian people saw it, were ridiculed for their Indian names, stripped of their tribal dress, and punished for speaking native tongues; eventually their elders were shamed out of believing in the ancestral spirit world, animal totems, and vision quests—a speaking landscape sacredly reciprocal with the people.

Culture after culture, beginning with Cortes' destruction of Tenochtitlán in 1521, witnessed deicide, as conquered tribes were forced to abandon their own religions and buckle on Christianity. The Indian encounters with missionaries are recorded with courteous irony. Red Jacket, the Seneca sachem, spoke to missionaries near Buffalo in 1805:

> [Y]ou say that you are right, and we are lost; how do we know this is to be true? . . .
>
> Brother, you say there is but one way to worship and serve the Great Spirit; if there is but one religion, why do you white people differ so much about it?

> . . . [W]e will wait a little while and see what effect your preaching
> has upon [other whites]. If we find it does them good, makes them honest,
> and less disposed to cheat Indians, we will then consider again what you
> have said. (Astrov, pp. 163–64)

The missionaries denied any "fellowship between the religion of God
and the works of the devil." They turned away, refusing to shake hands.
A century later, graced with humor and native courtesy, the bicultural
Hopi Don Talayesva could recant modern civilization and return to the
old ways on the desert:

> I had learned a great lesson and now knew that the ceremonies handed
> down by our fathers mean life and security, both now and hereafter. I
> regretted that I had ever joined the Y.M.C.A. and decided to set myself
> against Christianity once and for all. I could see that the old people were
> right when they insisted that Jesus Christ might do for modern whites
> in a good climate, but that Hopi gods had brought success to us in the
> desert ever since the world began. (Astrov, p. 248)

Pressures on Indians to assimilate date further back than southwest
mission ruins. In preparing for the 1876 Centennial in Philadelphia,
the Smithsonian Institution set about gathering Indian curiosities to be
displayed in the "Great Wigwam." One hundred Indians from eighteen
tribes were invited to encamp at the exhibition, but each had to be
judged satisfactory according to a thirteen-point checklist. Among the
requirements were these: every householder would be pleasant; he must
be one of the "cleanest and finest looking"; he must be influential in
the tribe; and he must speak English. He would be attended, the
invitation stated, by one wife "well skilled in household arts," a clean
child, a dog, and a pony.[23] That year, 1876, the government bartered
the Sioux out of the sacred Black Hills for five cents an acre. (George
Custer two years before had broken the Red Cloud Treaty leading
prospectors to gold "from the grass roots down," still the richest deposits
in North America.) Shortly after Custer charged fifteen thousand Sioux
and Cheyenne in villages on a Sun Dance retreat at the Little Big Horn,
the Centennial Indian invitations were rescinded.

A more insidious oppression threatens Indians today under melting-
pot policies of assimilation: direct and indirect federal coercion of tribes
to adapt to mainstream American culture. The disastrous "termination"
policies of the 1950s are currently being revived in congressional bills
to abrogate treaties, and "when someone says 'termination,'" an anthropologist of the Montana Blackfeet writes, "the Indians hear 'exter-

mination.' "[24] This essay then seeks to defend cultural independence, as reflected in the literatures of many hundreds of tribal societies extant in America.

The Indians, America's most diverse minority, hold the status, independently, of "domestic dependent nations" (Chief Justice John Marshall opinion of 1831, *The State of Georgia* v. *The Cherokee Nation*), that is, nations within a nation whose members are legally "wards" of the federal government, yet remain "sovereign." They occupy separate land bases of some fifty-three million acres, salvaged from the 140 million acres allotted under the 1887 Dawes Act.[25] The lands contain half of the uranium and one third of the strip-mine coal in the United States (the coal alone worth perhaps a trillion dollars), and yet some reservations suffer the worst hardship in America: incomes at half the poverty level, an average schooling of five years, the highest alcoholism and suicide rates in the nation, substandard housing and social services, high infant mortality, a higher incidence of tuberculosis and diabetes than any other minority in the country, and an average life expectancy of forty-four years.[26]

Historical ironies notwithstanding, traditional Indian literatures, taken mostly from religious and healing ceremonies, idealize the harmonious balance of spiritual and worldly concerns throughout the world. Within the context of this native vision, fueled by pastoral myths of the noble savage and a return to the Garden of Eden, both Indians and non-Indians tend to gloss contemporary reservation life and take comfort in visions of the way things used to be. We still fail to see the Native American as an individual with a tribal and individual identity. "To be an Indian in modern American society," Vine Deloria writes, "is in a very real sense to be unreal and ahistorical" (*Custer*, p. 2). The transparent "Indian," a film and fictional stereotype, lingers as a silhouette—the only minority anonymously enshrined on our currency, the Indian-head nickel. And the true history of national Indian affairs shapes an often bitter resistance to "the American way." D. H. Lawrence wrote:

> The desire to extirpate the Indian. And the contradictory desire to glorify him. Both are rampant still, to-day.
> The bulk of the white people who live in contact with the Indian to-day would like to see this Red brother exterminated; not only for the sake of grabbing his land, but because of the silent, invisible, but deadly hostility between the spirit of the two races. The minority of the whites intellectualize the Red Man and laud him to the skies. But this minority of whites is mostly a high-brow minority with a big grouch against its own whiteness.[27]

When America shadows Native Americans on its money and names professional teams the Warriors, Indians, Redskins, or Aztecs, the stereotype surely reaches down through the sentimental myth of the noble savage into "the bloody loam" of national history. The refracted image belies several million Indians whose lives were destroyed or who were violently "removed" from their native soil.[28] And today, there seem "so few of them left," Frederick Turner observes in his introduction to *The North American Indian Reader*, "so far away from the centers of population" (Turner, p. 9). This, too, is open for discussion, since Native Americans represent the fastest growing minority in America, having doubled in population between 1950 and 1970, and more than half now live off-reservation, many in major cities. If the people are few in number, proportionately, they are many in ancient diversity, and they stand large in the national consciousness. We would do well to appreciate their literatures as origins of cultural history in America.

I. Tribal Poetics

Except for the Mayans and the Aztecs, North American tribal peoples evolved without written languages, as oral cultures living mouth to mouth, age to age, passing on a daily culture. Their literatures survived as remembered myths and rituals, songs, poems, narrative tales, legends, and parables. Rich literary cultures came to the attention of ethnologists such as Frances Densmore, Washington Matthews, Ruth Benedict, Daniel G. Brinton, Francis La Flesche, Alice C. Fletcher, and others.[29] Once these oral works were translated into English, Americans began to recognize the importance of Native American literatures.

Since the early research in ethnology and folklore of almost a century ago, a new literary interest in Native Americans has developed, accelerated by the alternative cultural explorations in the 1960s. Anthologies of traditional Indian song-poems, dream visions, narratives, speeches, life stories, and religious rituals illustrate the remarkable variety and scope of literatures in hundreds of tribal cultures: George Cronyn's early work, *The Path of the Rainbow* (1918), was followed much later by Margot Astrov's *The Winged Serpent* (1946); A. Grove Day's *The Sky Clears* (1951); John Bierhorst's *In the Trail of the Wind* (1971), *Four Masterworks of American Indian Literature* (1974), and *The Red Swan* (1976); Thomas Sanders and Walter Peek's *Literature of the American Indian* (1973); Gloria Levitas' *American Indian Prose and Poetry* (1974); Frederick Turner's *North American Indian Reader* (1974); Alan Velie's *American Indian Literature* (1979); and two more experimental works,

Jerome Rothenberg's *Shaking the Pumpkin* (1972) and William Brandon's *The Magic World* (1971).[30] Indeed, a number of America's writers—from Thoreau, saying "Indians" with his dying breath, to novelists such as Cooper and Melville, Faulkner and Hemingway, Berger and Kesey, to contemporary poets Snyder, Merwin, Rexroth, Olson, Levertov, Rothenberg, Creeley, Kelly, Berg, Simpson, Wagoner, Norman, and Tedlock—have found a need to "go native," ingenuously or genuinely, seeking their more integral place in this land, their uses among people, their tribal language and audience, their raw material in the myth and history and imagination of America. "Not for himself surely to be an Indian, though they eagerly sought to adopt him into their tribes, but the reverse: to be *himself* in a new world, Indianlike" (Williams, p. 137). Non-Indians cannot be Indians, but they can discover or rediscover their own tribal place in this earth. It appears that modern American poets seek to revive a personal relationship with the spoken word, a natural environment, and a tribal audience. Their interest in America's earliest poetry signals an interest in the life and immediacy of their own "language of the tribe."[31] This can be "re-creative" translation, giving birth to songs in a new medium and cultural tongue, as Margot Astrov and Walter Benjamin call for.[32]

If the tribal poet has created an integrated context of beauty, ethics, and form, how can the translator re-create Native-American oral traditions—hundreds of indigenous literatures permeated with religion, mythology, ritual, morality and heuristics, national history, social entertainment, economics, magic formulas, healing rites, codes of warfare and hunting and planting and food gathering, visions and dreams, love incantations, death chants, lullabies, and prayers—in printed words for modern audiences? One language may be regarded as magically powerful, the other as only a functional means of transmitting ideas. "From what you say," Ikinilik told Knud Rasmussen, "it would seem that folk in that far country of yours *eat* talk marks just as we eat caribou meat" (Rasmussen, p. 195). Peter Nabokov reminds us that the first Cherokee shamans to adapt Sequoya's 1821 syllabary, the earliest "talking leaves" north of Mexico, hid their transcriptions in trees and attics for fear of exploitation.[33]

Translators must look two ways at once: they must carry over, as much as possible, the experiential integrity of the original, and they must regenerate the spirit of the source in a new verbal performance. Two artists, working in two languages, collaborate at the beginning and end; their work is neither simultaneous nor identical, but reciprocal, and directed toward different audiences. When the tribal ear listens ceremonially at one end of this continuum and the existential eye scans the printed page at the other end, questions of form and function, how and why one uses language, and the designs of literature naturally come into play. "Firmly planted. Not fallen from on high: sprung up from below," Octavio Paz, the Mexican poet, says. The voiced words—like the handmade object, the well-told tale, the finely wrought poem— speak of "a mutually shared physical life," not of art as icon, commodity, or art for its own precious sake. "A glass jug, a wicker basket, a coarse muslin huipil, a wooden serving dish: beautiful objects, not despite their usefulness but because of it."[34]

The most basic translative paradigm is that of one person listening to another telling a story. But consider the variables in *Black Elk Speaks*, perhaps the most ubiquitous text in Native American studies, "*as told through* John G. Neihardt (*Flaming Rainbow*)" (*BES*, title page).

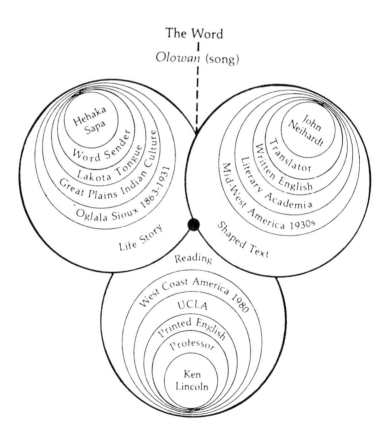

The Word
|
Olowan (song)

At any one moment (or "word") here, three overlapping sets of at least six variables come into play:

The *individual* in his or her own psychogenetic complex
The individual's *role* in the event at hand
The *medium* involved
The *space/time* of the event (synchronic moment)
The *cultural matrix* around the event (diachronic history)
The *performance* itself

Hehaka Sapa (Black Elk) sat on the South Dakota prairie for days with his family and friends in the spring of 1931, describing for John Neihardt his half-century as an Oglala Sioux healer. Ben Black Elk translated his father's spoken Lakota into English speech, as Neihardt asked questions. Then Ben Black Elk translated Neihardt's questions into Lakota, while Neihardt's daughter Enid recorded the conversation in stenographic notes. A *wicasa wakan* ("holy man"), partly blind, Black Elk sat at the vortex of an oral performance, as distinct from a written story, among his extended family. His narration was interspersed with comments from his friends Standing Bear, Iron Hawk, and Fire Thunder. Neihardt later transformed these "translations" into a written text, exercising poetic license with the notes. Readers half a century later assimilate the published account into their own experience. Spanning a century, the process moves from visionary-healer-singer-teller to poet-translator to literate reader; from spoken recall to written translation to reading a book; from the environmental anthropology (the where and when) of each person involved to the next; from the cultural traditions and histories of each to another; from informant to creative writer to reader. To note these passages stimulates care for the details of translation; it raises questions about how one moves toward, or slides from away from, genuine translations.

"The poem's form is the sound it makes when spoken," says H. S. McAllister.[35] Translations must risk distorting the forms of reality in song-poems, since the world does not lie flat on a page or fit within its margins. The page serves as a canvas, with dimensions, perspectives, and energies around words as objects in space, moving according to design among other objects in space. At the same time, this translation should not violate a second audience's expectations, vis-à-vis the boundaries of reality or the behavior of poetry: to push too hard on the re-creative metaphor is to lose song and shape through overstylization. A translation can miss the truth of place and cultural history by looking sideways in space, or mar the delicacies of re-creative poetry by mirroring itself. A poem may hang mobile in space like the leaves on a tree. It may serpentine through a Hopi rain dance in stately choral strophes, arrange itself in a Navajo origin myth as patiently as strata in a canyon wall, or burst freely around Plains drumming and chanting. A poem may lap quietly as lake ripples beaching on a Chippewa shore, or stalk powerfully through darkness over a broken Iroquois terrain. It may soar with the trickster Raven over the Pacific Northwest, or descend into itself, as *kachina* gods disappearing into a kiva. The original song in its human reality and the transplanted poem in its spatial equivalent are measured, shaped, imaged, pitched movements in space.

How do members of Indian cultures look upon their languages and literatures? A. Grove Day writes:

> The Indians made poems for many reasons: to praise their gods and ask their help in life; to speak to the gods through dramatic performances at seasonal celebrations or initiations or other rites; to work magical cures or enlist supernatural aid in hunting, plant-growing, or horsebreeding; to hymn the praises of the gods or pray to them; to chronicle tribal history; to explain the origins of the world; to teach right conduct; to mourn the dead; to arouse warlike feelings; to compel love; to arouse laughter; to ridicule a rival or bewitch an enemy; to praise famous men; to communicate the poet's private experience; to mark the beauties of nature; to boast of one's personal greatness; to record a vision scene; to characterize the actors in a folk tale; to quiet children; to lighten the burdens of work; to brighten up tribal games; and, sometimes, to express simply joy and a spirit of fun.[36]

Native Americans seem to believe that words make things happen. "In the beginning, the word gave origin to the Father," a Uitoto myth begins (Astrov, p. 20). The primacy of language interfuses people with their environment: an experience or object or person is inseparable from its name. And names allow us to see, as words image the spirits of things. Black Elk says of his Great Vision: "It was the pictures I remembered and the words that went with them; for nothing I have ever seen with my eyes was so clear and bright as what my vision showed me; and no words that I have ever heard with my ears were like the words I heard. I did not have to remember these things; they have remembered themselves all these years" (*BES*, p. 49).

A common language is essential. Oral traditions unite the tribal people, just as they poeticize the common speech. For the most part, tribal cultures still express themselves through spoken literatures, and the peoples' "literary history" is a function of memory, imagination, and daily and seasonal ritual. The arts of language remain communally open; the word is a tribal bond. According to Vine Deloria, the original names of twenty-seven different tribes meant, in various forms, "the people": "the people" (Arikara), "real people" (Cherokee), "the flesh" (Zuni), "men of men" (Pawnee), "the allies" (Lakota), "first people" (Biloxi), and "people of the real speech" (Winnebago).[37]

Scott Momaday tells of the Kiowa arrow maker who sat working in his tepee with his wife. He fashioned and straightened arrows in his mouth, and the best arrows carried teeth marks. Once at night he saw a stranger looking in from the darkness. The arrow maker said, in Kiowa, that if the outsider understood the language spoken in the tribe, he would give his name and be welcome. The stranger remained silent. Casually the arrow maker bent his bow in one direction, then another, and then killed the outsider with a single arrow.[38] Words are penetrant as arrows; the craft, ceremony, power, and defense of the tribal family depend on them. A well-chosen word, like a well-made arrow, pierces to the heart.

Oral tribal poetry remains for the most part anonymous, for tribal poets see themselves as essentially keepers of the sacred word bundle. They regard rhythm, vision, talent, nature, and words as gifts that precede and continue beyond any human life. Song-poets discover nature's poems; they never pretend to have invented a "poetic" world apart from nature; they believe they are permitted to husband songs as one tends growing things. The poets sing for their place in the tribe and in nature. They take no credit for having created their songs; instead they give thanks that the songs have chosen them. The anonymity leaves them both unassuming and dignified, twice honored. They give the songs back to those powers that granted them voice, humbling themselves before nature's tribal circle, their visions enriching the public rituals so vital to tribal health. Their aesthetics prove utilitarian, as they believe that tribal life needs beauty. Among the Pueblos "good" and "beautiful" are the same word.[39]

Tribal life centers on a common blood, a shared and inherited body of tradition, a communal place, a mutual past and present. The tribe's image is a circle. Black Elk questions why the grass is kept penned up with the people in cities, since the spirits have shown him the "sacred hoop" of the world: "You have noticed that everything an Indian does is in a circle, and that is because the Power of the World always works in circles, and everything tries to be round" (*BES*, p. 198). Daily relationships, at once personal and ceremonial, preserve this continuity; all tribal members are regarded as close kin, as a parent to a child or a brother to a sister. Tribal values include sharing material and spiritual wealth, remaining loyal to one's kin, caring about one's place in the world, maintaining an extended family, and being kind in the older sense of the word, that is, "of the same kind" and "kind" or generous within that bond. So to be giving and gracious remains natural among kind people.

Despite their separate histories, Native American tribes and literatures interconnect in a poetics that resists the European idea of the artist's primacy as word and world maker (*poietes*, "maker," in Greek), imposing order on nature through his craft, relying on the fixity of the printed word. Native American literatures, given their diversity, intersect in a common, organic aesthetics—a poetic kinship that unites people, other earthly creatures, the gods, and nature in one great tribe.

Rooted Words

Indian traditions place words organically in the world as animate and generative beings. Words are the roots of continuing tribal origins, genetic cultural sources within nature. Indian literatures are then grounded in language that brings into focus a single detail, as in the words of this Ojibwa song-poem:

> The bush is sitting under a tree and
> singing (Brandon, p. 96)

Secure within nature, the bush sings its own poetry "under a tree." The poem is landscaped with care toward the ecology that conditions singing, rather than the triumph of song. The language remains spare, neither more nor less than the evoked "thing" itself. Words as things carry their essential meanings, and the minimal world elicits the poet's attention to small detail, as it sharpens response to the larger world. In a Quechuan poem an insect orders the night's darkness, even death:

> The water bug is drawing
>   the shadows of the evening
>   toward him on the water (Brandon, p. 96)

The poems sing the origins of people, creatures, things, in local revelations, exactly where they exist. The people glimpse truths unexpectedly, out of the corner of the eye, as nature compresses and constantly surprises with its rich mystery. All things are alive, suggestive, sacred.

A Sioux holy man reverently addresses a stone as *Tunkashila*, a word that also means "Grandfather."[40] On the Great Plains, where everything exists in vast emptiness, an isolated rock provides the world's

cornerstone, a resting place for restless spirits, as in this fragment from
an Omaha ritual:

> unmoved
> from time without
> end
> you rest
> there in the midst of the paths
> in the midst of the winds
> you rest
> covered with the droppings of birds
> grass growing from your feet
> your head decked with the down of birds
> you rest
> in the midst of the winds
> you wait
> Aged one (Brandon, p. 83)

Nature here bases wandering spirits—winds, birds, grasses that come
and go, even droppings on the earthly origins. The rock's patience serves
as the poem's refrain: "you rest . . . you rest . . . you rest . . . you
wait / Aged one." Time is here a permanence of place.

Words do not come after or apart from what naturally is, but are
themselves natural genes, tribal history in the bodies of the people.
People are born into their tribal tongue when they enter the world.
They do not make up words any more than they make up nature. Singers
chant songs, drawing tonally on the voice as an interpretive human
instrument to give life to the words living in the mouth and body;
pitch modulates and brings out meaning; accent gives cadence to meanings
as they draw together. Instead of rhyming words (the poem as unifying
technique), the songs rhyme perceptions, moods, natural objects, the
world as word (the poem as unifying association). A lyric threads the
story through poetic time as chords tie the song together harmonically.
The Tewa sing to Mother Earth and Father Sky, and the image of a
weaver's loom appears:

> Then weave for us a garment of brightness;
> May the warp be the white light of morning,
> May the weft be the red light of evening,
> May the fringes be the falling rain,
> May the border be the standing rainbow. (Astrov, p. 221)

Formulaic repetition makes a ritual of the sky's interwoven lights, and

resonances between rhymed events stretch the song taut over the sky
loom ("fringes"—"falling rain"; "border"—"rainbow"). In a Navajo
night chant, the singer's craft is discovered in a natural "house made
of dawn":

> May it be beautiful before me.
> May it be beautiful behind me.
> May it be beautiful below me.
> May it be beautiful above me.
> May it be beautiful all around me.
> In beauty it is finished. (Astrov, p. 186)

The Navajo perceive nature through tribal correspondences:

```
cotton
        motion
                clouds
frog
    hail
            potatoes
                    dumplings
cloud water
        fog
            moss
smoke
    cloud
        rain
                acceptance
                    breathing in⁴¹
```

"Do you picture it," a Zuni asked Dennis Tedlock as he was translating,
"or do you just write it down?"[42]

Minimal Presence

The poetry suggests a philosophical awareness of things, their
resonances, their places. Space shapes objects just as silence determines
sound; objects in turn are defined at their circumferences, where they
cease to exist. Shadows and echoes silhouette origins. "Listen!" the poets
sing, invoking silence as the initial chord of a song-poem, the essential
words depending on the silence from which they originate. True poets
listen as they sing:

> There is in the Indian towns also a sense of timelessness and peace. No
> one who has watched the winter solstice ceremonies at Jemez can have
> failed to perceive the great spiritual harmonies which culminate in those
> ancient rites. None who has heard the deep droning concert of the singers
> and the insistent vibration of the drums can have mistaken the old sacred
> respect for sound and silence which makes for the magic of words and
> literature.[43]

The strengths of young and old cross in the poet, who can sense words
in the desert silence, pattern in the forest shadows, design in the falling
stars, the return of the summer sun at the winter solstice.

Poetry and morality fuse in storytelling, and listening provides an
occasion for learning tribal values. Morals lie inherent in the tales,
the performing context of the story, the participation of audience and
teller, and the season of telling.[44] The storyteller does not gloss the tale
or tell too much; the listeners imagine their places in the story.

Just as silence speaks to the mind, so space is fertile without
objects. "Nothing" can be suggestive presence, as echoed in the southwestern deserts or resonant on the Great Plains or shadowed in the
northern woodlands. Tribal people learn to know richness in a sense of
loss; they know through a necessary economy, tempered in poverty,
that more is not always better. The tribe depends on natural growth
cycles for survival, and to go over or under what is necessary threatens
the balance of nature and tribe. People in tribal cultures learn to give
in order to live: witness the ceremonial "give-aways" and potlatches
and rituals of sacrifice. Thoreau records that the Iroquois practiced a
"busk" ritual of burning all possessions every fifty years to begin anew.
Nature is ever alive with spirits, powers, mysteries, sacred objects, and
sacred spaces.

Sacred Play

A truly sacred world allows for a sense of mockery and play that
inverts reality's weight. Tribal kinsmen joke to lift their spirits, play
to loosen an encumbering seriousness; their play at once tempers and
includes the serious world. Seneca poetry, Jerome Rothenberg observes,
"works in sets of short songs, minimal realizations colliding with each
other in marvelous ways, a very light, very pointed play-of-the-mind,
nearly always just a step away from the comic (even as their masks are),
the words set out in clear relief against the ground of the (Meaningless)
refrain. Clowns stomp & grunt through the longhouse, but in subtler
ways too the encouragement to 'play' is always a presence."[45]

A storyteller mythologizes holy foolishness as a means of releasing light spirits into their own place, next to dignity. Sioux *heyokas* sport sacramentally as clowns, just as the Trickster gods play with men. To become a *heyoka* one dreams of lightning, the spiritual connection between sky and earth. Southwest *kachina* gods called "mudheads" use laughter to cleanse magically. Iroquois "False Face" wearers mimic the wrong ways to do things. Those touched by the gods at play—saints, clowns, priests, idiots, children, elders—become holy and foolish in one gesture (in like manner the English word "silly" traces a double lineage back to the Old English "saelig," meaning holy and foolish).

Laughter, song, dance, and chant move the tribe through public ritual into nature. In healing ceremonies and celebrations the people dance to draw life from touch with the earth; they grieve to voice sorrow openly. Black Elk, a *heyoka*, or "holy fool" priest, says,

> You have noticed that the truth comes into this world with two faces. One is sad with suffering and the other laughs; but it is the same face, laughing or weeping. When people are already in despair, maybe the laughing face is better for them; and when they feel too good and are too sure of being safe, maybe the weeping face is better for them to see. (*BES*, pp. 192–93)

Tribal stories pivot on contrasts and reversals, releasing sorrow, sparking laughter, inspiring invention, purging primal fears. They give humankind a range of characters and settings—from the animals and the earth to the gods and the sky. Black Elk laments that the sacred hoop of his tribe is broken and the flowering tree is withered after the Wounded Knee Massacre: "a people's dream that died in bloody snow" (*BES*, p. 2). Yet this *heyoka* healed his people over a lifetime with sacred play. A Nez Percé narrative poem is entitled "coyote borrows Farting Boy's asshole, tosses up his eyes, retrieves them, rapes old women and tricks a young girl seeking power" (Rothenberg, *Pumpkin*, p. 105). In a Cochiti story Coyote talks Beaver into exchanging wives, to Coyote's chagrin and his wife's pleasure (Brandon, p. 54). In a Hopi tale Coyote Old Man deflowers the tribal virgin, whom both gods and men have courted unsuccessfully; he escapes and parades his genitals on a distant hill; then the rain god hunts him down and kills him (Brandon, p. 44). The Maricopas tell how the Creator gave teeth of sun's fire to a gentle snake, as protection against a bullying rabbit, and the creatures in vengeance killed their Creator (Astrov, p. 26). In all these tales gods and spirits walk the earth at one with plants, animals, and human beings. Powers of transformation interrelate both animate and inanimate beings in a reverse form of spiritual anthropomorphism: instead of projecting human forms on animals and the gods, men take their personal characteristics, family names, and clan names from the animal and natural world— Black Elk, Crow Dog, Lone Wolf, Eagle Heart, Crazy Horse, Two Moons, Sun Chief, Star Boy, Sweet Grass Woman.

The natural world speaks for itself without shame or self-consciousness, dancing its life and language. The Makah sing:

> Mine is a proud village, such as it is,
> We are at our best when dancing.[46]

Decorous senses blossom in the "orchidean" Mayan and Aztec cultures, elegized by William Carlos Williams (*American Grain*, p. 27). As the dance plays itself through, Aztec flowers bloom on the poet's lips, singing: a word is a flower is the dawn is a quetzal is a dewdrop is human life—beautiful, sexual, changing, perishable. In the words of a Nahuatl poet, "The flower in my heart blossoms in the middle of the night" (Brandon, p. 32). Passion. Human sacrifice. The terror of beauty.

No single mood corners nature's temperaments. No single curiosity exhausts the possibilities of surprise. Given a respect for nature's range, tribal peoples are free to experiment with natural rules, to discover inherent truths by trial and error, to carry on their own investigation of traditions and moralities. Trusting tribal boundaries and a local sense of origin frees the people to explore their heritage and environment. The Pueblo moves over a space as small as a mesa top, down through kivas into the earth, among family and extended kin, back into a communal past working itself out in the present. A plainsman, in contrast, once roamed a thousand miles a season on horseback and felt at home in motion. The "traditional" freedoms, unconfined by a sense of space, empower a tribal member to celebrate life without restriction, disregarding momentary hardship, unafraid of dislocation, and without self-pity. Plenty-Coups, chief of the Crow, told the White "Sign-talker":

> I am old. I am not graceful. My bones are heavy, and my feet are large. But I know justice and have tried all my life to be just, even to those who have taken away our old life that was so good. My whole thought is of my people. I want them to be healthy, to become again the race they have been. I want them to learn all they can from the white man, because he is here to stay, and they must live with him forever.[47]

Sense Magic

The Indian poet sees the magic of the world through symbolic detail. Lame Deer, the Sioux medicine man, speaks of the attention of a natural visionary:

But I'm an Indian. I think about ordinary, common things like this pot. The bubbling water comes from the rain cloud. It represents the sky. The fire comes from the sun which warms us all—men, animals, trees. The meat stands for the four-legged creatures, our animal brothers, who gave of themselves so that we should live. The steam is living breath. . . . We Indians live in a world of symbols and images where the spiritual and the commonplace are one. To you symbols are just words, spoken or written in a book. To us they are part of nature, part of ourselves—the earth, the sun, the wind and the rain, stones, trees, animals, even little insects like ants and grasshoppers. We try to understand them not with the head but with the heart, and we need no more than a hint to give us the meaning. (*Lame Deer*, p. 108)

The world, as tribal seers know it, suggests endlessly. The seers feel the world "real" enough to be guided by and trust what they feel, seeing from "the heart's eye," as Lame Deer says. Seers heed intuitions, believe in a perceptual reality cognate with nature's reality. If dreams are unreal, Momaday's grandmother spirit cautions him, then so are the dreamers.[48]

A seer walks the Yaqui *brujo*'s "path with heart": " 'The world is all that is encased here,' [Juan Matus] said, and stomped the ground. 'Life, death, people, the allies, and everything else that surrounds us. The world is incomprehensible. We won't ever understand it; we won't ever unravel its secrets. Thus we must treat it as it is, a sheer mystery!' " Castaneda, the stumbling anthropologist and shaman's apprentice, must be surprised into knowledge. " 'We have exhausted nothing, you fool,' [Juan Matus] said imperatively. '*Seeing* is for impeccable men. Temper your spirit now, become a warrior, learn to *see*, and then you'll know that there is no end to the new worlds for our vision.' "[49]

"Go to a mountain-top & cry for a vision," the Sioux holy men counsel (Rothenberg, *Pumpkin*, p. 197).

The spirit world and the natural world intermingle through dreams, most intense in the traditional vision quest, whether that of a Papago on pilgrimage from the desert to gather sea salt, or an Eskimo shaman who drops to the bottom of the sea asking forgiveness from the earth daughter, or a Sioux warrior lamenting in a vision pit on a lonely mountaintop. Seers know the world with care, attune themselves with natural magic. Their healing aligns the people with the natural health and energy of the universe, the balance of all things. A medicine man ties the people's needs into the things of the world, releasing the spirits in things to move through the tribe. A thought is a spiritual act; a word has the magical power to actualize spirits.

Dreams relay visions from the spirit world; sacramental songs ritualize the dream myths, bearing visions into the world (a shaman is midwife to the gods). A Sioux *heyoka* sings:

> The day of the sun has been my strength.
> The path of the moon shall be my robe.
> A sacred praise I am making.
> A sacred praise I am making. (*BES*, p. 193)

Such song-poems are tribal conductors of dream power, and "sometimes dreams are wiser than waking," says Black Elk (*BES*, p. 10). The spirits and ancestors speak to the living in dreams, giving their daily lives a sacred strangeness. Incantations, dream visions, totems, and imitative magic set up conduits of well-being and power in forces believed beyond the limits of human beings in this world. Dreams heighten people's awareness—as does fear when it is regarded positively—proving medicinal, therapeutic, because cleansing and energizing the tribal spirit. The word medicine of a Navajo chant heals a supplicant asking health from the gods. The formula: chant, learn, be healed, remember:

> The singer stroked the patient's body
> and pressed his body to the patient's body.
>
> Have you learned? they asked him
> and he answered, Yes.
>
> They sang all night, and the patient learned
> and was well.
>
> Then he was told to be sure and remember all that
> he had been taught, for everything forgotten went
> back to the gods. (Brandon, pp. 64–65)

The healing power of these words is inspired by the gods, and yet it is communal, so that the sacred world is again seen as common in the mythic origins of religious thought. Black Elk's "great vision" has no healing power until his people perform it tribally and locate it ceremonially in their daily life. The Navajo sing from the Night Chant:

> In beauty
>   you shall be my representation
>
> In beauty
>   you shall be my song
>
> In beauty
>   you shall be my medicine

> In beauty
>> my holy medicine (Brandon, p. 62)

A singer works at dreaming and seeing but does not dwell on the work. The work ethic can be transcended by a dream ethic, an intuitive morality inspired by the spirit world. "Men who work cannot dream, and wisdom comes in dreams," warned the Nez Percé, Smohalla of the Dreamer Religion. "You ask me to plow the ground. Shall I take a knife and tear my mother's breast? Then when I die she will not take me to her bosom to rest" (Astrov, p. 85).

Tribal Song

>> I
>> the song
>> I walk here (Brandon, p. 3)

This Modoc chant is imagined apart from any song maker. The people come to it for life, tradition, medicine, play; the tribe lives in the song's daily presence. Such oral literature arises out of the common ceremonies of people speaking day to day, joining in tribal song. Many tribes speak of hearing the earth's heartbeat in their songs, as in the healing Brush Dance songs of northern California. The chanted rhythms rise with the heartbeat, drums, moving feet; through them the people dance to the earth's pulse. The singing lives in tribal time, in rhythm with nature's cyclic time—the seasons of planting, growing, harvesting, and returning to the living earth.

Oral poetry is kinetic ritual. The body dances and sings alive with the mind. Black Elk says of the grandfather stallion's song in his vision: "It was so beautiful that nothing anywhere could keep from dancing. The virgins danced, and all the circled horses. The leaves on the trees, the grasses on the hills and in the valleys, the waters in the creeks and in the rivers and the lakes, the four-legged and the two-legged and the wings of the air—all danced together to the music of the stallion's song" (*BES*, pp. 41–42). To know is to be moved by song, to be alert, quick— as the Yaqui *brujo* speaks of wisdom, "light and fluid" (Castaneda, p. 16). A man of knowledge dances his wisdom. The Papago, Maria Chona, remembers a cactus camp with her family and tribe:

> Everybody sang. We felt as if a beautiful thing was coming. Because the rain was coming and the dancing and the songs.

> Where on Quijota Mountain a cloud stands
> There my heart stands with it.
> Where the mountain trembles with the thunder
> My heart trembles with it.

That was what they sang. When I sing that song yet it makes me dance.
(Astrov, p. 201)

Song cadences balance one another and play in running rhythms; the song-poet groups words in parallel phrases and rhymes thoughts, as though words, also, gather tribally. A human condition rhymes with a natural phenomenon, man with animal origins, as in this Aztec poem:

> The divine *quechol* bird answers me as I, the singer,
>   sing, like the *coyol* bird, a noble new song,
>   polished like a jewel, a turquoise, a shining
>   emerald, darting green rays, a flower song of
>   spring, spreading a celestial fragrance, fresh
>   with the dews of roses, thus have I the poet sung. (Day, p. 176)

A Lakota singer laments:

> I considered myself a wolf
>   but the owls are hooting
>   and now
>   I fear the night (Brandon, p. 93)

or in war,

> Soldiers,
> You fled.
> Even the eagle dies. (Astrov, p. 124)

The sensibility here, in Frederick Turner's words, lies "rooted so deeply in things that it goes through them and beneath them" to ancient truths in the world (p. 15).

Poetry as Survival

The Sioux doctor Ohiyesa (Charles Eastman) says that Native American poetry survives as "a perilous gift." The people keep the songs alive by necessity and choice; the words live in the mouth, the torso, the heart, the limbs of the singer. As oral poetry, the song-poems must compel listeners immediately, or they will lose their audience, their right to be. The language is by definition, Momaday says, one generation from extinction. A Wintu singer chants:

> Down west, down west we dance,
> We spirits dance,
> Down west, down west we dance,
> We spirits dance,
> Down west, down west we dance,
> We spirits weeping dance,
> We spirits dance.[50]

While the chant drops "down" to "weeping," simultaneously it moves out toward life and against the descent of death. The poem ritualizes pain through repetition and accretion, stylizing grief in the movements of the dance, the pulse answering death's prone stasis. An old Kiowa woman sings as she prepares the earth for the Sun Dance. The older the old woman grows, the more she frees herself, by necessity, playing to live:

> We have brought the earth.
> Now it is time to play;
> As old as I am, I still have the feeling of play.

> (Momaday, *WRM*, p. 88)

And within the Sun Dance play lies a sense of ancient, sacred processional. Black Elk tells of his vision:

> But I was not the last, for when I looked behind me there were ghosts of people like a trailing fog as far as I could see—grandfathers of grandfathers and grandmothers of grandmothers without number. And over these a great Voice—the Voice that was the South—lived, and I could feel it silent. And as we went the Voice behind me said: "Behold a good nation walking in a sacred manner in a good land!" (*BES*, p. 36)

A warrior prepares for death with philosophical counsel and bearing. "Let us see, is this real, / This life I am living?" a Pawnee warrior chants, his battle a metaphysical question (Astrov, p. 109). Life stands as a warrior's perishable gift, the world his mystery and challenge. Fear inspires the Omaha, brings him to life in humility before his task:

Wa-kon'da,
here needy he stands,
and I am he. (Astrov, p. 95)

Requesting bravery and power from the spirits, a warrior respects "the power to make-live and to destroy," the interdependent powers that Black Elk, cousin to Crazy Horse, receives from his Grandfather in the western sky. Black Elk is given a bow and a wooden cup filled with rainwater—the terror of a thunderstorm, the gentle life force of its moisture (*BES*, p. 26).

The warrior meets death directly, honestly, with no illusions, confronting the defining fact of life, that is, not-life. His bravery grows out of his acceptance of his own smallness in the face of the universe, realizing that the spirits one day will take back the life given him for the moment. "Have pity on me," sings the Assiniboine warrior, crying his vulnerability (Astrov, p. 95). White Antelope, a Cheyenne war chief, stood with folded arms and sang this death song as he was ambushed and killed at the Sand Creek Massacre of 1864:

> Nothing lives long
> Except the earth and the mountains[51]

Tribal Circles

The tribal Native American finds power in natural circles: sun and moon, stars, nest, tepee, flower, rainbow, whirlwind, human contours, nature's seasonal cycles. The singers of a poetic tribal world live in the circular presence of spoken words. The mouth rounds out in speech and song; the printed page remains fixed, rectilinear. Black Elk[52] laments that Indians are penned up on islands (*BES*, p. 235), and Lame Deer questions the power of a society living in squares and plastic bags (*Lame Deer*, pp. 108–18).

The vision quest is circular, requiring solitude but not corners for hiding; the visionary leaves his tribe periodically in order to return. "Help yourself as you travel along in life," the Winnebago, Crashing Thunder, counsels. "The earth has many narrow passages scattered over it. If you have something with which to strengthen yourself, then when you get to these narrow passages, you will be able to pass through them safely and your fellow-men will respect you."[53] Like the warrior, the song-poet lives an individual for the sake of the tribe; his singing is a matter of life or death for the people. He does not celebrate himself separately but sings of his kinship in the tribal circle:

With low thunder, with red bushes smooth
as water stones, with the blue-arrowed rain,
its dark feathers curving down
and the white-tailed running deer—
the desert sits, a maiden with obsidian eyes,
brushing the star-tasseled dawn from her lap.

It is the month of Green Corn;
It is the dance, grandfather, of open blankets.

> I am singing to you
> I am making the words
>   shake like bells.[54]

II. Word Senders

He is a word sender. This world is like a garden. Over this garden
go his words like rain, and where they fall they leave it a little
greener. And when his words have passed, the memory of them
shall stand long in the west like a flaming rainbow.
—Black Elk on naming John Neihardt "Flaming Rainbow"[55]

The Lakota have no word for "poet" or "poem." The closest term,
olowan, means "song." *Piyalowan* means to repeat a song from four to
twenty-five times during a healing ceremony. *Piya*, or "renewing" the
song, by repeating it, is thought to renew the patient; a medicine man
is known as *wapiye* or "someone who renews" or "repairs."[56] In many
tribes illness comes from forgetting natural harmonies—something as
essential as the earth's heartbeat, for example. Ceremonial songs are
then used to reawaken the ritual designs necessary for health.[57] Medicinal
song-poetry is meant to cure by realigning the patient with natural
forces in the world. An ethnologist, William K. Powers, writes of the
Lakota:

> Given that music is part of the natural order, it is *there*, occupying a niche
> in the natural universe, with a human-like capacity to be born and die,
> to undergo changes, to be renewed—"cured" if you will (as the language
> suggests). Music is not so much composed from whole cloth as it is,
> metaphorically, reincarnated, just as is true, so the Oglala believe, with
> humans. The term *yatun* "to give birth to a song" is perhaps the closest

gloss to "to compose," but the connotation of *"tun"* is "to give rise to something *that has already existed in another form."* (Powers, p. 33)

The Lakota medicine man, or conjurer, renews things by singing the old songs, which are natural and as necessary as breath to the continuation of life.

Healer, visionary, teacher, artist: a Plains medicine man—or *wicasa wakan*, among the Lakota—is inspired by a sacred, natural world through dreams. His very identity is determined in vision questing. He converses with the energies of plants and animals and the earth itself. "The ability to make objects 'sacred,' thus giving them mysterious power, was said to belong only to men who had the ability to talk with such objects and to understand what they said," Densmore notes (p. 183, n. 1). The medicine man may appear as shaman or priest, holy man or witch doctor, but his tribal role remains therapeutic: he fills the people's spiritual needs with things of this world, connects religion and culture with medicine and morality as an umbilical cord ties a child to a parent.[58]

The medicine man releases spirits in things to allow them to move through this world; he fuses mind and matter, mends the split between ideas and objects. He doctors and blesses, counsels and laments, interprets signs and improvises stories, chants, and visions integral with tribal traditions. The people respect him as a wise man, a seer of heart and knowledge; he moves freely among the best and worst of the tribe, humbled and empowered by the natural spirits of his vision, carrying a medicine bundle and sacred pipe among the Lakota. As Lame Deer, a modern-day Rosebud Sioux, remarks, the *wicasa wakan* soars as high as the eagle and sinks as low as the bug (*Lame Deer*, p. 79). Whether traditional or iconoclastic, purist or reprobate, he is distinguished as one of power and vision, chosen by the spirits, destined to heal.

The origins of these "old ways" lie in natural things. Through ceremony, discipline, and sacrifice a medicine singer tries to release himself into the spirit world that is at the heart of reality. Standing Rock sun dancers told Frances Densmore: "An ordinary man has natural ways of doing things. Occasionally there is a man who has a gift for doing extraordinary things, and he is called *wakan*. Although this is a supernatural gift, he can use it only by effort and study. A man may be able to do things in a mysterious way, but none has been ever found who could command the sun and moon or change the seasons" (Densmore, p. 85, n. 2).

The medicine singer opens himself for spirits to move through to the world; he is like the curing conduit found in the pipe itself, and he serves as a medium between one level of reality and another. Black

Elk sees these complementary realities as the Red Road, north to south, and the Black Road, west to east, which intersect at the heart of the world. So, too, the words of a sacred song can be transmitted from places of silence into a language of audible movement—the rhythms and tones of drumbeat, dance, and chant. The eighty-year-old Red Weasel told of learning the Sun Dance from his uncle: "In regard to the songs, Dreamer-of-the-Sun told me that I may pray with my mouth and the prayer will be heard, but if I *sing* the prayer it will be heard *sooner* by *Wakan' Tanka*" (Densmore, p. 88).

In his term for a poet, "word sender," Black Elk creates an image of flight, of ideas traveling from one place to another by way of a shaman's sacred language. In the Kiowa traditions inherited by N. Scott Momaday, a modern poet, words are thought of as sacred arrows.

The Shadow of a Vision Yonder

"I was born in the Moon of the Popping Trees [December] on the Little Powder River [Dakota Territory] in the Winter When the Four Crows were Killed (1863)." Second cousin to Crazy Horse, fourth generation to bear his family name and medicine powers, Black Elk entered the world a holy man, *wicasa wakan*, born during the Indian Wars. Black Elk turned to the spirit world and experienced his first trance at five years old. The vision reappeared when he was nine, and he ritualized his "great vision" at seventeen with the tribe's participation: "I looked about me and could see that what we then were doing was like a shadow cast upon the earth from yonder vision in the heavens, so bright it was and clear. I knew the real was yonder and the darkened dream of it was here" (*BES*, p. 173).

Visionaries of all times, from Plato to Saint John to Black Elk, have questioned whether they stand on, inside, or beyond the world at such moments. The visionary can press for transcendence, as in the Christian tradition, or live spiritually in this world. Black Elk imagines the ideal: traveling the Red (spiritual) Road and the Black (worldly) Road simultaneously.

There seems to be consensus among holy men, scholars, and translators that the visionary truth of the other world, regardless of time or culture, can enter this world only through the special concentration of dream images, a language of many tongues speaking in one, and a fleeting sense of witnessing more than the ordinary mind can see or comprehend or tell. John Neihardt, Black Elk's intermediary, remembers "half seeing, half sensing" the blind holy man's story, translated across languages, cultures, and time itself, as if he were seeing "a strange and beautiful landscape by brief flashes of lightning." The dreamer's language remains sacred and symbolic, *wakan* the Lakota say, and not to be understood as ordinary words:

> Then I was standing on the highest mountain of them all, and round about beneath me was the whole hoop of the world. And while I stood there I saw more than I can tell and I understood more than I saw; for I was seeing in a sacred manner the shapes of all things in the spirit, and the shape of all shapes as they must live together like one being. And I saw that the sacred hoop of my people was one of many hoops that made one circle, wide as daylight and as starlight, and in the center grew one mighty flowering tree to shelter all the children of one mother and one father. And I saw that it was holy. (*BES*, p. 43)

The visionary sees and speaks "with a heart that is different," *cante' mato' kecaca*, with the fierceness of the bear's heart (Densmore, p. 120).

A concrete language of natural signs informs Neihardt's translation of the holy man's life story[59]: the six grandfathers "older than men can ever be—old like hills, like stars" (*BES*, p. 25), the sacred hoop "wide as daylight and as starlight" (*BES*, p. 43), the creation's "roots and leggeds and wings," the "bitten moon" waning, and the tribal clan name, Oglala, which means "scattering-one's-own" among the seven council fires of the Lakota, or "allies." Black Elk "signs" his name by drawing a man connected with a darkened elk. As in the old winter counts sketched on animal skins and ledgers,[60] history is told in images. To Black Elk the Battle of the Hundred Slain, which crippled his father, seemed "like something fearful in a fog" when the boy was three (*BES*, p. 8). His older friend, Fire Thunder, says of the 1867 Wagon Box Fight, "they shot so fast it was like tearing a blanket" (*BES*, p. 16).

Black Elk's people organized their year according to seasonal moons:

> Moon of the Red Grass Appearing (April)
> Moon When the Ponies Shed (May)
> Moon of Making Fat (June)
> Moon When the Red Cherries Are Ripe (July)
> Moon When the Black Cherries Turn Black (August)
> Moon When the Calves Grow Hair
>   or Moon of the Black Calf
>   or Moon When the Plums Are Scarlet (September)
> Moon of the Changing Season (October)
> Moon of the Falling Leaves (November)
> Moon of the Popping Trees (December)
> Moon of Frost in the Tepee (January)

Moon of the Dark Red Calf (February)
Moon of the Snowblind (March).

Place names derive from natural occurrences: Greasy Grass (Little Big Horn), White Clay, Wounded Knee, Pine Ridge, Rosebud. The state name, Nebraska, means among the Omaha "flat river" (for the Platte), and Dakota, obviously, is taken from the tribal name for the allied nation of bands. It is commonly acknowledged that over half the state names in America derive from Indian terms.[61] And within the context of Black Elk's life story the personal names of tribal friends who assisted him lend metaphoric presences: Standing Bear, Iron Hawk, Fire Thunder. There are mystical names as well. Neihardt is known as Flaming Rainbow; in his vision, Black Elk is given the sacred name Eagle Wing Stretches; and Curly, or Light-Haired-Boy, grows up among the Lakota as Our-Strange-Man, or according to his great vision, Crazy Horse.[62]

Black Elk tells his story in the animate language of Lakota oral tradition. Silence lies fertile around spoken words; gesture, mime, and human interaction help to act out the meanings in words; things speak themselves, as the natural world comes alive in its own animistic expression. The black stallion sings "in a sacred manner," and Black Elk remembers:

> The leaves on the trees, the grasses on the hills and in the valleys, the waters in the creeks and in the rivers and the lakes, the four-legged and the two-legged and the wings of the air—all danced together to the music of the stallion's song.
> And when I looked down upon my people yonder, the cloud passed over, blessing them with friendly rain, and stood in the east with a flaming rainbow over it. (*BES*, pp. 41–42)

Spiritual witness to visionary traditions centuries old and lamenter of his people's present condition, Black Elk tells Neihardt his story, testifying to his own dream out of a desire to help his tribe. It was not Black Elk alone but "the nation that was dying" (*BES*, p. 184); the holy man's story is less autobiography than healing tribal history.

Black Elk ritually humbles himself, as in preparing for a vision quest. He assumes no control of or credit for the powers that move through him; he is a force of wind and spirit, sun and moon. "Of course it was not I who cured. It was the power from the outer world, and the visions and ceremonies had only made me like a hole through which the power could come to the two-leggeds. If I thought that I was doing it myself, the hole would close up and no power could come through" (*BES*, pp. 208–09). Lakota traditions place a value in the spiritual openings inside things, the positive "nothing" that eastern religions seek within the material world. Open at the center and virtually a breathing sacrament, the medicine pipe is the core of a kinship system based on the circle as conduit into the spirit world, more precisely, the "sacred hoop" that encompasses all tribes under the sky and within the horizon. The circle is a balanced form, symbolizing unity among the people, and it is continuous, fusing endings and beginnings in history, so that time is envisioned as circular, rather than linear.[63] All points of the circle remain equidistant from a still center, standing for equality among all things, and unsegmented, representing the sharing of necessities in tribal life. The pipe stem forms a spine, the bowl a living body of ancestors in the earth, and the sacred smoke the breath of *Wakan' Tanka* entering the people. Like the *yuwipi* society of medicine men, whose name means "tying up," the pipe taps into the spirit world and unifies worldly and spiritual "realities," ties the individual to tribal ancestry, and aligns the Black Road of this life with the good Red Road of eternal life. An emptying out and opening up in all this allows a place for sacredness within the world.

In Black Elk's vision the gift-bearing grandfathers change back and forth from elders to stallions of the four winds. The grandfathers come from the cardinal directions, symbolized in the primary colors dark blue, white, red, and yellow. There is a "power to make over," the healing power of the black stallion's song, in these transformations. Black Elk envisions a world of interconnected, renewing life forms in overlapping images, from grandfathers who turn into horses that turn into elk, buffalo, and eagle. The earth grandfather grows backward from old age into the young Black Elk, reversing time.

A black stallion rides out of the west, where the life-giving rainstorms gather on the plains, and gives Black Elk a wooden cup of water and a bow, "the power to make-live and to destroy." These sacred objects represent the cup of the sky and the bow of lightning, a natural joining of holy man and warrior through the life-giving gift of rain and the striking power of storm. Black Elk and Crazy Horse, one remembers, were born cousins in a genealogy of holy men; "the power to make-live and to destroy" inheres in the black stallion's gifts. The white stallion from the north stands for the test of winter, a healing that takes place through hardship and endurance. This grandfather offers Black Elk a sacred white herb and a goose feather, that is, holy medicine and the power of winged flight. The sorrel from the east stands for renewal and enlightenment, the sunrise of spring after winter's northern trial. The spirit of dawn appears in the gifts of the daybreak star of understanding and the sacred red pipe out of the east. The fourth grandfather enters as a yellow or buckskin stallion from the south, summer's richness when the sun rises highest. This buckskin gives Black Elk a flowering staff and the sacred hoop, representing the tribal circle around its living cottonwood center, the axis of the sun dance. Siya'ka told Frances Densmore of the elk dreamer's hoop: "Part of the rainbow is visible in the clouds, and part disappears in the ground. What we see is in the shape of a hoop. This word [hoop] is employed by medicine-men and especially by dreamers of the elements of the air and the earth." He then sang:

> Something sacred wears me
> all behold me coming.
>
> Something sacred wears me
> all behold me coming.
>
> All behold me coming.
>
> A [sky] hoop wears me
> all behold me coming.
>
> All behold me coming. (Densmore, pp. 295–96)

The four winds of the sacred hoop represent the unifying number, four: the four colors, the four seasons, the four times of day (sunset, midnight, sunrise, and midday), and the four ages of man (old age, death, rebirth, and maturity—Sitting Bull's name derives from the first of the four ages). In *The Sacred Pipe*, the second of the Black Elk texts, the holy man explains that

> in setting up the sun dance lodge, we are really making the universe in a likeness; for, you see, each of the posts around the lodge represents some particular object of creation, so that the whole circle is an entire creation. . . . You see, there is a significance for everything, and these are the things that are good for men to know, and to remember.[64]

Black Elk's fifth grandfather is the father-sky eagle, and his sixth grandfather the mother-earth bay. Adding sky blue and earth green to the colors of the four winds makes an ancestral nimbus of six elders: before, behind, above, below, to one side, to the other side. The sacred hoop then extends a primal sphere around each member of the tribe, imaged in the daybreak star, six points around a central seventh point representing the self. There is an integration of four and three—earth and sky, object and spirit—as the number seven completes the sacred system: the seven council fires of the Teton Sioux, the seven bands in the rainbow.

> You have noticed that everything tries to be round. In the old days when we were a strong and happy people, all our power came to us from the sacred hoop of the nation, and so long as the hoop was unbroken, the people flourished. The flowering tree was the living center of the hoop, and the circle of the four quarters nourished it. The east gave peace and light, the south gave warmth, the west gave rain, and the north with its cold and mighty wind gave strength and endurance. This knowledge came to us from the outer world with our religion. Everything the Power of the World does is done in a circle. The sky is round, and I have heard that the earth is round like a ball, and so are all the stars. The wind, in its greatest power, whirls. Birds make their nests in circles, for theirs is the same religion as ours. The sun comes forth and goes down again in a circle. The moon does the same, and both are round. Even the seasons form a great circle in their changing, and always come back again to where they were. The life of a man is a circle from childhood to childhood, and so it is in everything where power moves. Our tepees were round like the nests of birds, and these were always set in a circle, the nation's hoop, a nest of many nests, where the Great Spirit meant for us to hatch our children. (*BES*, pp. 198–200)

In this vision, Black Elk says, everywhere is the center of the earth.

Yet sadly, with the *Wasichus* invading (Lame Deer translates *Wasichus* freely as "fat-takers"), "a strange race had woven a spider's web all around the Lakotas," eventually forcing them onto "islands" (reservations). "But there came a year when 'the sun died,' " Red Bird told Densmore (Densmore, p. 86), when the "Great Sioux Reservation" was abstracted in 1868, only to be partitioned twenty-one years later with nine million acres ceded to the "Great White Father." Pine Ridge Agency became the Place-Where-Everything-Is-Disputed. *Pahuska*, the "long-hair" Custer, forged the Bozeman Trail, or "Thieves' Road," into the Black Hills, discovering gold in 1874, violating Red Cloud's Treaty of 1868, and then "told about it with a voice that went everywhere. Later he got rubbed out for doing that" (*BES*, p. 79). Named for the sunsets at his birth, Red Cloud led the compromisers to Soldiers' Town, or Fort Robinson, and there they became hang-around-the-fort Indians, coffee coolers, "friendlies." Here in 1877 Crazy Horse, accompanied by the legendary seven-foot Touch-the-Clouds and Little Big Man, was betrayed and murdered: "And suddenly something went through all the people there like a big wind that strikes many trees all at once" (*BES*, p. 146). Twelve years later the Sioux Act of 1889 halved the Lakota lands again, and the government vainly set out to convert hunters into homesteaders. The last sun dance was held and the last buffalo killed in 1883. "So the flood of Wasichus, dirty with bad deeds, gnawed away half of the island that was left to us" (*BES*, p. 235).

"Well, it is as it is. We are prisoners of war while we are waiting here. But there is another world" (*BES*, p. 200). Despite the *Wasichu* greed for land and their desire to pen up grass and people in cities, despite the "other *Pahuska*," Buffalo Bill—commercializing warriors in his "Wild West" show—despite the despair of a conquered nation within a nation, Black Elk turns to the prophecy of his people's reemergence after "four ascents" (generations) of suffering: "But I was not the last; for when I looked behind me there were ghosts of people like a trailing fog as far as I could see—grandfathers of grandfathers and grandmothers of grandmothers without number. And over these a great Voice—the Voice that was the South—lived, and I could feel it silent.

"And as we went the Voice behind me said: 'Behold a good nation walking in a sacred manner in a good land!' " (*BES*, p. 36)

Momaday's Way

> They shape their songs upon the wheel
> And spin the names of the earth and sky,
> The aboriginal names.
> They are old men, or men
> Who are old in their voices,
> And they carry the wheel among the camps,
> Saying: Come, come,
> Let us tell the old stories,
> Let us sing the sacred songs.
> —from "Carriers of the Dream Wheel"

N. Scott Momaday's debt to Black Elk, across time and Plains cultures, includes an impressionistic reverence for the land, the elders, the old traditions, and the spirits alive in all these. In addition to the 1969 Pulitzer Prize novel, *House Made of Dawn*, Momaday, who teaches comparative literature at the University of Arizona, has written a collection of tales and lyric impressions, *The Way to Rainy Mountain* (1969); two volumes of poetry, *Angle of Geese* (1974) and *The Gourd Dancer* (1976); a family memoir of growing up in Oklahoma and New Mexico, *The Names* (1976); and numerous critical essays and reviews. As a modern poet and novelist, Momaday translates the old ways into a subjective idealism, believing traditionally in people being as they imagine and name themselves to be. In *The Gourd Dancer*, he tells of his grandfather, who was honored with the gift of a black stallion: "And all of this was for Mammedaty, in his honor, as even now it is in the telling, and will be, as long as there are those who imagine him in his name."[65]

In translating Plains oral tradition, Momaday believes that words condense and contain the remembered past; one powerful word, rightly recalled, gives access to detailed experiences that cluster magically within a focusing sound. Names lie at the heart of ritual language—each word chosen carefully to convey a holy sense of power, vision, and meaning: such names put human beings in touch with the spirits of the gods on earth. The "great Voice" that Black Elk felt was "silent"—a vision that "remembers itself" through the years—comes to life as Momaday listens over centuries to his own "grandfathers of grandfathers and grandmothers of grandmothers." In the quietness of natural things, the speakings of plants and animals and the elements, the continuation of the old ways, Momaday hears a poetry of natural order and beauty; he records Kiowa heritage in an elegant plain style that does not intrude on arts engrained in the world.

An unspoken poetry underlies Black Elk's vision of the "real" reality, a place unnamed, spiritual, and out of reach here and now. To name something as an act of possession, traveling the Black Road of this shifting world, is to touch real things, but to fix anything is potentially to lose it, demean it, and finally not to touch it at all. There is another, older poetry, a preverbal language of things in themselves. Down in the world, fossilized, lie more dependable truths: objects sacred with age that speak from old centers. Only the ancient, hard edges of things, severely defined, rescue them from a shadow world of confusions and half-perceptions and failed languages. In a poem for Georgia O'Keeffe, "Forms of the Earth at Abiquiu," Momaday asks for objects "clean and precise in their beauty, like bone," or none at all—old natural artifacts, aged and inviolable, having endured the wreckage of consciousness and time, now ageless.

Momaday's first book, the noncommercial "archetype" (his word) for *The Way to Rainy Mountain*, appeared in a limited edition of one hundred handmade copies with no title page, no pagination, no gloss, no footnotes—simply a rich calfskin cover with "The Journey of Tai-me" printed in dark blue letters in the lower right-hand corner, followed by a one-page opening, thirty-three tales, and seven woodcuts. The old stories stand by themselves. Instead of making something of an object through adornment, Momaday presents his art in natural objects and expressions—the richness of leather, the texture of handcrafted paper, the magic of language, the resonance of tribal heritage. Momaday combines

simplicity and natural beauty here, passing on the Kiowa tales in the
sacred spirit of Tai-me bringing life to the people. " 'Take me with
you,' the voice said, 'and I will give you whatever you want.' From
that day Tai-me has belonged to the Kiowas" (*WRM*, p. 36). *The Journey
of Tai-me* pays tribute to ancient and sacred art forms imprinted with
human hands, as the Navajo creation myths say, fingerprints "in the
trail of the wind" that shaped life itself.[66] Ancient and still living, the
parchment suggests an old woman's skin, her voice warm and thin as
an evening wind in Oklahoma summer.

Momaday included twenty-three of the thirty-three Tai-me tales
in *The Way to Rainy Mountain* and dedicated the book to his parents,
Natachee Scott and Al Momaday, themselves artists and writers. Scott
Momaday's own name signifies the joining of two modern-day Oklahoma
tribes that emerged from different backgrounds. The Cherokees on his
mother's side (one-eighth), an Appalachian agricultural people, endured
the long 1830s Removal from Georgia to forced acculturation on the
Great Plains. They were leaders among the Five "Civilized" Tribes of
the southeast, where the Cherokee scholar Sequoyah devised the first
native North American syllabary in 1821. By contrast Al Momaday's
people, the Kiowas, were a nomadic and essentially "wild" tribe of
buffalo hunters who migrated out of the northern mountains over three
centuries, to roam the lower Great Plains, where they had settled by
the mid-eighteenth century. According to plains lore, the Kiowa owned
more horses and killed more whites per capita than any other tribe;
they are still suing for their share of the Black Hills.[67] So with Scott
Momaday several traditions, cultures, and histories merge in one syn-
cretistic life. Farmer and hunter, temporizer and renegade, woman as
earth-mother and man as sky-father ("Mammedaty" means "walking
above") come together in a collection illustrated by Momaday's father,
told by his grandmother, peopled by his ancestors, set in the heart of
the continent, and informed by tribal and anthropological records.

If individual and collective identities of Indian tribes fragment
into myth and legend, memory and imagination, the "way" to Rainy
Mountain gathers and recomposes disseminated Kiowa "history." Each
facing page speaks across to the other, forming a unified set designed
as a collage that realigns four Kiowa perspectives: the *tribal* or folkloric
mode speaks through Aho, the grandmother muse; the *pictorial*, or
visual, mode is represented in the father's drawings to illustrate his
mother's stories; the *historical*, or public, mode draws heavily on James
Mooney's *Calendar History of the Kiowa Indians* (1898), Elsie Clews Parsons'
Kiowa Tales (1929), and Mildred P. Mayhall's *The Kiowas* (1962)[68]; the
personal, or impressionist, mode re-creates Momaday's pilgrimage from

Montana to Oklahoma, occasioned by Aho's death and the author's journey to find her alive in his imagination. As with the hundred-year-old Ko-sahn who ends the book, "there was no distinction between the individual and the racial experience, even as there was none between the mythical and the historical" (Momaday, "Land Ethic," p. 11). Momaday's intention, in *The Way to Rainy Mountain*, seems to be to tend and nourish a life that has passed through him; he is in this sense a keeper of tribal culture who arranges the mosaic of history, present and past, private and public.

Continuing a pilgrimage begun forty millennia ago, according to Bering Strait theories, Momaday's "way" moves through and toward "the history of an idea, man's idea of himself, and it has old and essential being in language" (*WRM*, p. 2). The carefully shaped and structured parts of personal history interact to compose a whole narrative sequence of tribal life. The writer remembers ancestors buried in the ground and "kinsmen in the sky," especially the seven star sisters whose origin myth takes place at *Tsoai*, or "Rock-Tree" (Devil's Tower near Sundance, Wyoming, a laccolith Black Elk's people called *Mato-tipi*, or "Bear-lodge"). The place name yields Momaday's first Indian name, *Tsoai-talee*, or "Rock-Tree Boy," as celebrated in his name poem, "The Delight Song of Tsoai-talee," from *The Gourd Dancer* (p. 27):

> I am a feather on the bright sky
> I am the blue horse that runs in the plain
> I am the fish that rolls, shining, in the water
> I am the shadow that follows a child . . .
> I am the glitter on the crust of the snow
> I am the long track of the moon in a lake
> I am a flame of four colors
> I am a deer standing away in the dusk
> I am a field of sumac and the pomme blanche
> I am an angle of geese in the winter sky
> I am the hunger of a young wolf
> I am the whole dream of these things . . .

What began three centuries ago as a people's migration toward a homeland ends in the early 1960s at Aho's resting place: "There, where it ought to be, at the end of a long and legendary way, was my grandmother's grave. Here and there on the dark stones were ancestral names. Looking back once, I saw the mountain and came away" (*WRM*, p. 12).

From Momaday's memory emerges a set of directional axes around Aho's house, corresponding with Black Elk's "sacred hoop" intersected by red and black "roads." In ancient astrology, a circle in quadrants, ⊕, symbolized the earth.

These coordinates seem more personal—perhaps even subliminal—and less formally tribal than Black Elk's vision; but the cultural meanings of space and time, the placement of the artist's life within the framework of Kiowa values and heritage, and the observances of all these according to the "four winds" offer essentially a re-*membered* experiencing of details that grant Momaday self-definition as a Native American. His method is to record details in passing, as if to graze them and trust the nicked edges to speak the whole.

Momaday maintains "a going forth into the heart of the continent," as his Kiowa ancestors came down from the mountains into their new homeland (*WRM*, p. 4). A hushed landscape is impressed on the imagination, waiting for the right accent to make coherent the design of things in the world (for such a cross-fertilization of visual and verbal arts, see *Colorado*, on which Momaday collaborated with photographer David Munsch; first published by Rand McNally in 1973). Momaday ends Aho's tales with this thoughtful statement:

> East of my grandmother's house the sun rises out of the plain. Once in his life a man ought to concentrate his mind upon the remembered earth, I believe. He ought to give himself up to a particular landscape in his experience, to look at it from as many angles as he can, to wonder about it, to dwell upon it. He ought to imagine that he touches it with his hands at every season and listens to the sounds that are made upon it. He ought to imagine the creatures there and all the faintest motions of the wind. He ought to recollect the glare of noon and all the colors of the dawn and dusk. (*WRM*, p. 83)

A "word has power in and of itself," Momaday writes in *The Way to Rainy Mountain*, giving origin to all things, granting an ability to deal with the world on equal terms, conferring identity through personal names. The grandfather Mammedaty, a peyote priest, observed the sacred text for the Native American Church, the Book of John: "In the beginning was the word." The "road man," or priest, in *House Made of Dawn* speaks of an original language of events in things themselves, the Word *"older than the silence and the silence was made of it."*[69] Words can be used to defend as well as to confer identity, and Aho wards off ignorance and disorder with the interjection, "zei-dl-bei," a negative twist on Black Elk's "wakan."

Borrowing from Kiowa traditions, Momaday imagines words as arrows in liquid space. Ko-sahn remembers the passing on of "the sacred

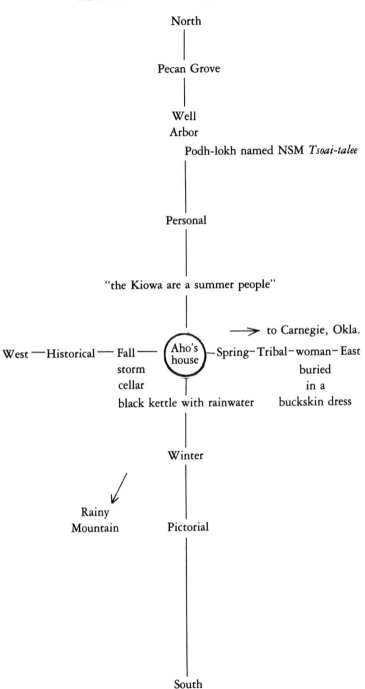

arrow" when White Bear told Momaday's clan, the Gourd Dance Society, "I have the sacred arrow. I am very old and can no longer dance. I want to pass the arrow on. The man to whom I give the arrow must dance with it; he must never touch its point to the ground."[70] The transfer is made one generation to the next, and "then the young man had the sacred arrow," Ko-sahn goes on, "and there was a great give-away. You know, the giving away of goods is an old, old custom among the Kiowas. It happens when a great honor comes to someone." With the "time and patience to their craft" old men in *The Way to Rainy Mountain* make arrows straightened in their teeth, and, like old words well made, these arrows are valued as hunting weapons, tools of defense, tribal craft, and trade goods. Reminiscent of the arrow maker and name giver, Pohd-lokh, whose photograph opens *The Names*, Old Cheney goes out each morning to chant the sun "up on land. There, at dawn, you can feel the silence. It is cold and clear and deep like water. It takes hold of you and will not let you go" (*WRM*, p. 47).

The women in Momaday's family bear names that ripple like flowing water: Aho, Keahdinekeah, Kau-au-ointy, Ko-sahn. The men's names burst softly in the back of the mouth: Mammedaty, Pohd-lokh, Guipahgo. The land, too, comes alive as the mountains gather to an epic roll call of "wilderness names: Wasatch, Bitterroot, Bighorn, Wind River" (*WRM*, p. 23). Rivers demarcate the land: "For more than a hundred years they had controlled the open range from the Smoky Hill River to the Red, from the headwaters of the Canadian to the fork of the Arkansas and Cimarron" (*WRM*, p. 6). Soft alliteration marks the names of trees that thicket Oklahoma creeks: "groves of hickory and pecan, willow and witch hazel" (*WRM*, p. 5). The names of flowers color the landscape—"a mountain meadow bright with Indian paintbrush, lupine, and wild buckwheat" (*WRM*, p. 23), the rain shadow of the Rockies "luxuriant with flax and buckwheat, stonecrop and larkspur" (*WRM*, p. 7). Even the crawling "relatives" are named for what they are and do: "dung beetles and grasshoppers, sidewinders and tortoises" (*WRM*, p. 27).

Momaday's focus on words at the center of *The Way to Rainy Mountain* (there are twenty-four sections) moves from sunset in Section XII to sunrise in Section XIII. To move forward in narrative sequence, starting with an ending, is to go backward in conceptual time, it appears, from an end to a beginning; and yet, in the larger picture of all the tales, time is circular: from sunrise to sunset to sunrise again. The end (sunset) moves toward the beginning (sunrise), as a mythic regression reverses linear history. It is going backward, looking forward. At the end of the "golden dawning" of Kiowa history, 1740 to 1833,

Momaday traces back to his tribal origins, reordering the sun's journey from sunset to sunrise. So, too, the Navajo Night Chant ceremonies begin at sunset and end with rebirth in the sunrise eight and a half days later,[71] and Native American Church services take place from after sunset to the sunrise. To re-member is to overcome time and carry the past forward, to journey into the present. And in all this, words are resonant as arrows through a still dawn.

A traditional Kiowa tale, told in Parsons (p. 15), reemerges in *The Way to Rainy Mountain* when the people learn to speak with the storm spirit, a mythic horse incarnating the tornado. Al Momaday represents the storm's four primordial elements in land and sky inversions. The horse's earth body thrusts backward in a fishtail and diagonally downward in a wind whip; these vectors are paralleled by a lightning bolt struck from the horse's forelock, bridled to the mouth, and flaring over the head in a mane of flames. The serpent's tail and lightning bridle converge in the tornado's vortex from sky to earth. The Kiowas talked to the storm horse, legend has it, saying, "Pass over me," just as the sun twins spoke to smoke in the giant's cave, "thain-mom" meaning "above my eyes," and now "they are not afraid of *Man-ka-ih*, for it understands their language" (*WRM*, p. 48). All things talk. By speaking with the world the Kiowas tribalize it. The bridle of lightning, tying a mane of fire through the horse's mouth to its hoof, seems to illustrate the striking power of words, the concreteness of words as actions. As with Black Elk's cup and bow from the storm winds, lightning and rain translate into the hunter's need for arrows and the food gatherer's dependence on moisture. Momaday remembers a felt language, a literal touching of objects in order to understand them; next to Aho's south porch stood a great iron kettle that "rang like a bell when you struck it, and with the tips of your fingers you could feel the black metal sing for a long time afterward. It was used to catch the rainwater in which we washed our hair" (*WRM*, p. 81).

The Kiowas tell a folktale of a handsome young man blinded by the wind for his recklessness; the tribe then ostracizes him with his wife and child, forcing them to hunt for their own food. The man's wife betrays and abandons him, reporting that his arrows have missed, but the hunter, although he is blind, knows "the sound an arrow makes when it strikes home" (*WRM*, p. 58). Alone, the hunter has only the game he hunts and has to eat grass to keep alive. In seven days a band of Kiowa takes him in, and by firelight he hears a woman telling of her dead husband. "The blind man listened, and he knew her voice" (*WRM*, p. 58). At sunrise the bad woman was "thrown away." In addition to describing the "hard lives" of Kiowa women and men, the tale illustrates the integrity of tribal words and the penalty for misusing them, cognate, it seems, with the hunter knowing instinctively, as well as by sound, a true arrow or a true voice. The young hunter is punished for abusing tribal codes; through a rite of *humilitas* he is given a second chance to honor the tribe, and he proves that he hears the truth. The woman lies twice, and twice guilty, is "thrown away."

The circle of tribal time binds all things together. The Kiowa Sett'an ("Little Bear") winter and summer counts, from 1833 to 1892, envision time as circular, beginning in the lower right-hand corner and spiraling to the center.[72] In 1848 when scarce game brought all the people together, hunting in a "great circle" that closed in on the center, "by necessity were the Kiowas reminded of their ancient ways" (*WRM*, p. 19). Completing a sacred circle with no beginning or end, Momaday returned to Rainy Mountain in the springtime of Aho's death, granting him rebirth as a Kiowa grandson. "Carriers of the dream wheel" turn and center their voices on tradition, just as Momaday turns again to childhood memories of Tai-me: "There was a great holiness all about in the room, as if an old person had died there or a child had been born" (*WRM*, p. 32). The return is timeless. As a boy Momaday's father went with his grandmother, Keahdinekeah, to make a cloth offering and pray at the *talyi-da-i* shrine:

> The holiness of such a thing can be imparted to the human spirit, I believe, for I remember that it shone in the sightless eyes of Keahdinekeah. Once I was taken to see her at the old house on the other side of Rainy Mountain Creek. The room was dark, and her old age filled it like a substance. She was white-haired and blind, and, in that strange reversion that comes upon the very old, her skin was as soft as the skin of a baby. I remember the sound of her glad weeping and the water-like touch of her hand. (*WRM*, p. 35)

When all else is taken or given away, the people still remember and imagine, tell old stories, and sing the sacred songs, filling the air with their voices. Not to do so means to die:

> Botone was the last Tai-me man. He was the only man who could open the bundle. But he forgot about Tai-me. You know, the Tai-me man is not supposed to leave Tai-me after sundown. Botone forgot about that. Once he went chasing after women and left Tai-me alone at night. After that, Botone died. But before he died he told his daughter of a dream that he had had. While he lay asleep he heard a voice that said: "You forgot about me. Now I am going to forget about you." And sure enough, that was Tai-me. Botone died. (*The Journey of Tai-me*, Tale 21)

Words live as visionary medicine beyond their "carriers" or "senders," as Black Elk would have it. After one hundred years Ko-sahn remembers in her childhood an "old, old woman" who brought the "bag full of earth on her back" to start the annual sun dance. This was all "a long time ago," and the remembering concentrates two hundred years in Ko-sahn, the "ancient one" whose aged voice keens as she begins "to speak and sing":

> We have brought the earth.
> Now it is time to play;
> As old as I am, I still have the feeling of play.

Momaday hears another voice beneath her words, attuned with the "silent" song Black Elk "feels" on the vision mountain. At rest in her grave, Aho settles into "the shadow of a vision yonder." In the beginning of the book Momaday returns to his grandmother's burial, and he places "Rainy Mountain Cemetery" at the end:

> Most is your name the name of this dark stone.
> Deranged in death, the mind to be inheres
> Forever in the nominal unknown,
> The wake of nothing audible he hears
> Who listens here and now to hear your name.
>
> The early sun, red as a hunter's moon,
> Runs in the plain. The mountain burns and shines;
> And silence is the long approach of noon
> Upon the shadow that your name defines—
> And death this cold, black density of stone. (*WRM*, p. 89)

By grief and custom unable to speak her name in death, the mourning poet sees the engraved name "Aho." Not being able to speak to her or hear her, estranged from her by death, Momaday listens beneath the "wake" and senses his grandmother's spirit, her soul like her name living on in the shadows cast by a red sun. Indeed, Aho's grandson is testimony to her continuing life. To sense someone's shadow is to summon that person's soul (Indians referred to Edward Curtis, a pho-tographer, as "the Shadow Catcher.")[73] People are silhouettes of darkness, the poem tentatively offers, temporal on the plain, existing by reason of passing under a running sun. Word senders name and imagine and resurrect the tribe not through possessing things of life but by way of open passages through the things of the world: a word as an engraved opening in stone, a spirit alive in silence, a verbal shadow.

III. Contemporary Native America

> "There are some things I have to tell you," Betonie began
> softly. ". . . long ago when the people were given these ceremonies,
> the changing began, if only in the aging of the yellow gourd
> rattle or the shrinking of the skin around the eagle's claw, if only
> in the different voices from generation to generation, singing the
> chants. You see, in many ways, the ceremonies have always been
> changing."
>
> Tayo nodded; he looked at the medicine pouches hanging
> from the ceiling and tried to imagine the objects they contained.
>
> "At one time, the ceremonies as they had been performed
> were enough for the way the world was then. But after the white
> people came, elements in this world began to shift; and it became
> necessary to create new ceremonies. . . . things which don't shift
> and grow are dead things."
>
> —Leslie Silko, *Ceremony*

"I go backward, look forward, as the porcupine does," the ninety-
four-year-old Swampy Cree Jacob Slowstream says as he begins Howard
Norman's *Wishing Bone Cycle*. In over three hundred tribes and a million
peoples, there are several hundred writers adapting older tribal literatures
to modern forms of poetry and fiction. Leslie Silko (Laguna Pueblo) has
won critical acclaim for her first novel, *Ceremony* (1977), about a southwestern half-breed who returns from the Korean war to search for himself.
Silko is also a successful poet in *Laguna Woman* (1974) and *Storyteller*
(1981). Simon Ortiz (Acoma Pueblo) has written poetry and prose in
Going for the Rain (1976), *A Good Journey* (1977), and *Howbah Indians*
(1978). Before his death in 1977, D'Arcy McNickle (Flathead) completed
his third novel, *Wind from an Enemy Sky*. Gerald Vizenor (Chippewa)
has published the more experimental fiction of *Wordarrows* (1978) and
Darkness in Saint Louis Bearheart (1978). The works of sixteen young
Indian poets are presented in *Carriers of the Dream Wheel* (1975), edited
by Duane Niatum, and Kenneth Rosen's *The Man to Send Rain Clouds*
(1974) presents a range of promising Indian fiction. [74]

Trickster's Bones

Jaime de Angulo notes that the Pit River Indians called the first
California whites *enellaadwi*, or "wanderers" (less politely, "bums"),

since they appeared homeless.[75] In the mythologies of hundreds of Native American tribes a figure known as Trickster, an uncivilized wanderer, scavenges on the fringes of tribal kinship systems. Trickster is accountable for the world's wrongs—a personification of disorder, a god-beast less than divine but more than animal, moving in and out of the tribal world.

Trickster's humor and teachings are still alive and grinning in the Swampy Cree oral poetry of Howard Norman's *Wishing Bone Cycle* (1976). Norman grew up among the Canadian Swampy Cree, speaking their language and apprenticed to a storyteller. He continues to know the villagers of Otter Lake, while developing his skills as poet, ethnologist, and translator. Very simply, Norman presents details and lets them narrate the poems themselves; he allows the natural world to tell its own story. Norman once heard a new parent sing:

> Little snail
> curled up
>
> leaving a snail shape
> in the blanket
>
> when I lift you[76]

The poems crystallize through an economy in presentation:

> I can't travel
> away from you
>
> rolling pine cone
>
> Each time I go to leave
> my shoes hide
> in your dreams (Norman, p. 126)

Norman's translation registers as an act of essentially selecting, editing detail and word and event, and then placing the parts in spare composition as verse. The poems come into focus so natural and succinct that any other way of casting the insight would string out as explanation.

The Wishing Bone Cycle opens with an origin myth improvised by Jacob Nebènegenesábe ("Slowstream"). One spring a snow goose alighted near Lake Winnipeg, only to be eaten by a lynx. Just as the lynx was down to cracking the marrow bones, a man scared him away and found the magic bone with which he could wish anything up and change himself into any form. Now, bones are inside things, and so they are naturally the last to get to and the last to go. These Trickster bones then carry the secret of cultural survival, the framework of tradition. The wishing bone, in particular, protects the heart and its dreams, and it is Trickster's play around the core of things that preserves the sweet marrow of life. This winged bone quickens the world with changes and sets up alternatives; it represents what we "like" in flights of imagination, rather than what grounds us. Significantly forked, implying both options and divisions in a continuum, a wishing bone symbolizes the delightful, yet problematic, duality in this world of changes. A humor of twists and turns, contrasts and inversions, transforms everything into something surprising in Trickster's world. "I couldn't think straight so thought crooked," says the wishing-bone man transformed into a snake (Norman, p. 15).

Trickster sometimes goes by the name of "Imitator." What Norman terms "mimicry" in nature's mirroring kinships, cognate with the imagination adapting humorous guises, runs throughout the tales. Here is an animal wit at play, an improvisational alertness akin to protective coloration: masking and mimicry keep animals alive, literally, in a world of natural laws that threaten and mislead. Trickster is treacherous, always out for himself, but all other creatures know his game. If they forget or fail to attend carefully, Trickster fools them, steals from them, even kills them. Staying alive requires wit, cleverness, self-protection, self-assertion.

A good story contains information and attitudes useful to life in the north. "The best storyteller is one who lets you live if the weather is bad and you are hungry."[77] Thus, Trickster plays his games well, bungling only when his vanity gets the upper hand. He's a worthy, though devious, comic adversary in a predatory world with variable codes of allegiance; sometimes he honors his word, but never as a matter of form. All values are open to redefinition as Trickster acts out the serious play of hunting, eating, loving, defecating, gaming and fighting, civilizing, and surviving death; he gambols to regenerate the world, to change or make over a reality that is always in flux. The Trickster's imagination stays alert in all this, inverting, reversing, changing shape, and surprising. The tales crane our necks to see other sides to old truths about the essential interplay of danger and necessity in the world. Listeners are "puzzled / but interested," like the wolves stalking a man changed into a moose farting in a hammock large as a valley—led on, curious with delight and apprehension, in a metamorphic world (Norman, p. 27).

In all the poems there exists a world alive to people, for better or worse, as they walk in and out of themselves, taking on the environment, seasons, weather, the animals and plants around them. Trickster teaches comically, by negative example, that this shifting world bears careful study, that the behavior of things is often other than it appears, that masking and duplicity remain basic to nature, and that we survive despite this trickery, perhaps even learning from it. We come to count on Trickster in this world of recurrent difficulties, stay careful of him, depend on him to keep us alert, laughing, and keen to the rules of survival. The unknowns in all this necessary tricking make us conscious of the contingent variables and critical play in a deceptive natural world. The acted-out dangers, comic or close to the bone, serve to wake us up. The tales lead us to a cautious empathy with the world, where skepticism grounds sympathy and keeps the heart honest.

New Old Ways

Beyond bloodline, tribe, government role, and national movements, being Indian is an idea of oneself, Momaday believes, a self-realizing act of the imagination that moves through a taproot into the ancestral past deep in the land. In the emerging literatures of Native America, being Indian is giving voice to the elements feeding that ancient root, and there are hundreds of tribal and regional and genetic variants. The poets gathered in UCLA's Native American Series represent some of these many voices: Norman Russell's *indian thoughts: the children of god* (1975), J. Ivaloo Volborth's *Thunder-Root* (1978), Barney Bush's *My Horse and a Jukebox* (1979), William Oandasan's *A Branch of California Redwood* (1980), and Paula Gunn Allen's *Shadow Country* (1982). In their varying styles and subjects the five poets reflect a cross-section of current Indian writing in America. Norman Russell develops traditional themes, J. Ivaloo Volborth adapts tribal ways of seeing, Barney Bush talks his poetry in narrative blues lyrics, William Oandasan experiments with fusional forms, and Paula Gunn Allen measures the shadows in free verse between Indian and non-Indian, that thresholding where the majority of Native Americans now live and ponder their Indianness.

Return

Norman Russell, a part-Cherokee life scientist at Oklahoma Central State University, listens with care to speak gracefully and accurately of nature and traditional Indian themes. Russell's *indian thoughts* opens with poems honoring the ancestral spirits in rooted trees; he next addresses the animals as extended kin; then he ritualizes sacrifice among living things; and he ends with an expression of respect for winged creatures. The poet selects natural details to convey his insights as the poems tell stories and sing. He moves attentively through a natural setting, learning the wisdom of trees, the secret of mosses, the instinct of animals, the freedom of birds.

> in the sand
> the willow speaks
> saying water
> saying dig here
> saying do not despair
>
> for the willow
> follows the ways
> of lost rivers (Russell, p. 9)

Russell traces a poetic lineage to the ancient tribal knowings of trees, the living bridges between sky and earth that speak as first beings in nature and embody the origins of life: many cultures honor the tree of life, of wisdom, of good and evil, of sacrifice, of the family. The tree is grounded in nature, upright (like human beings), communal; it reaches to the heavens while drawing life from the earth and speaking through the wind. Listen, the juniper whispers, "and i will tell you all the wisdom." To see in these poems is to voice nature with spirit and craft in a language of the senses:

> if it is alive
> then it must have a voice
> i listen
> it seems to me that it is speaking to me (Russell, p. 38)

The poet's voice is quiet, genuine, still edged and keen to his subjects. As a Papago woman once told Ruth Underhill, "The song is very short because we understand so much" (Astrov, p. 200).

Russell's voice takes no advantage over natural detail. To see is to hear, in order to speak. Responding in kind with nature, the poems do not explain: they reveal. Most natural beings remain quiet, suggesting their meanings: "the deer makes no sound / and yet his doe always hears him" (Russell, p. 17). Seen voices, felt in stillness, compel a reader to listen with the poet's alertness—intuitive, sensate, and conscious.

Russell's poems suggest that lowering the self is a way of heightening the senses. Instead of limiting human nature, this humility extends one's resources throughout nature, just as extended kinship projects the family bonds throughout the tribe of "leggeds, wings, and roots." Human life is part of a larger life cycle and is dependent on the whole.

If the self can become one with all living things, it can take on another "nature," rich in power and meaning. As sensate beings, we draw our life from the earth itself, an "earth household," as Gary Snyder says. The poet Russell believes that we are the natural "children of god." He wrote to me in 1974:

> I have been writing my Indian poems for perhaps 8 years now, and have written perhaps 2000 of them on many subjects. My aim has been essentially to recreate (or create) a whole society of people, with respect, understanding, wisdom, and peace among themselves and their environment. I believe this society did exist on this continent, though there is no historical (written) record of it. I think it had to. And I think it will come again.

Renewals

J. Ivaloo Volborth is a young American woman drawn to tribal Native America. Her father of Apache descent, her mother Comanche, she grew up on the industrial eastern seaboard, severed from Indian life. As a school dropout in New York City, "far from Mescal Mountain," she imagined the bull roarers, the water drums, and the rain-making Sky-Boy gods in the rubber and steel pulse of the city. Her poems work essentially as personal transformations, in this regard, rediscoveries of a magic native identity in this earth—traditions rooted in indigenous peoples, their tongues, their lands, legends, and gods. The poet's needs tie into an imagined tribal family, powerfully alive at the heart of this Turtle Island, as she sings of the mix of cultures and tongues in her own gathering Indian identity. In this context *Thunder-Root* taps down into the Sky-Boys' lightning within the earth, deeper than concrete and confused bloodlines, tribal dislocations, dispirited adaptations.

The poems occur at quiet times, the dusk of need and desire and the stirrings of dreams. In "Native Winter" the water spiders have gathered the lake shadows, the crows have ceased their gossip, and

> The-One-Who-Scatters-Leaves-Across-The-Snow
> has departed. (Volborth, p. 37)

Here, without, Volborth hears her muse, "the flute player / rising in my ear." Everywhere there is the poet's stillness, a waiting and listening for images that focus the day's confusion into lunar clarity:

> From rattling sleep
> my reed fingers

> brush past willows,
> slide along green robes
> of moss covered stones
> and find their way
> to fluid pools
> where Moon-seeds have fallen. (Volborth, p. 44)

The poems emerge as acts of tenuous courage drawn from the darkness; the night, shadows, and the edges of reality lay the ceremonial grounds, as though after-images of daily life spirited the poet's imagination. "In the great night my heart will go out," Owl Woman, a Papago healer chanted, "Toward me the darkness comes rattling, / In the great night my heart will go out" (Astrov, p. 196). Volborth's songs to the night, as in Native American death chants, seem pulses of a heart affirming life, delicate and fading, magical and fearful. "It is a good day to die," the old warriors once sang of their mortality.

Thunder-Root begins with dream songs to mark the night: abalone horses circling the moon's rim, sleeping beetles and a wet-nosed coyote about to sneeze, Coyote the dreamer collecting fragments along a shore. These three movements—translucent image, comic disruption, dream quest—pattern the collection. The poems take us to a birthplace of poetic sightings; images dawn fresh and luminous. The poet sets up continuities between objective reality and imaginative recesses. Says Don Talayesva, "I studied clouds and paid close attention to my dreams in order to escape being trapped by storms too far from shelter" (Astrov, p. 250).

Volborth chants of Moon-Rim-Runners, creatures on the lunar edges of things, who sing of thresholds, pilgrimages, magical transformations—Old Shadow Woman lifting her painted breasts in a dusk chant, and Grandfather

> going home,
> back to his Mother,
> to sit in the shadows
> of her painted breasts. (Volborth, p. 8)

The poems often rest on the edges of not being there; the images appear, flare, and recede, as the concrete world fades into the breath of songs coalescing from mists of daily words.

The poet works in single-tone poems of slender cadence, sculpted in the manner of Japanese haiku and song-poetry of the Northern Plains; she sees in patterned fragments, sketching line by line as the images gather:

> Old Woman bent by heavy snow,
> in the weight of her breath
> a Sky-Loom appears. (Volborth, p. 31)

A word strikes a note, then another, and the poet holds still for resonances, overtones, echoes:

> Iron-Door-Woman,
> behind downy plumed clouds.
> Crows await your eyes. (Volborth, p. 49)

The waiting time is essential, consonant with the wordless canvas around each image that takes shape. All is dependent on a suggestive minimal stroke, and in the distance, a sky-clear terrain.

Volborth moves by instinct, without gloss, to the primal origins of things. She speaks of seeing the shape and texture of a poetic detail as in a dream, then listening for the tones in the image. She does not so much think about the poems as let the images surprise her; she accepts living among them, shaping her dreams into lyric terraces. The reader peers through a water-glazed lens, "a moon domed sea," at the calligraphy of a finely tuned imagination. The word "abalone," she told me, began to glow as she examined the iridescent, mother-of-pearl layers of a seashell, and then suddenly, as if by magic, she could hear the opalescent ripples in "ab-a-lo-ne." Then she sang of abalone horses circling the moon's rim.

There is another facet to Judith Volborth's poetry—an animal wit, a subtle play, a sneeze to disrupt the meditative rest. These poems' refrain might well be the mad dogs' laughter:

> "Enough!" cried Coyote jumping in circles on his hind.
>   But the mad dogs of four-quarters
> continued to yelp and laugh at Coyote.
>   "Coyote dared dream on Red Ant Hill."
>   "Coyote dared dream on Red Ant Hill." (Volborth, p. 12)

Coyote gives the poet a mask to sing our native place in the dream world, matching wit with the gods, fabling our bestial selves through extended animal kin—Lone Hare, Dancing Bear, Night Otter—even Black-Coat, the pestilent missionary. Volborth has charmed the traditional figure of the Coyote trickster, an inspired clown and bestial god, into a lyric singer whose howl, rightly heard, is the music of wild, gentle things:

Molten Moon
drips down into the pine needles.
Coyote tracks embers
all along the embankment.
"Yipyip-Eeeeooowww!" (Volborth, p. 13)

The poet finds patterned release in Coyote's antics, melody in his yelp, design in his running, whirling, and spinning. Attuned to the wheeling moon, this lyrical Coyote is not simply a fool of license and comic exaggeration but a singer and a player, clever and sensible in his own tangents, ludicrous often, yet appealing as a Native American akin with all creatures. Still brother to the shy poet in her retreat, Coyote tells Turtle Medicine, "I've waited this long already" for the world to quiet down so he can get some sleep, for the lice to go away, for Black-Coat to shut up. And yet he waits. Coyote can be patient, chanting shadows while the molten moon drips into pine needles; the goal is a mind of liquid illumination, a poet's incandescent clarity of vision.

Volborth sings of a lean scavenger, the drone of fat-bellied flies, an empty buffalo head

In the buffalo's skull
the drone of fat-bellied flies
makes a lean Coyote impatient. (Volborth, p. 25)

The lessons involve going without in a world of changes, the landscape scoured, the poet a child alone. Volborth sings her own "Animal Thirst," crouching below, looking up to life:

Empty wind,
milky tit
in hollow sky:
my furry reach
too small. (Volborth, p. 38)

The attitude is supplicative, expressive of the humbling and loss of self on the vision quest. "Pity me, for I want to live," the sun dancers chant, staring into the sun, helpless figures of pierced flesh on a vast plain. "And here I stand / with an empty bridle," the poet sings below the abalone horses circling on the moon's rim:

Pass the whirl of Moon-Rim-Runners,
journey into the den
where The-Hump-Backed-Flute-Player

>   has left his notes in cold stone,
>   past soaring graves and dust hawks
>   where clinks of bone rattles are heard.

"Come," she calls to us,

>   enter where the ghost of my tongue
>   seeds out skeletal words,
>   where Bull-Roarers rage
>   the windless cries
>   of your frothy tears. (Volborth, p. 51)

Indian Blues

Poet, teacher, consultant, speaker, Barney Bush, a Shawnee-Cayuga in his early thirties, comes out of southern Illinois, Oklahoma, and New Mexico. His first-person lyric voice sings the contemporary Indian blues—bars, loves lost, Indians in the cities, powwows, booze, drugs, cops, suicides. He lives on the edges of a Native American pain, singing through the broken lines in his peoples' lives.

In a generation of rough-cut Indian realists—James Welch, Leslie Silko, Simon Ortiz, Ray Young Bear—Bush writes as a narrative chanter of conversations that make up our everyday lives:

>   —we both know—
>   about how nights turn cold
>   the leaves fall too soon
>   and the grey mystery
>   of glancing at each other
>   over pool tables and
>   jukeboxes (Bush, p. 39)

His poetry sounds distinctively contemporary. Instead of identifying, in the older tradition, with a single tribal origin or fixed sense of place, Barney Bush works toward an Indian consciousness of all tribes and all places that would bind Native Americans together. He seems, first of all, a human being who reaches down for definition as an Indian—but with a present-tense twist, a traveler's knowing of the way things are in country and city. He stays aware of what it means to live off the reservation, as most Indians do now, and long to go home again:

>   I thought about how
>   you walked

> cowboy boots, chokers
> Oklahoma, Pine Ridge
> and an eagle feather
> I don't remember promising
> you (Bush, p. 21)

Here is a lamenter's song, an updated ritual of the vision quest, "the long ride home" to Indian self-definition, wistful at times, and other times gently sad or comic. "The blues is an impulse to keep the painful details and episodes of a brutal experience alive in one's aching consciousness," Ralph Ellison comments, "to finger its jagged grain, and to transcend it, not by the consolation of philosophy but by squeezing from it a near-tragic, near-comic lyricism."[78] To lament and to laugh at once, out of the pain and the pride of being Indian, is the poet's trickster talent, the holy laughter of the Lakota *heyoka* or Southwest *kachina*, and according to Vine Deloria in *Custer Died for Your Sins* (pp. 146–67), this tribal humor provides a binding "cement" for contemporary Indian consciousness.

Barney Bush writes of his own Indian-ness in the heart of America, of ancestral visions clouded by urban despair, of a sense of something lost though possibly recoverable—a traditional past, set against city time and the descent of history, nascent in tribal names, family ties, Indian places, powwows in "Milwaukee, Chicago, Minneapolis"—all Indian sacred grounds and names.

The Prologue to these poems speaks of a rock breathing and blowing leaves, while "Richard is laughing / with the otter / foaming whirlpools." Although the way remains difficult, strewn with broken stones of pain, a horizon away from home, the poet still senses a whirling energy of correspondences and animal-human freedoms in the natural world of Native America; and this imaging of likenesses throughout creation is related in spirit to the pleasures of pure laughter, an energy of delight, motion, transformation, and renewal that enables people to endure the pain of being alive: "laughing all the way / out to Volcano Cliffs about / Indians 49ing in the rain" (Bush, p. 49).

And in refrain there's the going home again: "By bits and pieces I made / it home," hitchhiking on Christmas day (Bush, p. 29), "backtracking," as the Blackfeet poet James Welch has it, to a place and people always there by the side of the asphalt road. Barney Bush finds his way back with a mind of fall, a seasonal anticipation of exacting times and the need to return home before winter. With cousins, beer parties, piñon fires, and a shared blanket until the wind calls him away, the poet lives through the hard seasons beadworking and playing cards all night. He writes love poems to someone in the north country, voicing the individual side of the contemporary Indian story, recalling wild, good times and living as Lame Deer, the Lakota stand-up holy comedian, sees "an *ikce wicasa*, a common, wild, natural human being" (*Lame Deer*, p. 149). Barney recalls a friend, mending broken bones in a hospital and wanting breaded pork chops: "You goddamn crazy Indian" (Bush, p. 23). *My Horse and a Jukebox* comes alive with coyote's Oklahoma bark, loping gait, scruffy hide, and midnight laughter. And while coyote yaps in the half-shadows Barney sings with the wind, "I been out drinking / all night long, way-ya hey-ye" (Bush, p. 31).

In all this coming and going, loving and parting, with shadows sinking into the lake, we hear a drumming pulse, water-muted—an unspoken, felt Indian accent in the spaces between people, the distances that separate things and memories and places we want to carry with us. "You heard it's tough to be an Indi'n," Lame Deer once said in his backyard, "but the whole world is a tough thing for ever'body."

These poems reach down to a buried image, an interior Indian, coming to life through a daily trust in songs and poems and stories: "Feel that crazy / Chippewa sitting inside / my heart." Given the disparity between present time and times past, the tenuous correspondences between the young and the old-young, the new and the ancestral, the past and the present-past carried with us, Barney Bush talk-sings his Indian ways going home in the fall of America:

> for we know we are
> part of the shadows
> that sink deep into the
> lake after the sun
> has gone. (Bush, p. 43)

Fusions

William Oandasan's *A Branch of California Redwood* opens chanting a new day to return us to the oral origins of the printed word, the poem as song. He brushes dreams of ancient breath in a willow basket, glimpses grandfathers lancing game in a chert arrowhead, and hears three hundred centuries of Native America whisper in an old woman's "TATU." The poems begin as darkness just lifts into a new blue day— not the blues of Western autumnal estrangement but native meditations, the cool harmonies of sea reflecting sky. In the coastal cultures of his father's Filipino past and his mother's Yuki homeland where he was raised, this son can look up to the sky for quiet inspiration and down to the sea for his sources, where all colors merge and again emerge.

Born in 1947 in Santa Rosa, California, William Oandasan comes to us a writer of fused peoples and backgrounds (northern California, the Philippines, Canada, the southwest, Chicago, now Los Angeles). As a young poet, acculturated in modern literacies among older oral forms, he searches for a blending of voice and value in schooling himself a native in America. Ideally, a poet would make use of our composite place and heritage in this land, reciprocal assimilations. As we each come from two parents, divided genders, separate personalities, and merge differences through love, care, trust, the traditions of shared time, so we fuse separate tribes, variant backgrounds, diverse sets of cultural tools. One complements another one, from geographic, tribal, and genetic localities; the ancient mutualities among life forms decide our common ecology and values. And so with poetic forms reflecting our lives and lands. From his mother's Round Valley songs to free verse to *senryū* to city surrealisms, Oandasan carries the old ways forward into a new day, "fusions of dream and reality, red hope."

"Round Valley Songs," the first of three sections in *A Branch of California Redwood*, returns to a Yuki fullness in the earth, grandmothers of grandmothers telling stories of valley, water and ripe acorns, poppies, redwoods and jade dreams. As "rounds," the songs turn melodically back into themselves, too, observing the traditional continuities of the sacred circle. To hear so naturally, with poetic care, requires the patience to wait, an older sense of time and stillness, as rivers know the valleys they steadily carve, as stones know their heaviness in the earth, as trees know their seasons of harvest and hibernation in endless forests. Even more demanding comes the quiet waiting on the reservation today, while invisible lines cut across land and lineage:

> north by south, west from east
> an invisible but historical line
> slices across the valley's lives
> as sharply as bloodlines (Oandasan, p. 16)

In this once most densely populated region of Native America, California's north coastal valleys, old men struggle with eels in their sleep and young men lie down in drink, while an old woman moans alone outside an off-reservation bar.

In the adapted haiku of *senryū*, improvisational spaces open for the journey.

full moon;
woods on one side   town on the other
the path between   (Oandasan, p. 48)

This opening takes place in a ceremony "at the wood's edge," the traditional ground where colonists and Indians first treated, then and still "the path between." The contraries of in and out, fire and dark, change and continuity modulate through quick, limpid changes in Oandasan's poems, gently intoned, brushed, left to themselves amid a play of natural surprises.

promise
of autumn—turned
inside out   (Oandasan, p. 58)

And as the poet renews ways of seeing and speaking, a break in form reveals new possibilities in the poem:

still another apple blossom,
pierced by frost (Oandasan, p. 50)

The poems converge in a unified set of voices, given many directions coming and going. For the Gaelic bard W. B. Yeats, the leaf, the blossom, and the bole compose one "great-rooted blossomer," the whole synchronous with its growing parts. In the traditions of native dance and song, William Oandasan's roots leaf forth in *A Branch of California Redwood.*

Southwest Shadows

Laguna mother, Lebanese father, Lakota grandfather, a life on the margins of mainstream and Indian, somewhere in between American respectabilities and Native American closures Paula Gunn Allen writes in the shadows of visions, "fingering silence and sound" with a poet's touching measure. She sings desire, need, grief, confusion, and rage over a horizon note of loss. *Shadow Country*: that marginal zone of interfusions, neither the shadower nor the shadowed, both and neither, in liminal transition.

In the halfway house of mixed ancestry, Paula Allen does not so much live in a tribe as try to articulate her sense of the tribal and still live, without rhetorical claims, choosing Native American definitions, defining Native America in her life. Allen knows only too well the tribal sense of alienation, the corresponding necessity for mutual assimilations, America and Native America.

Rediscovering traditional Indian ways, Paula Allen also records new adaptations, shattering old stereotypes of blood warriors and demure squaws, reconstituting new images of real people from the Indian debris. Her poems voice the polychromatic shock of Indian modernism, in Fritz Scholder's paintings, for example, where cowboy Indians slouch with cigarettes and dark glasses, Coors beer and American flag shawls, ice cream and umbrellas on horses.

With a girl-child's sensitivity to pain, Allen is concerned with a woman's self-images and self-esteems. Men stand in the distances, women foregrounded. In "Off Reservation Blues" she dreams the Lady of Laguna, locked in a tower of defeated fantasy, earth-fearing, behind glass and above a white-skinned figure who waves but cannot hear:

> night was coming
> and I had to speak
> raise my hand and hit the glass
> I groaned
> sound too soft to hear

The grief language of her mute body registers speechless acts. She braves see-through barriers of sex, race, class, education, language, "civilization," consciousness itself in its many definitions—out of that breed no (wo)man's land of pained inarticulations, potentially revolutionary on the poet's tongue. Existing wholly in neither Indian nor non-Indian classifications, she assimilates both as best she can.

Such a poet on the diagonal can write of "Relations" from the underside: Trickster's contrary perceptions, knowing the world from bottom up, inside out. Trickster knows a ground sense down *in* things, as poets plead and cajole, a study of thought in its origins, and felt thought

> of dead poets, dead buffalo, dead coyotes, dead waters, dead ground,
> where understanding hangs in the balance,
> precariously.

Not-knowing, knowing forbidden or dangerous things, knowing obliquely, keeps this woman desperately alive, a chill in her courage to look down under words.

> cántas encantadas, wondering, de la luna, del sol, del muerte,
> de la vida

(forgotten and lost) where song is a one-time shot, where
pain and bearing in blood make the herbs of understanding bloom
on this once new earth that is dying once again

Dying also wakens the poet, her agony a birthing resurrection, her loss
a new awareness. She knows by the shadows where we are: like memory
in after-image, but more presently tense, absently, darkly with us.

> There are no shadows
> to tell us where we are,
> but memory of yesterday's
> perfect songs, when tomorrow was sure,
> a time of met images and kept fires:
> winter dreams that almost disappeared
> in scattered light.

Here and following in canceled lines from "The Return" the price of
knowledge is shaded by loss, the gap between being and knowing-of-
being. Allen's clarity, within confusions openly embraced, comes by
way of her need to regain that still place of earth-integrated acceptance.

> This winter or next
> we will go home again
> back to our own time and earth
> and know the silence of change and bone,
> of easy disappearance and of flight.

"The Trick Is Consciousness," Allen says in the chapbook, *Coyote's
Daylight Trip* (Albuquerque: La Confluencia, 1978), but an inverting
trick at times, unpredictable. To know is painful too often, not to know
can be innocent wonder.

> The key is in remembering, in what is chosen for the dream.
> In the silence of recovery we hold
> the rituals of the dawn,
> now as then.
>
> Watch   *(Coyote's Daylight Trip*, p. 39)

The "silence of recovery" reconciles all: that looking back to witness,
without questioning, without pain, momentarily. Traveler of memory,
betrayal, secret love, the night that covers and forgives all in mystery,
Coyote—the back-tracking romantic—reminisces dreams of truths in
all lights, day or night.

At cost, there is clarity in looking back, by way of an inner moon of remembrance. This is not the "real" world of things imposed on the poet but lyric counterstressing of freedom and will, the mind reimagining its own world. The fall is always back there, under dreams of spring. Allen sees a changed America, unknown to her now, remembered lyrically as "native" for indigenous peoples, acknowledged different, yet not wholly understood in pained awareness.

Paula Allen writes with the complete and myriad sensitivities of a woman with children, with a husband; in love, out of love; married, divorced, redefined: old women with weavings and potteries, new women with separations and new definitions. "No you can't use me," an Indian mother defies abuse,

> but you can share
> me with me as though
> I were a two-necked wedding jar
> they make, over in Santa Clara—
> some for each of us
> enough ("Indian Mother Poem")

Often, a woman's teasing opacity tints the poems, refusing linear logics and singular openings, in search of shared questions that place the poet, many-minded and multiply emotional, among her literary shadows (echoes of Whitman and his descendents Pound, Williams, Olson, Creeley, Snyder).

A woman's work and love lie at the heart of this poet's living, food and water, clothing and shelter, birthing and continuation in "Womanwork":

> some make potteries
> some weave and spin
> remember
> the Woman/celebrate
> webs and making
> out of own flesh
> earth

IV. Blackfeet Winter Blues

> Meaning gone, we dance for pennies now,
> our feet jangling dust that hides the bones

of sainted Indians. Look away and we are gone.
Look back, tracks are there, a little faint,
our song strong enough for headstrong hunters
to look ahead to one more kill.
       —James Welch, "Blackfeet, Blood and Piegan Hunters"

Among the most talented young Indian writers today is James Welch, a Blackfeet/Gros Ventre poet and novelist born in 1940 in Browning, Montana. Raised Native American and educated in American schools, Welch sifts the debris of two cultures in conflict. The Indian traditions lie in ruins amid the wreckage and garbage of Western materialism: junked cars, tar-paper shacks, blown tires and rusting radiators, discarded bathtubs, shattered glass . . . and the memories of Indians past. The haunting traditional names still carried by Blackfeet—Speak-thunder, Earthboy, Star Boy, Bear Child—remind the people of times that might have been, of old myths half remembered and half made up. Times change, traditionalists "look back" to worn "tracks," idealizing a mythic past out of reach even in "the old days," and "stumble-bum down the Sunday street," as in the poem "Grandma's Man." Parts refuse to mix, and differences are the rule, incompatibles, incongruous groupings: "alone, afraid, stronger," the poems say, in "a world of money, promise and disease."[79]

The contemporary world desecrates sacred things, past and irrecoverable, as Indian memories warp in pained fantasies. Heart Butte, a holy place for vision quests, is littered with dreaming drunks, Moose Jaw winter-locked, Havre lined with bars and tale-telling fishermen. Between boilermakers and double scotches lost men brag of epic catches. The White "airplane man" of *Winter in the Blood* bagged a thirty-pound pike once in Minnesota; the Blackfeet narrator mutters in Montana:

> "You'd be lucky to catch a cold here."
> "Caught some nice little rainbows too. Pan size."
> "There aren't any rainbows."[80]

Welch's understatement puts a drag on artificial lures, letting dialogue plane itself in the low-keyed, delayed metaphysics of naturalism. "Not even a sucker," the narrator flatly contends, in the Milk River.

Welch refuses to create any illusions that would ameliorate pain; he begins with the bone of *what is*, the "blood" definition by tribe, and asks no more. Searching through "a dream of knives and bones," in creative antagonism the artist pieces together a skeleton of the present—

a structure inside things heard in the death rattle of the old ways. "Only an Indian knows who he is," Welch argues in an interview, "—an individual who just happens to be an Indian—and if he has grown up on a reservation he will naturally write about what he knows. And hopefully he will have the toughness and fairness to present his material in a way that is not manufactured by conventional stance. . . What I mean is—whites have to adopt a stance; Indians already have one."[81] The Blackfeet were born into a winter that was always severe, a northern and western climate of mind in seasons of exacting change: "A damned, ugly cold. Fall into winter" (*WB*, p.159). It breeds "hunger" that "sharpens the eye," says the blind grandfather, squatting "on the white skin of earth," the Tiresian seer of *Winter in the Blood* with fingers "slick, papery, like the belly of a rattlesnake" (*WB*, p. 78).

Long considered among the fiercest "hostiles" on the Great Plains, the Montana Blackfeet held out as the last northern tribe to negotiate a truce with Washington. The popular historian George Grinnell wrote in 1892: "Fifty years ago the name Blackfeet was one of terrible meaning to the white traveler who passed across that desolate buffalo-trodden waste which lay to the north of the Yellowstone River and east of the Rocky Mountains."[82] During "the winter of starvation," 1883–84, more than a quarter of the Blackfeet died of hunger as the government systematically exterminated the last of the buffalo herds in one season. By 1894 the Indian commissioner thought to make reservation-loving, potato-farming, beef-eating, hymn-singing Christians out of nomadic buffalo hunters who worshiped the sun:

> Sun dances, Indian mourning, Indian medicine, beating of the tomtom, gambling, wearing of Indian costumes . . . selling, trading, exchanging or giving away anything issued to them have been prohibited, while other less pernicious practices, such as horse-racing, face-painting, etc., are discouraged.[83]

Two generations later but no less "hostile" in spirit, James Welch resists the "Big Knives," asking in "The Renegade Wants Words": "Were we wild for wanting men to listen / to the earth, to plant only by moons?"

The key to Welch's art seems an adversary sense of reality—attitudes that resist, counter, and invert a conventional position in the world. The ethnologist Clark Wissler records one of the earliest Blackfeet creation parables, told and retold from ancient times, about Old Man (Na'pi) and Old Woman (Kipitaki)—the original wedded contraries, sometimes personified as the sun and the moon (literally, the "night-sun"). In the beginning, in making "things-as-they-are," Old Man gets the first say, and Old Woman has the second. Old Man is a trickster, a sacred clown, and he thinks that people should do no hard work; Old Woman, ever pragmatic, reverses the idea, in order to cull the good workers from the bad. Old Man wants to place people's eyes and mouths vertically on their faces; Old Woman places them crossways. Old Man figures people need ten fingers on each hand; Old Woman says that's too many, they'll get in the way. When Old Man suggests placing genitals at the navel, Old Woman argues that childbearing would be too easy and that people wouldn't care for their children. So the "order" of things interweaves divine nonsense and corrective sense; Old Woman sounds the worldly countervoice to Old Man's naiveté. The epistemology appears to be a dialectic of absurd first impressions countered by hard truths, as though initially the imagination distorts the world comically, then must be corrected by a firmer sense of why things are as they are.

The tale continues: Old Man and Old Woman are finally stumped by the problem of life and death. Old Man proposes a gambling solution to the question. He'll toss a buffalo chip on the water; if it floats, people will die a few days, then live forever. If it sinks, they die for good. "No," Old Woman objects, "we'll throw a rock on the water." So death comes to be, the draw in a fickle game of inversions, and people lose. "If people didn't die forever," Old Woman reasons, they wouldn't "feel sorry for each other, and there would be no sympathy in the world." Old Man must agree.

The parable ends with a coda: Old Woman bears a daughter, who dies, and she wants to change the order of things. "No," Old Man says, "we fixed it once."[84]

This Blackfeet origin myth seems to illustrate the contrary nature of a world in which men and women are fated to act as counter-fools. Reason finds its limitations wedded to foolishness. People are destined to live out adversary designs, an interplay between men and women, life and death, comedy and tragedy. Absurdist fantasy recoils from an exacting sense of reality, and neither rules. The sinking stone of death is life's only fixed point. Play here is for keeps.

Dispossession

Welch's first novel, *Winter in the Blood* (1974), opens in a highway borrow pit, the ditch beside the road to the deserted Earthboy homestead: "In the tall weeds of the borrow pit, I took a leak and watched the sorrel mare, her colt beside her, walk through burnt grass to the shady side of the log-and-mud cabin. It was called the Earthboy place, although no one by that name (or any other) had lived in it for twenty years"

(WB, p. 3). In this windy, vacant space, once fertile and peopled, the earth has been dredged to crown a highway over land where Indians lived in harmony with things, or so the myths remember. The tenant farmers have moved away, but their names haunt the place like ghosts of the dispossessed past that is symbolized in the borrow pit. Words no longer are integral with the things they name but are what things are "called." Judeo-Christian names with lost referents—Agnes, Teresa, John, Moses—and out-of-place Indian names drift among incongruous place names—Malta and Moose Jaw, Havre and Heart Butte, State Highway #2 and the Milk River. The narrator confesses a lost identity, "I was as distant from myself as a hawk from the moon" (WB, p. 4), and his mother complains of his dead father, "He was a wanderer— just like you, just like all these damned Indians" (WB, p. 26).

The thirty-two-year-old narrator remains nameless and faceless throughout the story. The persona of the alienated wanderer in one respect serves as a modernist rhetoric of fiction for invisible men. Welch ironically updates the Blackfeet tradition that forbids people to speak their own names to others, just as Kroeber's "Ishi," the last surviving California Yahi, could name himself only "a man."[85] Yet to be without a name or kin among dislocated referents and dispossessed cultures grants one a measure of anonymous freedom. "No name," too, becomes the reader's ancient mask, seeing through the narrator's mind and pain and numbness. Unable to look at and label the narrator, the reader looks through him.

Human suffering in Welch's fiction correlates with the muted desperation of other modern works, from Eliot's *The Waste Land* to Pinter's *No Man's Land*, as the Indian sense of lost history and cultural crisis echoes through an urban cold war; Red and White refugees cry out the need to simplify, to recover the essentials, to trace an archaeology of cultural roots, to find a design down in things. Williams declared, "Lost, in this (and its environments) as in a forest, I do believe the average American to be an Indian, but an Indian robbed of his world" (Williams, *American Grain*, p. 128). As Peter L. Berger wrote in *Pyramids of Sacrifice*, the year Welch published *Winter in the Blood*, "The loss of collective and individual security carries with it the constant threat of isolation as well as meaninglessness. In their cumulative result, these processes add up to a pervasive condition of 'homelessness'—man is no longer 'at home' in society, in the cosmos, or ultimately with himself. . . . Both the oppressions and the discontents of modernity have engendered passionate quests for new ways of being 'at home' socially, religiously, and within the individual psyche. The central mythic motif in these quests is the hope for a *redemptive community* in which each individual will once more be 'at home' with others and with himself."[86]

"No headstone, no name, no dates. My brother . . .": so says the narrator of *Winter in the Blood* as he stands before his family grave sites. Only a white priest would tax a person with a "Christian" name nailed to an Indian surname—John First Raise, the mock adventist father, and Moses First Raise, the death-exiled brother.[87] The narrator knows only dead portents of redemption. Brother "Mose" lies in bondage under the packed, dead earth of the deserted Earthboy allotment on the Blackfeet promised land. "Earthboy calls me from my dream": the novel begins with a shard, a fragment broken from a poem, "Dirt is where the dreams must end." And somewhere behind Earthboy's fall lingers a pastoral memory of the creation and a dark and "dirty" Adam, whose name once meant "red earth." "Earthboy: so simple his name / should ring a bell for sinners." "And the Lord God formed man of the dust of the ground, and breathed into his nostrils the breath of life; and man became a living soul" (Gen. i.7). Now exiled from Eden, face down in dirt, Earthboy tastes the fruit of Adam's disobedience: the bruised snake eats dust, women ruled by men conceive in sorrow, men farm a dead land.

> cursed is the ground for thy sake
> in sorrow shalt thou eat of it all the days of thy life;
> Thorns also and thistles shall it bring forth to thee;
> and thou shalt eat the herb of the field:
> In the sweat of thy face shalt thou eat bread,
> till thou return unto the ground;
> for out of it wast thou taken;
> for dust thou art,
> and unto dust shalt thou return. (Gen. iii.17–19)

John First Raise stretches dead drunk beneath a Styrofoam cross; the dirt over his grave has fallen a foot into the earth, as though the dead keep dying. The family name swirls in dust, estranged from mother earth, and "white" kids taunt "dirty" Indians "comic" in their dark poverty:

> Bones should never tell a story
> to a bad beginner. I ride
> romantic to those words,
> those foolish claims that he
> was better than dirt, or rain
> that bleached his cabin

white as bone. Scattered in the wind
Earthboy calls me from my dream:
Dirt is where the dreams must end.

In a disquieting mixture of surreal poetry and bone-dry prose *Winter in the Blood* opens with Indians falling from Turtle Island.[88] Riding the Earthboy homestead, an unregenerate quarter section of land drawn and quartered by the barbed wire of white allotment, foreshadows an unending Indian fall.

Welch's Milk River runs muddy, polluted, fished out. When the Game Commission stocks the waters, the fish don't die, but simply disappear, as does the Game Commission. The "airplane man" flies into the promised land as a parodied White avatar on the lam from the FBI. This fugitive Fisher King touches down, casts in sterile waters, barhops on the banks of the tumid river, recruits an Indian sidekick for the price of a faded blue Falcon to replace his twenty-three-year-old white swayback, "Bird," and the two attempt an escape under a full moon into Canada, where Sitting Bull with his renegade Lakota and Chief Joseph with his fleeing Nez Percé tried to outrun the cavalry in 1877. The historical irony of an Indian helping a white man flee America salts the narrator's disbelief: "I can't figure out why you picked me—maybe I should tell you, those guards like to harass Indians. They can never figure out why an Indian should want to go to Canada" (*WB*, p. 104).

Descriptions startle and quicken in flintlike strokes: the narrator's frozen father accents "a blue-white lump in the endless skittering whiteness" of the borrow pit (*WB*, p. 26); his grandmother's eyes swell "black like a spider's belly" (*WB*, p. 43); his lover's breasts spread "like puddings beneath the sheet" (*WB*, p. 93). These images derive from the idioms of working ranch hands, waitresses, bartenders, day laborers, selectively compressed in a work of art not made up but salvaged from a reality of T-shirts and Levis, Pepsi and potato chips, a balking horse that "crowhops" and "sunfishes" and "hunkers" beneath a rider (*WB*, p. 73). With penetrating attention, the narrator records a world of common, working things: his stepfather in high rubber farming boots, his mother rubbing Mazola oil into a wooden bowl, a *Sports Afield* ad for a fish lure that calls fish "in their own language," a John Deere tractor and Farmall pickup haying a field, an American Legion punchboard that pays in chocolate-covered cherries, a girlfriend's teeth in crème de menthe green, a "coarse black hair on the white pillow" in a hotel room where a vacuum cleaner hums "somewhere far away." The unreal nonsense of bar banter refracts the contrary reality between men and women: the narrator winks at himself in the wall mirror, the barmaid scowls back, the two spar, and then they screw in a hotel bed. The next chapter opens with the narrator in delirium tremens.

Realistic details prove the accuracy of this fiction. The narrator watches a young tough pick lint from his black shirt; he sees his girl friend's brother blow a flake of dandruff from a pocket comb. The morning after a drunk he says, "I drank a long sucking bellyful of water from the tap" (*WB*, p. 64). The narrative voice stays close to the bone, edged and braced with the sting of a Plains death chant:

> It could have been the country, the burnt prairie beneath a blazing sun, the pale green of the Milk River valley, the milky waters of the river, the sagebrush and cottonwoods, the dry, cracked gumbo flats. The country had created a distance as deep as it was empty, and the people accepted and treated each other with distance.
>
> But the distance I felt came not from country or people; it came from within me. I was as distant from myself as a hawk from the moon. (*WB*, p. 4).

The novel's forty-two chapters are chiseled like petroglyphs, isolated on stark planes. Scenes seem strung on a wire of pain just short of breaking, as the reader sees in glimpses. Moment by moment the narrative almost fails to cohere or go on. "What use," the narrator as a child cried at his brother's death, yet he went on, answering despair with survival. Getting through is the novel's staying power.

On the surface the plot makes a mocking pretense of balance and unity. Seven was a mystical number for the Blackfeet; it represented the traditional union of odd and even, as Edward Curtis points out; the Blackfeet called Ursa Major "Seven," and all sacred things were painted with a red earth called "seven paint." [89] There are seven primary characters in the novel—the nameless narrator, Teresa (his Christian mother), an Indian grandmother (unnamed), Agnes (the narrator's Cree girl friend), Lame Bull (his stepfather), the airplane man (a white "brother" in khaki), and Yellow Calf (the narrator's real grandfather, unknown until the end)—doubled by seven incidental characters—Doagie (the absent half-breed "grandfather"), Dougie (the "brother"-in-law caricature), Marlene and Malvina (bar girls), Ferdinand Horn and his wife in turquoise-frame glasses, and Long Knife (the one-day hired hand). The narrator's girl friend deserts him, and his mother marries a squat, half-breed farmer; the narrator dredges local bars for his stolen razor and rifle, "my sack of possessions that I no longer possessed" (*WB*, p. 69), the airplane man picks him up and implicates him in a bizarre escape; the plot falters. Then, in quick sequence, the grandmother dies, the blind hermit indirectly admits to blood union with her from that first 1883 "starvation winter," the deaths of the brother and father emerge in tragic memory, and the novel ends with the death of the narrator's old horse, Bird, farting in a muddy rain, after the gallows humor burial of the grandmother:

> The hole was too short, but we didn't discover this until we had the coffin halfway down. One end went down easily enough, but the other stuck against the wall. Teresa wanted us to take it out because she was sure that it was the head that was lower than the feet. Lame Bull lowered himself into the grave and jumped up and down on the high end. It went down a bit more, enough to look respectable. (*WB*, p. 198)

This anticlimactic, dark comic ending is structurally anticipated halfway through the novel when an old man in a bar rolls his own smoke, strikes a farmer's match on his fly, and pitches face down into a bowl of oatmeal, "deader'n a doornail" (*WB*, p. 100). This fiction teeters on the borders of believability, absurdly off balance, tragedy pushed toward a cartoon of reality.

If the fiction seems disjointed, the poetry dismembered by conflict, Welch tenuously holds his art together with pain and beauty, a severe, exacting courage to face the truth. Words splinter like the broken bones of a man's innocence—a language of hard bitter things, driving winds, a winter in the blood. The narrative voice immerses itself in real talk that cuts abrasively: the bartender takes a minute off "to bleed my lizard," and Bird drops "a walking crap" on the way to Yellow Calf's cabin. "Poor sonofabitch," the narrator remarks of an anonymous Indian figure shoveling an irrigation ditch in the rain (*WB*, p. 48).

Men wander as homeless bastards in this novel, and women prove bitchy. With white-rimmed red eyes a cow bawls for her lost offspring. Fathers are nowhere to be found. Welch pathetically images the breakdown of animal-human kinship: the narrator struggling home flanked by a sorrel mare and her colt; the heifer and her errant calf at Mose's death; the cow stuck in the mud. Against a natural setting characters are portrayed in action without psychological flourishes. Grandma rocks and smokes, saying nothing, plotting to knife the Cree girl friend who reads movie magazines, imagines herself Raquel Welch, and leaves with the rifle and razor. (The historian Grinnell writes that in the old days the Blackfeet punished a warrior's primary wife, "sits-beside-him," for infidelity by cutting off her nose or ears; a second offense would mean death [Grinnell, p. 220].) The narrator finds the girl, but she won't go back with him, and he can only advise her to find a skill. "Learn shorthand," he says. "It's essential." The narrator's own brand of shorthand stays close to a precise, elemental reality: homely witticisms, bar talk, street truths, country know-how—no more or less than Montana reservation life itself. As the hermit grandfather says of good housekeeping, "It's easier to keep it sparse than to feel the sorrows of possessions" (*WB*, p. 77).

Northern Montana is a land, Grinnell notes, where a good crop could come through once in four or five years. Farming is still something of a bad joke on a reservation that includes Glacier County; winter temperatures can fall fifty degrees below zero, not taking wind chill into account. Welch's seasons of birth, growth, and harvest—seasons of green, yellow, and red—leach to a searing white, and winter snow shadows are "blue like death." When "Christmas comes to Moccasin Flat," the poet laments, "drunks drain radiators for love / or need, chiefs eat snow and talk of change, / an urge to laugh pounding their ribs." Welch's fictional figures drink chintzy distillations of "white man's water"—whisky boilermakers, crème de menthe, Coke, vin rosé, pop-top beer, and grape soda. (The first alcohol sold to the Blackfeet in the 1870s was laced with such snakebites as black chewing tobacco, red peppers, Jamaica ginger, and black molasses[90].)After a time the blues of *Winter in the Blood*—tones of distance, separation, and loss—blanch to a winter monochrome. Just so, the women (Malvina, Marlene) and men (Dougie, Doagie) blend into blurred images that recede from the narrator's vision: the small blue details ironically diminish in the distance; the cows eat "blue-joint stubble" on the late fall prairie when "things grow stagnant, each morning following blue on the heels of the last" (so-called Indian summer is an illusion of a Plains fall); Teresa's black hair turns "almost blue" with age; the Cree girl friend appears in a "short blue dress" exposing her thighs in a bar; the airplane man wears a blue neckerchief and a blue and white striped sports coat; Marlene's faded blue jeans, panties loose inside, bunch on a hotel room floor; a tourist professor's carsick daughter wears a blue and white beaded Indian headband; Ferdinand Horn's wife wraps a light blue hankie around her can of grape soda.

Winter in the Blood is a regional novel with a Blackfeet sense of place. In this manner the particular winter locale and landscape reveal a universal state of mind, "a mind of winter," as Wallace Stevens says in "The Snow Man." Observations drop pointed and dispassionate in a lean, scoured environment. Distance tends to slur distinctions and the vastness of space hyperbolizes objects. Wallace Stegner, also raised in Blackfeet country along the 49th parallel, writes of northwestern life in *Wolf Willow*: "This world is very large, the sky even larger, and you are very small. But also the world is flat, empty, nearly abstract, and in its flatness you are a challenging upright thing, as sudden as an exclamation mark, as enigmatic as a question mark. It is a country to breed mystical people, egocentric people, perhaps poetic people. But not humble ones."[91] In such a homeland one of Welch's artistic principles is ironic displacement, underscoring the distance and disparity between things, the tension between distortion and truth, past and present, fantasy and reality. The story takes place in the heat of late summer, yet down under lies the coldness of winter in the blood. Old Bird and Yellow Calf, a hundred years old, feel the coming freeze wedged in their arthritic bones.

> Then, toward the end of September (when everyone was talking of years past), fall arrived. . . . At night the sky cleared off, revealing stars that did not give off light, so that one looked at them with the feeling that he might not be seeing them, but rather some obscure points of white that defied distance, were both years and inches from his nose. And then it turned winter. Although it had not snowed and no one admitted it, we all felt the bite of winter in our bones. (*WB*, p. 115)

It is a slant-rhyming land without perspective, "a country like this far off," as in the poem "Verifying the Dead," directly before the eye, yet unreachable as the sky. The narrative tone here, akin to the mother's "fine bitter voice" and "clear bitter look, not without humor" (*WB*, p. 154), is laced with the irony of sensing a mystery without resolution— the riddling mode of the absurd. This is Na'pi's reality, full of tricks and doubling meanings and blue humors. "I began to laugh, at first quietly, with neither bitterness nor humor," the narrator says, at last confronting his blind grandfather. "It was the laughter of one who understands a moment in his life, of one who has been let in on the secret through luck and circumstance" (*WB*, p. 179). The rule here: know things as they are; never inflate or exaggerate. "I never expected much from Teresa," the narrator says of his mother, "and I never got it" (*WB*, p. 27). At the end he's cursing his broken horse, a mud-stuck cow, "this greedy stupid country," and "a joker playing a joke" on us all. "The deep rumble of thunder, or maybe it was the rumble of energy, the rumble of guts" punctuates this winter humor and recalls an earlier moment when he first knew his grandfather. "I thought for a moment. Bird farted. And then it came to me . . . ." (*WB*, pp. 191, 179). It is finally dispossession that pervades the novel, from the narrator pissing in the highway borrow pit (where his father froze to death ten years before and his brother was thrown from a horse and killed) to his tossing a tobacco pouch with an arrowhead, the old medicine, into his grandmother's open grave. The narrator characterizes himself as "servant to a memory of death" (*WB*, p. 45). If burial of a hundred-year-old woman in the dead earth marks the conclusion, the agony of going home patterns the Indian quest, never easy, now tormented:

> Again I felt that helplessness of being in a world of stalking white men. But those Indians down at Gable's were no bargain either. I was a stranger to both and both had beaten me.
>
> I should go home, I thought, turn the key and drive home. It wasn't the ideal place, that was sure, but it was the best choice. Maybe I had run out of choices. (*WB*, p. 135)

The grandfather, Yellow Calf, tells of another delayed homecoming in the family a century before: "We had wintered some hard times before, winters were always hard," he remembers of 1883–84, "but seeing Standing Bear's body made us realize that we were being punished for having left our home. The people resolved that as soon as spring came we would go home, soldiers or not" (*WB*, p. 174). But this century-old theme—like old men and old cocks and old Bird, the cow horse that "had seen most everything"—is full of twists (*WB*, p. 13). Welch's realism checks any reassuring resolution. Yellow Calf and Standing Bear's widow had formed a bond in hunger; and for a hundred years the people stayed winterbound, distant from home, from themselves, from the regenerative earth.

"I'm sorry," the narrator says; his grandfather answers, "No need— we can't change anything. Even the deer can't change anything. They only see the signs" (*WB*, p. 80). The deer are not happy "about the way things are" in a world they see "by the moon" to be "cockeyed" (*WB*, p. 77). The people must learn again to "lean into the wind to stand straight," the old man counsels (*WB*, p. 79), to move toward an adversary to keep upright. The narrator feels salt in the cut of time: to see and register the incontrovertible signs of reality, to know and yet be without power to change anything, to survive sparely. "No man should live alone," the lone grandson says unwittingly to his blind grandfather (*WB*, p. 78). Welch adapts the adversary wisdom of Na'pi, the creator-fool whose name literally translates as "dawn-light-color-man"—time's silvering fiber as old age begins to see from the bottom of night (Grinnell, p. 256). The truth of things, says Yellow Calf, the blind seer, has "no need to be flattered. I am old and I live alone" (*WB*, p. 76).

Foxy Shaman

They shook the green leaves down,
those men that rattled
in their sleep. Truth became
a nightmare to their fox.

He turned their horses into fish,
or was it horses strung
like fish, or fish like fish
hung naked in the wind?

Stars fell upon their catch.
A girl, not yet twenty-four
but blonde as morning birds, began
a dance that drew the men in
green around her skirts.
In dust her magic jangled memories
of dawn, till fox and grief
turned nightmare in their sleep.

And this: fish not fish but stars
that fell into their dreams.

This poem, "Magic Fox," opens *Riding the Earthboy 40* (1971),
Welch's collected poetry, in a dreamed reality that cannot settle between
likenesses and things in themselves. Truth is a fox's game refusing to
make sense. To "ride" a plot of earth implies a precarious stability from
the start. "And the rolling day, / it will never stop? It means nothing?"
Welch asks in "Getting Things Straight." The poet's shamanic mystery
comes under question: truth turns to nightmarish magic, love swirls
with nervous leaves in a dance of memories, and poetry shifts on a
dangerously unstable set of images. The traditional death chant, to meet
the rattling darkness, has been transformed into the sounds of elderly
men snoring leaves off the sun dance tree of life. Even the Trickster's
cousin, fox, Welch's quick-witted totem (later paired with the wheeling
hawk, a symbol of the circling needs of hunger and the hunt), is not
sharp-eyed or sharp-clawed enough to unravel what is here the unreality
of reality. There are no fixed points: all is in disquiet, falling. Trickster
has doubled back on himself with a self-defeating wit.

We know that the stars did slip and fall in a nineteenth-century
nightmare sky. Following the 1833 Leonid meteor showers, smallpox
killed two thirds of the 20,000 Blackfeet in 1837, and there were
successive plagues in 1845, 1857, and 1869 (Ewers, pp. 65–66; Curtis,
p. 6). The horses were shot by cavalry or led away like so many bagged

fish on a string (as the buffalo were slaughtered and reservations staked). The sacred sun dance tree was torn down, to be replaced by the cross and the flagpole. And the poet-shaman, haunted by nightmares of a past that skews the present, is now discredited, with a "blonde" memory of his people's seduction and fall. He wakes to the dangers of a shamanic medicine that failed, the instability of magic and metaphor, remembering that in the old days a medicine man who failed could be ostracized or even killed. The "all-face man," as the Blackfeet shaman was known, can find no tribal mask now, no patronage among his people, and his power goes underground, a "holy ghost" questioning itself along "Arizona Highways," or lost in the alcoholic antiways of "Blue Like Death":

> You see, the problem is
> no more for the road. . . .
> the way is not your going
> but an end. That road awaits
> the moon that falls between
> the snow and you, your stalking home.

The Blackfeet poet's voice descends from the shaman's tongue, mysterious and ritualistic, chanting "finicky secrets" like a nighthawk, in strange, concentrated phrases, in paradox and parable; his images seem refracted from ordinary associations, as a nightmare is filtered through the dark side of day-to-day life. His words, as in "Counting Clouds," are difficult, contrary:

> A long way to come—
> this rain so old my bones
> crackle no before you speak.
> A way to come: downwind
> before the sudden clouds appear,
> turn you statue—no, I say,
> no to the north and no, no
> to your crummy mirror.

Grinnell notes (p. 284) that a medicine doctor for the Blackfeet was literally "a heavy singer for the sick." His terribly familiar voice cast insights into the shadows of people's lives, as the poet-shaman says of the nighthawk's secrets, "And another: man is afraid of his dark." Fear feeds a shaman's power; he teaches how to live with the unknown and uncontrollable, how to use the threatening world as a source of courage. In a traditional song-poem, a Pima sings,

> There I run in rattling darkness
> cactus flowers in my hair
> in rattling darkness
>   darkness rattling
> running to that singing place (Brandon, p. 37)

Along with courage born of fear, the poet-shaman also knows the alembic of anger. In "The Versatile Historian" Welch calls out for "mountains to bang against," a rhythm that rages everywhere among images. In "Surviving" he remembers,

> The day-long cold hard rain drove
> like sun through all the cedar sky
> we had that late fall. We huddled
> close as cows before the bellied stove.

Just as the old warrior songs moved the tribe into battle, the new poem, "In My Lifetime," drums the people to arms against the self-defeat of acculturated poverty:

> With thunder-
> hands his father shaped the dust, circled
> fire, tumbled up the wind to make a fool.
> Now the fool is dead. His bones go back
> so scarred in time, the buttes are young to look
> for signs that say a man could love his fate,
> that winter in the blood is one sad thing.
>
> His sins—I don't explain. Desperate in my song,
> I run these woman hills, translate wind
> to mean a kind of life, the children of Speakthunder
> are never wrong and I am rhythm to strong medicine.

Na'pi may have created man-the-fool in his own image, ironically, while Thunder gave the tribe a medicine bundle to pray for saving rain: the bundle is still opened each spring after the first thunder is heard (Ewers, p. 172). A contemporary Blackfeet, "blood to bison" and "desperate in my song," Welch inherits the original speech of Thunder in the poem, "In My Lifetime" (see, too, the end of Eliot's *Waste Land* where the thunder speaks a first language). The poet drinks wind of the sacred run after wild game, chants the old earth rhythms, drums the sky for rain, and translates breath into the rhymes of poetry. His rites of passage carry the running meter of Speakthunder into the crafted meters of a shamanic poet's vision quest. "Toward Dawn" opens with these words:

"Today I search for a name." And in "Getting Things Straight" the lamenter in his quest asks the traditional four questions of the "circling" hawk: Is hunger the life need? Who feeds the hawk? Am I his prey? Is he my vision? Riding toward "Crystal" in a night of drunken insight, when horses begin to sing, coyotes prowl in the blooming moonlight, and places mean their names, the poet does not so much "try to understand" as to witness "Crystal's gray dawn."

Traditional Indian verse ritualized the relationships between things through the use of corresponding ideas and objects. In contrast to the parallel phrasing of old chant formulas, Welch clusters images discordantly, using internal rhyme and rhythm to hold lines together. In "Counting Clouds" the poet couples the eidetic imagery and spiritual tension of surrealism, distantly related to the vision quest, with a Blackfeet attention to the land and the people:

> Once I loved this gravy land
> so famous in my blood
> my hair turned black
> with love. A way to think:
> so cold the sun could call me
> friend.

This palimpsest of modern style and Indian tradition is paralleled in the visual art of Oscar Howe, a Lakota painter who fuses the hallucinatory energy of Indian visions with cubist forms (see in particular *Medicine Man* and *Dakota Eagle Dancer*, 1962). Under intense compression, disquiet between old and new forms stirs the reader's sense of involvement; ideas call to a receding past, attempt rhyme, and grope for clarity. The poems impact as surreal conversations, densely imagistic, that follow structured stutters of the mind. An image suspends thought in midair; an ellipsis, colon, or hyphen trails an idea beyond recorded speech; a full-stop jolts the rhythm to halt in midline, as in "Going to Remake This World":

> Moose Jaw is overcast,
> twelve below and blowing. Some people . . .
> Listen: if you do not come this day, today
> of all days, there is another time
> when breeze is tropic and riffs the green sap
> forever up these crooked cottonwoods.
> Sometimes,
> you know, the snow never falls forever.

Welch writes a poetry of startling half-lines and broken forms (not

unlike John Berryman's *Dream Songs*). Conversational syntax and diction
tense against formal line lengths, so that verses enjamb or break at
midpoint; fragments of images splinter in commonplace rhythms, broken
lines of thought, and abrupt full stops. And within lines ideas implode
in rhyme: "Look away and we are gone. / Look back. Tracks are there. . . ."
Beginning with the idea that Fox *could* be related to Native American
Trickster figures such as Coyote (but Fox is more a European import
than a traditional Indian trickster), Welch explores the possibilities of
near-rhyme crisscross in the words "dance" and "fox" and "catch" and
"fish" in "Magic Fox," and carries the method through as a unifying
technique to the closing poem, "Never Give a Bum an Even Break":
"—instead he *spoke* / of a role so *black* the *unc*le died / out of *luck* in a
westend *shack*" [italics mine]. The near rhymes and sharp repetitions
of explosive sounds, a forced yoking of old and new ways, remind us
of "a woman blue as night" stepping from the medicine bundle and
singing of a slant-rhyming world "like this far off" in "Verifying the
Dead," the old ways gone but echoed on in Blackfeet blues:

> Have mercy on me, Lord. Really. If I should die
> before I wake, take me to that place I just heard
> banging in my ears. Don't ask me. Let me join
> the other kings, the ones who trade their knives
> for a sack of keys. Let me open any door,
> stand winter still and drown in a common dream.

This ironically assimilated "Lord's Prayer" in "Dreaming Winter" jars
against the older Blackfeet belief that the shadows of souls go to rest
in the "Sand Hills" on the Saskatchewan border (Grinnell, p. 273).

The old stories scatter as shards of ancient earthenware. Welch
recalls in "Blackfeet, Blood and Piegan Hunters":

> We ended sometime
> back in recollections of glory, myths
> that meant the hunters meant a lot
> to starving wives and bad painters.
>
> Let glory go the way of all sad things.

The fall of Icarus appears as a sign to the drunken Indian who envisions
"his future falling" in "Two for the Festival." The poet comes stumbling
on "awkward rhymes" cradling a blind toad (the "all-face" toad was
associated with a medicine man whose coiled hair likened him to a
horned toad), the magic fox and his surreal truth, and "thirteen lumpy

stones" (a reduction of the sacred "buffalo stones," once powerful hunting medicine). All this medicine power—totems, beasts, myths, chants— in no way prevents the fall of either Icarus or the Indian. Fox hugs his stones in fear. One more drink and the drunk goes home, dreaming of middle-class Christian keys to heaven, of a salvation that has nothing to do with neolithic knives and bones. Welch mocks the Indian's fantasy of possessing New World riches, of opening "any door," of standing "winter still" in white American prosperity and drowning "in a common dream" of melting-pot, self-help democracy. In "Harlem, Montana: Just Off the Reservation,"

> Booze is law
> and all the Indians drink in the best tavern.
> Money is free if you're poor enough.
> Disgusted, busted whites are running
> for office in this town.

Deafy, the silent cigar-store stereotype, can't hear the world anymore behind his "drum-tight ear," so he pretends he's "dumb" in "There Are Silent Legends":

> Though wind has shut his ears for good, he squats
> for hours at the slough, skipping stones, dreaming
> of a moon, the quiet nights and a not quite done
> love with a lady high in costly red shoes.

Bleeding from a smile, nose smashed straight and teeth scrubbed away with stones, wearing the mask of American camaraderie, the "civilized" savage acquiesces, head down, penitent, and "happy for the snow clean hands of you, my friends" in "Plea to Those Who Matter." And, back on the reservation, unregenerate Indians are "Surviving":

> That night the moon slipped a notch, hung
> black for just a second, just long enough
> for wet black things to sneak away our cache
> of meat. To stay alive this way, it's hard. . . .

Though self-wounded by these double-edged ironies, Welch counters the American myth of White plenty by giving thanks for Blackfeet seasons of loss, a mind of late fall and winter. The "noble savage" in "Directions to the Nomad" "instructs stars, / but only to the thinnest wolf." And "In My First Hard Springtime" the poet challenges:

> Starved to visions, famous cronies top Mount Chief
> for names to give respect to Blackfeet streets.
> I could deny them in my first hard springtime,
> but choose amazed to ride you down with hunger.

An essential paradox of Indian ritual (and now, inversely, of tribal history in America) lies in an old concept of *humilitas*, the power of loss.[92] "Pity me," the sun dancers cry in flesh-piercing ceremonies; the vision seekers chant "Listen" to the spirits. In Indian traditions the ritual loss of self brings spiritual gain, as winter warms the blood, hunger sharpens the eye, and the lonely vision quest leads the dreamer back into the tribe. So in "Thanksgiving at Snake Butte" the Indians ride to the crest of a holy mountain and find petroglyphs left crudely, without pretense, by their wandering ancestors, "driven by their names / for time":

> On top, our horses broke, loped through
> a small stand of stunted pine, then jolted
> to a nervous walk. Before us lay
> the smooth stones of our ancestors, the fish,
> the lizard, snake and bent-kneed
>
> bowman—etched by something crude,
> by a wandering race, driven by their names
> for time: its winds, its rain, its snow
> and the cold moon tugging at the crude figures
> in this, the season of their loss.

The old ones lived out their names, imaged the needs of their seasonal losses, hunted for their lives, and depended on the animal in themselves to know when more is less under a "snow-fat sky." Bowed in rituals of blood sacrifice, "bent-kneed" bowmen climbed lonely buttes to lose themselves into their world's uncompromising truths. Thanksgiving, then, cuts two ways at once like a double-edged knife: the seasonal and positive ritual loss in the old ways of finding strength in abstinence, designed to meet necessity; and the historical, cultural loss ensuing from the first Algonquians giving thanks with the Pilgrims in 1621. Algonquian speakers who migrated westward before the invasion, the Blackfeet were at odds with the "Big Knives" from their first encounter on the plains. "No one spoke of our good side, / those times we fed the hulking idiot, / mapped these plains with sticks / and flint," Welch recalls in "The Renegade Wants Words."

During a "quick 30 below" blizzard in "Christmas Comes to Moccasin Flat,"

> Christmas comes like this: Wise men
> unhurried, candles bought on credit (poor price
> for calves), warriors face down in wine sleep.
> Winds cheat to pull heat from smoke.

Blackfeet children beg for legends, "a myth that tells them be alive," and Medicine Woman, spitting at her television to predict the end of day by the five o'clock news, translates the old Christian and Indian stories: "a peculiar evening star" bringing light to people in need, "something about honor and passion, / warriors back with meat and song." The original Savior (the Ghost Dancers of the late 1880s imagined an Indian Christ returning) perhaps appears more mythically alive to "warriors face down in wine," hungry friends awaiting supplies, children leaning into a grandmother's stale breath, and Charlie Blackbird feeding his fire against the dark cold of winter. In the late 1880s Ghost Dancers joined hands, danced in circles, and chanted until they fell down in visions:

> The whirlwind! The whirlwind!
>
> The new earth comes into being
> swiftly as snow.
>
> The new earth comes into being
> quietly as snow.[93]

In "Legends like This" Welch sees the crucified Savior as a renegade poet flanked by two other hostiles, "dying in the sight of God," who never bothered to learn their true names. Resurrected as renegade poets of the lost tribe, they "burned His church / and hid out for a long, long time."

The interwoven Christian, Indian, and Homeric fragments of myth, then, seem archaic dreams of the past, broken relics for exiles who suffer the losses of the present. In "Spring for All Seasons" the poet sees that "Our past is ritual, / cattle marching one way to remembered mud." The narrator at the end of *Winter in the Blood* recalls: "Somewhere in my mind I could hear the deep rumble of thunder, or maybe it was the rumble of energy, the rumble of guts—it didn't matter. There was only me, a white horse and a cow" (*WB*, p. 191). Not questioning the

source—signaled by the voice of spring thunder, or animal flatulence—
Welch's Blackfeet carry on, surviving the present.

The old Blackfeet ways taught the people how to survive in a severe
northern climate, how to grow stronger in seasons of loss. Accurate
translations of these ways in poetry and prose guide modern Native
Americans through an imposed winter of white culture and steel them
against the "sentimental crap" of country and western songs in junction
bars.

The pain of truth opens the people's eyes in "The World's Only
Corn Palace":

> Some looked away; others in their throats
> began to laugh, not loud, but blue,
> a winter blue that followed
> mongrels out the door. With knives
> those killers carved initials on his heart
> till his eyes grew white with wonder.

The last section of *Riding the Earthboy 40*, "The Day the Children
Took Over," tempers the hand-to-hand struggles of the opening "Knives"
section, pulls back from the "renegade" bitterness of the second section,
and moves beyond the third section's image of a poet weaving styptic
spider webs (the old medicine for wounds) "to bandage up the day" in
"Snow Country Weavers." With winter in their blood the children
redefine a season of cold beauty "in their own image," as a time of
counterplay "to create life." A psychic cultural storm locks conventional
mothers, lovers, statesmen, and priests in the arms of their losses.[94]
These closing poems register a spirit of reconciliation and defiant reaf-
firmation—the warrior's serious play with the odds against his people.
Militants, like Montana weathers, move the tribe against white assimilation
in "Call to Arms": "The eyes were with us, / every one, and we were
with the storm." Instead of retreating into the sentiment of defeat,
"cattle marching one way to remembered mud," Welch brings a warrior's
courage forward, under pressure of necessity, to battle against coercion
from mainstream America: "None looked behind, / but heard the mindless
suck of savage booted feet." And "Gravely" the old ones die: "we
watched her go the way she came, / unenvied, wild—cold as last spring
rain."

Na'pi's mask reappears in the final poem, "Never Give a Bum an
Even Break," a title borrowed from W. C. Fields. If Thunder gave the
original medicine bundle to invoke spring rain for the Blackfeet, Welch's
bundle of chants opens in the "fall" of Indian time and finally drums

up a spring "comic rain" to thaw the grip of winter (see also the regenerative "comic" rain at the end of *Winter in the Blood*). Resistant to White society, the poet still is hostile—leaving middle-class mirrors and waiting with a fellow bum to blow up "one of the oldest bridges in town," perhaps an underground bridge of extended kinship to the "other side," severing the illusory goodwill tie between Red and White cultures.[95] The old scores of history must be settled—the broken treaties, the lands stolen by "a slouching dwarf with rainwater eyes," the present poverty and despair, the condescending acculturation policies, the termination threats—or Indians must create new roles, as the poet adapts to a changing world by shifting to new forms of tribal medicine. The emergent roles may transcend a history of grief and anger. But, for now, the "all-face" poet remains the contemporary shaman, the warrior, the vision seeker in a White freezing desert, chanting his angers, nightmares, laments, and conflicts as verbal "masks / glittering in a comic rain." This is Welch's Native American art, purged of losses, regenerating, reintegrating in the world as it is:

> We are the sovereign and free children of Mother Earth. Since before human memory our people have lived on this land. For countless generations, we have lived in harmony with our relatives, the four-leggeds, the winged beings, the beings that swim, and the beings that crawl. For all time our home is from coast to coast, from pole to pole.
>
> We are the original people of this hemisphere. The remains of our ancestors and of our many relatives are a greater part of this land than any others' remains. The mountains and the trees are a part of us. We are the human beings of many nations, and we still speak many tongues. We have come from the four directions of this Turtle Island. We are the evidence of the Western Hemisphere, the carriers of the original ways of this area of the world, and the protectors of all life on this earth.
>
> Today we address you in the language of the oppressor, but the concepts predate the coming of the invaders. The injustice we speak of is centuries old. We have spoken against it in our many tongues. We are still the original people of this land. We are the people of *The Longest Walk*.[96]

Notes

1 Earlier portions of this essay appeared in *The Southwest Review, The American Indian Culture and Research Journal, UCLA Native American Series,* and *MELUS.* This material and other critical studies will appear in the author's forthcoming *Native American Renaissance,* scheduled for publication in spring 1983 (Berkeley: Univ. of California Press).

[2] John Neihardt, ed., *Black Elk Speaks, Being the Life Story of a Holy Man of the Oglala Sioux* (1932; rpt. Lincoln: Univ. of Nebraska Press, 1961), p. 25; hereafter cited in text as *BES*.

[3] Knud Rasmussen, *Across Arctic America: Narrative of the Fifth Thule Expedition* (New York: Putnam, 1927), p. 164.

[4] See Vine Deloria, *Custer Died for Your Sins: An Indian Manifesto* (New York: Macmillan, 1969), p. 13; hereafter cited in the text. As a Standing Rock Sioux, former president of the National Congress of American Indians, and legal counsel for Indian affairs, Deloria is in a position to arbitrate figures that vary from two hundred to six hundred extant "tribes." *Wassaja* (7 [Jan.-Feb. 1979]) published a Federal Register list of February 1979 that named 280 "tribal reservation entities" having a government-to-government relationship with the United States and another 40 Indian groups petitioning for federal acknowledgement through the Bureau of Indian Affairs. The statistics for aboriginal population are even less firm. Harold E. Driver cites Kroeber (1934, 1939) with the lowest estimate of 4,200,000 for the North American continent in 1492 and Dobyns (1966) with about 60,000,000. Driver revises to perhaps 30,000,000 for the continent. See Harold E. Driver, *Indians of North America* (Chicago: Univ. of Chicago Press, 1969), pp. 63–64, and Henry F. Dobyns, "Estimating Aboriginal American Population: An Appraisal of Techniques with a New Hemispheric Estimate," *Current Anthropology*, 7 (1966), 414. Dobyns' most liberal estimate is that ten to twelve million Indian people lived north of the Rio Grande, constituting roughly two thousand cultures in which a thousand languages were spoken. In response to this controversy, Alfonso Ortiz, the Tewa anthropologist, wrote to me that "no responsible anthropologist known to me believes that there were several thousand aboriginal cultures in Native America north of the Rio Grande, nor were there a thousand languages spoken. Five hundred languages and as many cultures is a commonly agreed estimate. On population eight million is the most liberal upper estimate with any following at all. True, the figures keep getting revised upward slowly as retrieval and sampling techniques improve, but until they do even more, anything beyond what I cite is at best conjectural" (letter received from Ortiz, 25 Jan. 1979). The 1980 national census reports California leading all states with 201,311 American Indians, Oklahoma next with 169,000, Arizona with 152,000, and New Mexico fourth with 101,000.

[5] Driver, pp. 527–28. Driver uses Bureau of Indian Affairs and United States Census figures.

[6] Jorge Luis Borges, "The Oral Poetry of the Indians," in *Literature of the American Indians: Views and Interpretations*, ed. Abraham Chapman (New York: New American Library, 1975), p. 277.

[7] Barre Toelken, "Seeing with a Native Eye: How Many Sheep Will It Hold?" in *Seeing with a Native Eye: Essays on Native American Religion*, ed. Walter Holden Capps (New York: Harper, 1976), p. 17.

[8] See *American Indian Culture and Research Journal*, 2, No. 3–4 (1978), 1–46. See also *Contemporary Issues of the American Indian* (Minneapolis: National Indian Education Assn., 1974). The Modern Language Association is preparing a book of sample course curricula for teachers of Native American literatures, edited by Paula Gunn Allen.

[9] Claude Lévi-Strauss, *Tristes Tropiques*, trans. John Weightman and Doreen Weightman (1955; rpt. New York: Atheneum, 1974), pp. 47–60.

[10] Anthony F. C. Wallace, *The Death and Rebirth of the Seneca* (New York: Random, 1969), p. 3.

[11] D'Arcy McNickle, *Native American Tribalism: Indian Survivals and Renewals* (New York: Oxford Univ. Press, 1973), p. 72.

[12] See Francis Haines, *The Buffalo* (New York: Crowell, 1970), and Tom McHugh, *The Time of the Buffalo* (New York: Knopf, 1972).

[13] Edward S. Curtis, *The North American Indian: The Indians of the United States and Alaska*, III (1908; rpt. New York: Johnson, 1970), 11.

[14] Constance Rourke, "The Indian Background of American Theatricals," in Chapman, p. 257.

[15] Lawrence C. Wroth, "The Indian Treaty as Literature," in Chapman, p. 327.

[16] Margot Astrov, ed., *American Indian Prose and Poetry* (New York: Capricorn, 1962), p. 87; first published in 1946 as *The Winged Serpent*. All further references to this work are cited in the text.

[17] Dee Brown, *Bury My Heart at Wounded Knee* (New York: Holt, 1970), p. 424.

[18] McNickle, p. 51.

[19] Francis Jennings, *The Invasion of America: Indians, Colonialism, and the Cant of Conquest* (Chapel Hill: Univ. of North Carolina Press, 1975), p. 30.

[20] William Brandon, ed., *The Magic World: American Indian Songs and Poems* (New York: Morrow, 1971), p. 115.

[21] Chapman, p. 16.

[22] James Mooney, *Calendar History of the Kiowa Indians: Extract from the Seventeenth Annual Report of the Bureau of American Ethnology* (Washington: Smithsonian Institution, 1898), p. 154.

[23] Robert A. Trennert, "The Indian Role in the 1876 Centennial Celebration," *American Indian Culture and Research Journal*, 1, No. 4 (1976), 7–13.

[24] Malcolm McFee, *Modern Blackfeet: Montanans on a Reservation* (New York: Holt, 1972), p. 64.

[25] See Vine Deloria's argument for a pan-Indian political coalition based on separate land bases and tribal sovereignty in *Custer*, pp. 243–67.

[26] Howell Raines, "American Indians Struggling for Power and Identity," *New York Times Magazine*, 11 Feb. 1979; Edgar S. Cahn, *Our Brother's Keeper: The Indian in White America* (Washington: World, 1969).

[27] D. H. Lawrence, *Studies in Classic American Literature* (1923; rpt. New York: Viking, 1966), p. 36.

[28] William Carlos Williams first wrote on American violence as a mythic act of regeneration soaked into "the bloody loam" of the country's history in *In the American Grain*, (1925; rpt. New York: New Directions, 1956); hereafter cited in text. Richard Slotkin has developed a "mytho-poetic" reading of American cultural archetypes through a study of colonial and frontier literary history in *Regeneration through Violence: The Mythology of the American Frontier, 1600–1860* (Middletown, Conn.: Wesleyan Univ. Press, 1973). New studies on Indian stereotyping and image making are causing Americans to revise myths about civilization and savagery: among many recent statements see Hugh Honour, *The New Golden Land* (New York: Random, 1975); Wilcomb E. Washburn, *The Indian in America* (New York: Harper, 1975); Frederick W. Turner III, introd., *The Portable North American Indian Reader* (New York: Viking, 1973); and Fredi Chiappelli et. al., eds., *First Images of America: The Impact of the New World on the Old*, 2 vols. (Berkeley: Univ. of California Press, 1976).

[29] Certain works of folklore, ethnology, anthropology, and biographical history are helpful in studying Native American culture: Paul Radin, *The Trickster* (1956) and *The Autobiography of a Winnebago Indian* (1920; 1963); Theodora Kroeber, *Ishi* (1961); Ruth Underhill, *The Autobiography of a Papago Woman* (1936); Luther Standing Bear, *My People the Sioux* (1928); Frank Waters, *Pumpkin Seed Point* (1969) and *The Book of the Hopi* (1963); Charles Eastman's reflections on Lakota childhood, especially *The Soul of the Indian* (1911); and Hyemeyohsts Storm, *Seven Arrows* (1972), to name only a few not cited elsewhere in this essay. An entire branch of American literature, written by non-Indians, focuses on American Indians: captivity narratives, explorers' accounts, artists' impressions, Fenimore Cooper's Leatherstocking Tales, frontier and western sagas, Mari Sandoz's *Crazy Horse* (1942), Stanley Vestal's *Sitting Bull* (1932), Thomas Berger's seriocomic *Little Big Man* (1964), Claire Huffaker's *Nobody Loves a Drunken Indian* (1967), Dan Cushman's *Stay Away Joe* (1952)—a favorite on reservations—and Arthur Kopit's play *Indians* (1969), a surreal drama of Buffalo Bill's "Wild West." Leslie Fiedler's critical study *The Return of the Vanishing American*

(1969) offers the most lively discussion of these materials, while Richard Slotkin
lays the mythic-historical groundwork in *Regeneration through Violence* (1973).

[30] The most complete annotated bibliography on American Indian literature will appear
in an anthology of traditional song-poetry edited by Alfonso Ortiz and Margaret
Ortiz, *To Carry Forth the Vine* (forthcoming, Columbia Univ. Press). See also Arlene
B. Hirschfelder, *American Indian Authors: A Representative Bibliography* (New York:
Assn. of American Indian Affairs, 1970).

[31] See Kenneth R. Lincoln, "(Native) American Poetries," *Southwest Review*, 63 (Autumn
1978), 367–84.

[32] Astrov, p. 5; Walter Benjamin, *Illuminations*, trans. Harry Zohn, ed. Hannah Arendt
(1955; rpt. London: Collins, 1973), p. 80.

[33] Peter Nabokov, "American Indian Literature: A Tradition of Renewal," *ASAIL Newsletter*,
2 (Autumn 1978), 37.

[34] Octavio Paz, *In Praise of Hands: Contemporary Crafts of the World* (Boston: New York
Graphic Society, 1974).

[35] H. S. McAllister, " 'The Language of Shamans': Jerome Rothenberg's Contribution to
American Indian Literature," *Western American Literature*, 10 (Feb. 1976), 299.

[36] A. Grove Day, *The Sky Clears: Poetry of the American Indians* (Lincoln: Univ. of Nebraska
Press, 1964), pp. 4–5.

[37] Vine Deloria, *God Is Red* (New York: Grosset and Dunlap, 1973), pp. 365–66.

[38] N. Scott Momaday, *The Way to Rainy Mountain* (Albuquerque: Univ. of New Mexico
Press, 1969), p. 46; hereafter cited as *WRM*.

[39] Octavio Paz argues that the beauty in art is good and useful in pretechnological cultures
where the arts are functional crafts; pottery, weaving, wood and metal work, song-
poetry, and story telling carry the touch of human hands (*In Praise of Hands*, pp.
45–52). W. H. Auden felt that cooking was the only functional art, both necessary
and aesthetic, left to western technological cultures.

[40] John (Fire) Lame Deer and Richard Erdoes, *Lame Deer, Seeker of Visions* (New York:
Simon, 1972), p. 266.

[41] Jerome Rothenberg, ed., *Shaking the Pumpkin: Traditional Poetry of the Indian North
Americas* (Garden City, N.Y.: Doubleday, 1972), pp. 310–11. I have adjusted the
line spacing.

[42] Dennis Tedlock, *Finding the Center: Narrative Poetry of the Zuni Indians* (Lincoln: Univ.
of Nebraska Press, 1978), p. xxxi.

[43] N. Scott Momaday, lecture, UCLA, May 1970.

[44] See Barre Toelken, "The 'Pretty Languages' of Yellowman: Genre, Mode, and Texture
in Navaho Coyote Narratives," in *Folklore Genres*, ed. Dan Ben-Amos (Austin: Univ.
of Texas Press, 1976), pp. 145–70.

[45] Jerome Rothenberg, "Total Translation: An Experiment in the Presentation of American
Indian Poetry," in Chapman, *Literature of the American Indians*, p. 295.

[46] John Bierhorst, ed., *In the Trail of the Wind: American Indian Poems and Ritual Orations*
(New York: Farrar, 1971), p. 45.

[47] Frank B. Linderman, *Plenty-Coups, Chief of the Crows* (Lincoln: Univ. of Nebraska Press,
1962), as quoted in Shirley Hill Witt and Stan Steiner, eds., *The Way: An Anthology
of American Indian Literature* (New York: Knopf, 1972), p. 16.

[48] N. Scott Momaday, "An American Land Ethic," *Sierra Club Bulletin*, No. 55 (Feb.
1970), p. 9.

[49] Carlos Castaneda, *A Separate Reality: Further Conversations with Don Juan* (New York:
Simon, 1971), pp. 105, 264, 187; hereafter cited in text.

[50] D. Demetracapoulou, "Wintu Songs," *Anthropos*, 30 (1935), 483–94.

[51] George Bird Grinnell, *The Fighting Cheyenne* (1915; rpt. Norman: Univ. of Oklahoma
Press, 1956), p. 178.

[52] Black Elk speaks of traveling with Buffalo Bill's "Wild West" show to New York and
"across the Big Water": "Afterwhile I got used to being there, but I was like a
man who had never had a vision. I felt dead and my people seemed lost and I
thought I might never find them again. I did not see anything to help my people.

I could see that the Wasichus did not care for each other the way our people did before the nation's hoop was broken. They would take everything from each other if they could, and so there were some who had more of everything than they could use, while crowds of people had nothing at all and maybe were starving. They had forgotten that the earth was their mother" (p. 221). Black Elk had gone with Buffalo Bill "because I might learn some secret of the Wasichu that would help my people" (pp. 218–19), but the pilgrimage failed. "Well, it is as it is. We are prisoners of war while we are waiting here. But there is another world" (p. 200).

53 Paul Radin, *The Autobiography of a Winnebago Indian* (1920; rpt. New York: Dover, 1963), p. 80.

54 Anita Probst, "Red Rock Ceremonies," in *Carriers of the Dream Wheel*, ed., Duane Niatum (New York: Harper, 1975), p. 164.

55 Niehardt, *John G. Neihardt, Flaming Rainbow* (three recordings of Neihardt readings), United Artists, UA-LA 157-J3, 1973.

56 Frances Densmore, *Teton Sioux Music* (1918; rpt. New York: Da Capo, 1972), p. 245; William K. Powers, "Oglala Song Terminology," *Selected Reports in Ethnomusicology* (Univ. of California, Los Angeles), 3, No. 2 (1980), 32. Densmore translates *wapiye* as "one who repairs," and Powers defines the term as "one who renews." Further references to these works appear in the text.

57 Charlotte Heth, *Songs of Love, Luck, Animals, and Magic: Music of the Yurok and Tolowa Indians*, New World Records, NW 297, 1977.

58 Some Lakota still practice the custom of preserving the infant's umbilical cord in an effigy; see Lame Deer and Erdoes, p. 145.

59 On the issue of Neihardt's role as editor and translator, see Sally McCluskey, "*Black Elk Speaks*: and So Does John Neihardt," *Western American Literature*, 6 (Winter 1972), 231–42, and Robert F. Sayre, "Vision and Experience in *Black Elk Speaks*," *College English*, 32 (Feb. 1971), 509–35. The collaborative bond was so strong between the two men that Neihardt, toward the end of his life, was not sure of any firm line between Black Elk's story and his own translating.

60 See Amos Bad Heart Bull, *A Pictographic History of the Oglala Sioux*, ed. Helen H. Blish (Lincoln: Univ. of Nebraska Press, 1967); Ben Kindle's Oglala Sioux oral winter count is reproduced in Turner, pp. 135–57.

61 National Geographic Society, *The World of the American Indian* (Washington, D.C.: National Geographic Society, 1974), p. 153.

62 Mari Sandoz, *Crazy Horse* (1942; rpt. Lincoln: Univ. of Nebraska Press, 1968).

63 See Toelken, "Seeing with a Native Eye," pp. 15–18.

64 Joseph Epes Brown, *The Sacred Pipe* (1953; rpt. Norman: Univ. of Oklahoma Press, 1975), p. 80.

65 N. Scott Momaday, *The Gourd Dancer* (New York: Harper, 1976), p. 37; hereafter cited in text as *GD*.

66 See Bierhorst, p. 39: "It was the wind that gave them life. It is the wind that comes out of our mouths now that gives us life. When this ceases to blow we die. In the skin at the tips of our fingers we see the trail of the wind; it shows us where the wind blew when our ancestors were created."

67 Mildred P. Mayhall, *The Kiowas* (Norman: Univ. of Oklahoma Press, 1962), pp. 110, 184.

68 Momaday quotes James Mooney's *Calendar History of the Kiowa Indians* (Washington, D.C.: Bureau of American Ethnology, 1898) extensively in *The Way to Rainy Mountain* and is heavily indebted to Mayhall's first chapter in *The Kiowas*. The openings to the books by Momaday and Mayhall are strikingly similar in tone and evocation of landscape. Elsie Clews Parsons' *Kiowa Tales* (New York: Stechert, 1929) opens with the "Split Boys" tale, a sacred origin story much the same as Aho's tale of the sun twins. Momaday has cut the excesses from Parsons' versions, tightened the structure, and spliced the various parts of his collection together with personal and ethnographic materials that frame the story-telling and give it clearer lines. *The Way to Rainy Mountain* shows the effect of poetic shaping and placement, a

simple grace that illuminates the tales. The synthesizing method here leaves the impression of mosaic composition; the carefully shaped and structured parts interplay to make the whole. The artist is responsible not so much for making up something new as for composing the given elements of Kiowa heritage and personally carrying on those traditions.

69 Momaday, *House Made of Dawn* (New York: Harper, 1968), p. 97; hereafter cited in text as *HMD*.

70 Momaday, *The Journey of Tai-me*, Tale 29, copy no. 80, special collections vault, Univ. of California, Santa Barbara.

71 See John Bierhorst, ed., *Four Masterworks of American Indian Literature* (New York: Farrar, 1974), p. 281 and Mircea Eliade on "conquering time" in sacred mythic ceremonies, *Myth and Reality*, trans. Willard R. Trask (New York: Harper, 1963), pp. 75–91.

72 See Mayhall, p. 15, and Mooney, pp. 254–364. Mooney lived with Sett'an, and his work includes a full-page plate of the Sett'an calendar.

73 Curtis' 40,000 photographs, 10,000 sound recordings, and miles of motion pictures covering eighty different tribes and thirty years of his life's work were first published as 272 rare editions of a twenty-volume set under the patronage of J. Pierpont Morgan. *The North American Indian* was reissued forty years later to the general public. "I do not think like a photographer," Curtis said; he tried to bring "art and science together in an effort to reach beneath the surface of what appears to be." T. C. McLuhan produced a brilliant two-reel film, "The Shadow Catcher" (1974 NEA), on the life and work of Edward Curtis. It is a fitting introduction to the field of Native American studies.

74 The present generation of Indian writers seems to have eliminated the need for non-Indian go-betweens, as in Oliver La Farge, *Laughing Boy* (1929); John Neihardt, *Black Elk Speaks* (1932); Leo Simmons, *Sun Chief* (1942); or Hal Borland, *When the Legends Die* (1963). A collaborative, bicultural model now works both ways at once, as in Richard Erdoes and John (Fire) Lame Deer, *Lame Deer, Seeker of Visions* (1972); Howard Norman and Jacob Slowstream, *The Wishing Bone Cycle* (1976); Dennis Tedlock, Andrew Peynetsa, and Walter Sanchez, *Finding the Center: Narrative Poetry of the Zuni Indians* (1972); or Margot Liberty and John Stands in Timber's *Cheyenne Memories* (1967). Harper and Row has initiated a Native American Publishing Program, while the universities of Nebraska, Oklahoma, and New Mexico continue to print standard texts in the field. Charles R. Larson has just published the first critical study of Indian novelists, *American Indian Fiction* (Albuquerque: Univ. of New Mexico Press, 1978). Hundreds of tribal newspapers are supplemented by the national publications *Wassaja*, *Many Smokes*, *Sun Tracks*, and *Akwasasne Notes*. Scholarly periodicals such as *The Indian Historian*, *American Anthropologist*, *Ethnohistory*, *American Indian Quarterly*, and the UCLA *American Indian Culture and Research Journal* promote academic studies. Among major universities, New Mexico, Arizona, Arizona State, San Diego State, UCLA, California at Berkeley, Minnesota, and Dartmouth support active Indian studies programs; UCLA offers a master's program in American Indian studies.

75 Jaime de Angulo, *Indians in Overalls* (1950; rpt. San Francisco: Turtle Island, 1973), p. 63.

76 Howard A. Norman, trans., *The Wishing Bone Cycle: Narrative Poems from the Swampy Cree Indians* (New York: Stonehill, 1976), p. 121; hereafter cited in text. Howard Norman recently has gathered and translated the "opposite thinking" Cree tales that fearfully complement Trickster's comic inversions, *Where the Chill Came From: Cree Windigo Tales and Journeys* (San Francisco: North Point, 1982).

77 William Smith Smith, quoted in Norman, p. 172.

78 Ralph Ellison, "Richard Wright's Blues," *Antioch Review*, 5, No. 2 (Summer 1945), 198–211; rpt. in *Shadow and Act* (1953; rpt. New York: New American Library, 1966), p. 90.

[79] All poems by Welch quoted in the text are from *Riding the Earthboy 40* (1971; rpt. New York: Harper, 1976).

[80] James Welch, *Winter in the Blood* (1974; rpt. New York: Bantam, 1975), p. 56; hereafter cited in text as *WB*. Since this article was written, Welch has published a second novel, *The Death of Jim Loney* (New York: Harper, 1979). See Kenneth Lincoln, review of *The Death of Jim Loney*, in *American Indian Culture and Research Journal*, 4, Nos. 1-2 (1980), 179–86.

[81] James Welch, "The Only Good Indian," *South Dakota Review*, 9 (Summer 1971), 54. Revised and enlarged, this eventually became *Winter in the Blood*.

[82] George Bird Grinnell, *Blackfeet Lodge Tales: The Story of a Prairie People* (1892; rpt. Lincoln: Univ. of Nebraska Press, 1962), p. 177; hereafter cited in text.

[83] Malcolm McFee, *Modern Blackfeet: Montanans on a Reservation* (New York: Holt, 1972), p. 52.

[84] Clark Wissler and D. C. Duvall, "Mythology of the Blackfeet Indians," *Anthropological Papers of the American Museum of Natural History*, 2, No. 1 (1908), 19–21.

[85] Theodora Kroeber, *Ishi in Two Worlds: A Biography of the Last Wild Indian in North America* (Berkeley: Univ. of California Press, 1961), pp. 127–28.

[86] Peter L. Berger, *Pyramids of Sacrifice: Political Ethics and Social Change* (1974; rpt. Garden City, N.Y.: Doubleday, 1976), pp. 23–24.

[87] Luther Standing Bear recalls the first class of Carlisle Indian schoolboys being assigned Christian names from a list written on a blackboard. Names were chosen with a pointer and taped on their shirts. "Soon we all had the names of white men sewed on our backs," he remembers; the procedure stood in stark contrast to the Lakota tradition of finding a name on the vision quest or in an act of bravery. *My People the Sioux* (1928; rpt. Lincoln: Univ. of Nebraska Press, 1975), p. 137.

[88] Alan Velie has documented the surrealist influences of Cesar Vallejo and James Wright on Welch in "James Welch's Poetry," *American Indian Culture and Research Journal*, 3, No. 1 (1979), 19–38.

[89] Edward S. Curtis, *The North American Indian: The Indians of the United States and Alaska*, III (1908; rpt. New York: Johnson, 1970), 66.

[90] John C. Ewers, *The Blackfeet: Raiders of the Northwestern Plains* (Norman: Univ. of Oklahoma Press, 1958), p. 258; hereafter cited in the text.

[91] Wallace Stegner, *Wolf Willow* (1955; rpt. New York: Viking, 1973), p. 8.

[92] See Dennis and Barbara Tedlock, eds., *Teachings from the American Earth: Indian Religion and Philosophy* (New York: Liveright, 1975).

[93] Paiute Ghost Dance Song, quoted in Brandon, p. 129.

[94] See Ewers, Chapter Eight, "All in Fun," on the traditional Blackfeet winter sports such as sliding and sledding, ice tops, and blanket tossing games.

[95] See, in particular, the anthropologist's identification as an extended kin with "neolithic" cultures in Claude Lévi-Strauss' *Tristes Tropiques* and The Savage Mind.

[96] *Wassaja*, 6, Nos. 7–8 (Aug.-Sept. 1978), 9–10. The statement begins an address to the United States Congress in 1977 made by the tribal coalition of traditional elders on the Longest Walk. To protest the abrogation of treaties the people reversed Manifest Destiny by walking for half a year from the West Coast to the East Coast.

Worlds Made of Dawn: Characteristic Image and Incident in Native American Imaginative Literature

Lester A. Standiford

In any culture, myth, legend, and folklore serve to explain the unexplainable, to promote cultural continuity and survival, and also to entertain. In this regard, Native American oral literature is no different. The Oklahoma Cherokee storyteller Asudi explains the function of his art in this way: "That's the way you heard things, and if you didn't pay attention, you wouldn't know anything. If you had paid attention, you would know."[1]

And if contemporary Indian imaginative writers have taken on a nontraditional language and a more complex mode of expression, it is only because they must adapt the basic techniques of their essential function to a changing world. The voice of Wah'Kon-tah, the great spirit that moves through all being, must be passed on, whether we call the vehicle myth or art. Furthermore, if we of this cacophonous age are to hear that voice, we must learn how to pay attention. Asudi's alternatives are unmistakable.

In one regard, ours is a particularly rewarding time to inquire into the literature of the Indian Americans, for it is a period of great publishing activity on the part of the Native American authors themselves. While there have been previous bursts of interest in ethnological transcriptions of oral literatures and flurries of collected translations of primitive poetry over the past hundred years, including A. Grove Day's *The Sky Clears*, William Brandon's *The Magic World*, and Jerome Rothenberg's *Shaking the Pumpkin*, it was not until 1968 that a written imaginative literature of the contemporary Indian American was founded. In that year, N. Scott Momaday, a Kiowa writer, published *House Made of Dawn*, a novel that won the Pulitzer Prize for 1969.

Momaday's work appeared simultaneously with a rebirth of political and social consciousness on the part of Indian Americans in the late 1960s, most forcefully expressed by Vine Deloria, Jr., in his 1969 manifesto, *Custer Died for Your Sins*. Since that time, the work of Indian imaginative writers has progressed along with the public's burgeoning interest in the social and political affairs of their people. In 1974 James Welch, a Blackfeet–GrosVentre writer, saw his first prose work, *Winter in the Blood*, referred to as "A nearly flawless novel about human life," by Reynolds Price in the *New York Times Book Review*.[2] Welch and Momaday have also written well-received collections of poetry, and other young poets and fiction writers, among them, Grey Cohoe, Durango Mendoza, Simon Ortiz, Gerald Vizenor, Phil George, Emerson Blackhorse Mitchell, Patty Harjo, Leslie Silko, Alonzo Lopez, Ray A. Young Bear, Bruce Ignacio, Duane Niatum, and Harold Littlebird, have placed their work in our most respected magazines and anthologies.

In other words, we are witnessing the birth of a contemporary Indian American Literature, an imaginative literature that resembles the oral literatures of the Native American tribal cultures in some ways yet speaks through the contemporary American literary medium as a distinct and powerful force. It is important that we seek a greater understanding and appreciation of that literature.

During one of those earlier periods of interest in primitive Indian literature—better referred to as traditional Indian literature, for our purposes—Louis Untermeyer reviewed a collection of translations from Indian oral poetry, calling it a document valuable chiefly for its ethnological interest, saying that it proved to him that "the harsh aborigine can commit poetry as trite and banal as many an overcivilized paleface." He concluded his review by noting that "as a collection for the mere man of letters it is a rather forbidding pile—a crude and top-heavy monument with a few lovely and even lively decorations."[3] Untermeyer's review brought a response from Mary Austin, a long-time student of Indian oral literatures, who wrote: "Mr. Untermeyer describes himself as a 'mere man of letters,' . . . but it begins to be a question in America whether a man is entitled to describe himself as a man of letters at all who so complacently confesses his ignorance of and inability to enter into the vast body of aboriginal literature of his country."[4]

Fifty years later, Vine Deloria, Jr., added a postscript to the matter of outside inquiry into the nature of things Indian. Writing in *Custer Died for Your Sins*, he in effect imposed a check on all researchers: "Perhaps we should suspect the real motives of the academic community. . . . Their concern is not the ultimate policy that will affect the Indian people, but merely the creation of new slogans and doctrines by which they can climb the university totem pole."[5]

It is between these poles that our inquiry is best directed, when we attempt to learn and enjoy without enforcing old assumptions on

those new aspects of a literature that draws from sources outside the
Anglo-American heritage. It is a very recent and still tenuous change
in Anglo attitude that allows for an objective view of any so-called
emergent or minority literature as being equal in value to the familiar.
But it is a healthy change and one that forces a new perspective, as we
see in this bit of Indian humor that Deloria relates in *Custer*: Two
Indians are viewed hidden in the forest, watching the arrival of the
Pilgrims at Plymouth. One turns to the other with a look of great
sadness and says, "Well, there goes the neighborhood" (p. 148).

Before going further, I would like to make it clear that I am not
interested in segregating literature into any permanent, exclusive cat-
egories. I am, however, interested in bringing as much exciting contemporary creative work to the attention of the widest possible audience.
I believe that many readers either feel distanced from works identified
as Indian American or become patronizing toward them. In either case,
the reader loses. While my remarks on the background and makeup of
contemporary Indian American imaginative literature may appear to be
aimed at enhancing its "emergence," I hope that they also serve to
delineate the shape of imaginative literature in general and to illuminate
the particular strengths of a group of writings from which any reader
or writer might gain. A greater understanding of the origins and characteristic image and incident patterns of any literature brings a reader
closer to that body of works. This understanding should also work
against the tendency to patronize the work by accepting it more for its
sociological value than for its status as imaginative art.

For those who would object at the outset that a "minority" literature
should be granted its own distinct set of artistic criteria based on political
contingency, let me quote from Gary Snyder's "The Yogin and the
Philosopher," in which he distinguishes between the philosopher, who
speaks "the language of reason and public discourse," and the poet/
yogin, "who marries word and song together."[6] Snyder goes on to draw
all poets together, saying: "The long 'pagan' battle of western poetry
against state and church, the survival of the Muse down to modern
times, shows that in a sense poetry has been a long and not particularly
successful defending action. Defending 'the groves'—sacred to the Goddess—and logged, so to speak, under orders from Exodus 34:13, 'you
shall destroy their images and cut down their groves' " (p. 3). Poetry
is involved in a battle, all right, but not in behalf of anyone's politics;
the battle is against politics itself.

In this view, poetry becomes a voice apart from the rhetoric of
church and state. Poetry *is* its images and its groves, speaking not in
service of church or state but in service of itself. I will be speaking of

contemporary Indian American poetry and fiction according to this archetypal concept of the poet as shaman who "speaks for wild animals, the spirits of plants, the spirits of mountains, of watersheds" (Snyder, p. 3). If you must have a notion of the worldly function of the poet, base it on this example from Snyder's remarks: "The elaborate, yearly, cyclical production of grand ritual dramas in the societies of Pueblo Indians . . . can be seen as a process by which the whole society consults the non-human powers and allows some individuals to step totally out of their human roles to put on the mask, costume, and mind of Bison, Bear, Squash, Corn, or Pleiades; to re-enter the human circle in that form and by song, mime, and dance, convey a greeting from the other realm. Thus a speech on the floor of congress from a whale" (p. 3).

Another way to explain the distinction is to point out that a poet who is lured away from the images and the groves to speak as a philosopher on the floor of Congress will weaken and wither as does any magician who leaves off contact with the touchstone. But poetry that speaks with the voice of the whale resounds with the true power of Indian American imaginative literature. It is the power referred to by William Carlos Williams when he described poetry as capturing the universal in the local.

We might at this point deal with a related controversy regarding the access of the "outsider" to Indian American literature. Some contemporary "minority" writers argue that their work is not intended for outsiders, particularly Anglos, and that it is in fact unintelligible to the reader who has not experienced life in the way of the intended audience. In his introduction to *Shaking the Pumpkin: Traditional Poetry of the Indian North Americans*, Jerome Rothenberg responds that "it has become fashionable today to deny the possibility of crossing the boundaries that separate people of different races & cultures: to insist instead that black is the concern of black, red of red, and white of white. Yet the idea of translation has always been that such boundary crossing is not only possible but desirable. . . . The question for the translator is not whether but how far we can translate one another. Like the poet who is his brother, he attempts to restore what has been torn apart."[7]

Of course, a short-sighted view of the application of minority literatures would exclude even those members of a group whose place might be validated by blood heritage but whose life experience lies largely outside the normal experience of the group. Should the Anglo farmer, for example, be discouraged from reading *Moby-Dick*? In addition, the experience of the modern Indian has moved away from the traditional tribal ways toward the experience of many Americans, even when the Indian is most insulated from the mainstream. William Kittredge makes this point in his review of a number of modern translations from the oral literatures of the tribes: "The other day I talked with a friend raised in the Pipe Region on the Pine Ridge Reservation in South Dakota, close to the site of Wounded Knee, and asked if he thought the young people could ever go back to the old ways. He told me no, that nobody could ever be Indian again in that sense. Too many things have been lost."[8]

And if the experience of the modern Indian is similar in some respects to that of many others who live in the United States, when a literary work is written in English, the amalgam of tribal experience and American experience provides an entrée for any English-speaking reader. As G. W. Haslam puts it, "language, unlike clay or pigment, is not a neutral medium; it imposes its own unique perceptual pattern and rhythm of expression. As a consequence, many literary forms are simply not transferable to English."[9] Thus a haiku written in, or translated into, English is no longer a haiku; the form is integrally bound to the dense suggestive power of the Japanese language in the same way that traditional oral poetries of the Indian American are bound to their original languages. Haslam has described the native languages as "essentially polysynthetic . . . composed of word-like bursts of sound each of which reflects meaning approximating that conveyed by an entire English sentence" (p. 15). What results in English may be a pleasurable success, but the work is undeniably a hybrid. In the haiku, it becomes an *Ameriku*; the Native American poem becomes an Indian American poem. Furthermore, the hybrid is likely to be most successful when it draws its influence from the original but does not attempt to copy it. The following Chippewa war song, when accompanied by its original music and coming in the context of other, more explicit, war-preparation lyrics, would have fully conjured up the sense of stoic bravery to its tribal audience, but it well may need explaining to the modern Anglo-American audience:

> in the coming heat
> of the day
> I stood there.[10]

Still, a modern Indian American writer can integrate such a simple natural image into a slightly longer context to suggest unspoken meanings to any reader. Consider this portion of Ray A. Young Bear's "One Chip of Human Bone":

One chip of human bone.

it is almost fitting
to die on the railroad tracks

. . . .
there is something about
trains, drinking, and being
an indian with nothing to lose.[11]

Because of the well-meaning liberals' desire to "give the downtrodden a break" and, for some, their drive to expiate their own sense of guilt, it may seem difficult at first to understand that the only standard by which to judge an Indian American work composed in English is that same artistic standard of unity of subject, style, and perceived intention that is generally applied to a work by Ernest Hemingway or Joyce Carol Oates. The only new knowledge necessary is an understanding of the cultural influences operating behind themes and styles of the Indian American works. With this goal in mind, let us turn to the question of a common Indian experience and its manifestation in current poetry.

N. Scott Momaday, when asked to describe the Indian voice in contemporary literature, gave this deceptively simple answer: "The phrase 'American-Indian writer' I understand to indicate an American Indian who writes. It does not indicate anything more than that to me."[12] But it should be remembered that the term "Indian" is itself a misleading white man's term that many Native Americans believe usurps distinct tribal identities. (Many blacks believe that slave names perform a similar disservice.) When Christopher Columbus arrived in the New World, he believed that he had reached India and accordingly labeled the inhabitants he met. It is estimated that at that time there were more than 2,000 independent tribes in the present United States, speaking languages of 50 distinct language families; and while more than 300 tribes and some 250 dialects remain,[13] the label "Indian" remains the common generic and conceptual term among non–Native Americans. Yet, as Harold Fey and D'Arcy McNickle explain, "To be an aboriginal of the Americas is to be Sioux, or Cree, or Mohawk, or Navajo—a tribesman. Among those who live most intimately with tradition, to talk about 'Indian issues' or 'Indian aspirations' is to talk a dangerous kind of nonsense. One might offend someone by seeming to speak for him."[14]

Nonetheless, a rising political awareness has led to the recognition of a common set of socioeconomic problems that extant tribes share, so that a certain pan-tribal feeling exists regardless of the difficulty of defining that elusive term. Such groups as the National Indian Youth

Council, established by young Native Americans who found their tribal elders too accommodating to the whites, and the Indians of All Nations, the militant group that occupied Alcatraz in 1969, represent the emergence of a new "Indian" consciousness.

Thomas Sanders and Walter Peek liken the process of defining a Native American to that of defining a Jew: it becomes largely a self-identification process. As Jews know they are Jews because they recognize themselves as part of an identifiable sociohistorical heritage, so do Indians know they are Indians because of their ties to the land, the remaining fragments of their oral literature, and their lingering awareness of heroic forbears.[15] Sanders and Peek cite La Donna Harris' reply to a group of University of South Florida students who asked her the difficult question during a 1972 campus lecture: "I can't define the Indian for you any more than you can define what you are. Different governmental agencies define him by amount of blood. I had a Comanche mother and an Irish father. But I am Comanche. I'm not Irish. And I'm not Indian *first*. I'm Comanche first, Indian second. When the Comanche took in someone, he became Comanche. He wasn't part this, part that. He was *all* Comanche or he wasn't Comanche at all. Blood runs the heart. The *heart* knows what it is" (Sanders and Peek, p. 11).

Perhaps the most popular concept of Indian identity for all Americans springs from the tragic political history of nearly all the tribes. Archaeological theory agrees that settlement of the North American continent began at least as early as 10,000 B.C. when tribesmen crossed the Bering Strait and moved southward. The movement is generally agreed to have ended with the arrival of the Eskimos approximately two thousand years ago.[16] Thus, while the claim of some Indian writers that civilization actually began on this continent may be romantic speculation, archaeologists have established beyond a doubt that the Indians were the original settlers on the land and that they maintained advanced systems of government and cultural institutions. Benjamin Franklin used the smoothly functioning Iroquois Confederacy as a model in attempts to end bickering among delegates to the Albany Conference (Sanders and Peek, p. 6), and Mayan literature had developed by the sixteenth century to include "history, science, lives of great men, astronomy, astrology, prophecy, theology, ritual, legends, fables, medicine, grammar, 'certain songs in meter,' and 'comedies for the pleasure of the public,' "[17] all of which the good Bishop Landa of Yucatan burned as part of the church's conversion efforts.

Despite the achievements of the Native Americans, the arriving white man tended to classify Indians as either romantic simpletons or bloodthirsty savages, depending on political expediency. The familiar "vanishing American" concept has its roots in the white man's refusal to recognize the Indians' claim to their territory or their right to life. Because most Indian tribes recognized only "use" or territory rights to the land which remained under the ownership of the Great Spirit, they were unable to understand the white man's concept of land as a salable commodity. Fey and McNickle describe the ensuing battles as clashes between an aggressive, acquisitive, materialistic society and a society that put the safety and welfare of the group above individual ambition. As the arriving Europeans valued a person for the amount of property he or she owned, the Indian with the most standing in the community was the one who gave the most to others (Fey and McNickle, pp. 19–20). In accordance with General Philip Sheridan's observation that "The only good Indians I ever saw were dead,"[18] the population of Native Americans within the United States had dropped from an estimated 900,000 in 1492 to 250,000 by 1900 (Fey and McNickle, p. 10).

The "Indian Campaigns," or "White Man's Wars," depending on one's point of view, have been recently recounted in terms sympathetic to the tribes by such writers as Fey and McNickle, Dee Brown, and William Brandon. While some critics have objected particularly to Brown's clear preference for the Indians' side of the story, there is no argument among Indians themselves, who feel that the book is long overdue in the face of hundred of years of Anglo-dominated interpretations of battles with "heathen," "brutish," "depraved savages," a one-sided saga that culminated in the twentieth-century Hollywood stereotype. David F. Beer's illuminating survey of the Indian image in early American literature charges that from the beginning, European Americans wrote of the Native Americans only for the allied purposes of religious conversion and political exploitation.[19] Beer cites the remarks of Captain John Smith as the model of literary inaccuracy that predominated into the twentieth century: "They are inconstant in everything, but what fear constraineth them to keep. Crafty, timorous, quick of apprehension and very ingenious, some are of disposition fearful, some bold, most cautious, all savage . . . they are soon moved to anger, and so malicious that they seldom forget an injury" (p. 208). Beer summarizes the progression of the early European-American literary view by saying, "From the initial poorly informed reports on the Red Man emerged the bigoted and ethnocentric literary attitudes of the pious and land-hungry Puritans. Soon to follow were the commercial and greatly fictional captivity narratives, and the turn of the century 'histories' of the Indian wars (never the 'White,' or 'Settlers' or 'Colonists' wars)" (p. 216).

In return for their lands, native tribes were shunted onto reservations often composed of marginal land,[20] which were in turn reduced in size, until today the per capita land base of the Sisseton Sioux has been valued at $19.12.[21] Nonetheless, reservation land remains the center of existence for most Native Americans, for it is estimated that 400,000, or 80%, of the identifiable Indians in the United States live on reservations or in similar tribal settlements (Fey and McNickle, pp. 10–12). This land, along with its allied political organization, is the means by which the tribes' existence is formalized; and as Fey and McNickle put it, Indians "are no more prepared to legislate themselves out of existence . . . than is any other group of people sharing a common history, a common language, and a system of commonly accepted goals in life" (p. 13). The peremptory action alluded to in this statement of allegiance to reservation land is the intermittent policy of "termination" employed by the government through its Bureau of Indian Affairs (BIA). Termination has its origins in the Federal Allotment Act of 1887, which attempted to turn Indians into "good American settlers"; the Act gave individual Indians title to small areas of land, anywhere from 10 to 640 acres, with all remaining acreage declared surplus land that the Department of the Interior was free to sell for white development. In this fashion, some 90 million of the 140 million acres designated as reservation land in 1887 were lost to the Indian by 1934, when the Indian Reorganization Act stopped the practice of allowing reservation land to pass out of the hands of individual tribe members.

Yet, once again, in the 1950s the BIA moved toward termination of reservation holdings in an attempt to force the Indians away from their tribal ways and into the mainstream of American life. During this time, the lands of the Menominees of Wisconsin and the rich timber holdings of the Klamaths of southern Oregon were in fact broken up into individual holdings, most of which were then acquired by white business interests.[22]

Because of this history of political oppression, it should come as no surprise that political reaction is a common theme in modern Indian literature, oratorical and imaginative alike. Leaving aside traditional instruments of war, today's most combative Native Americans have turned to the word. Vine Deloria, Jr.—with such books as *Custer Died for Your Sins, We Talk—You Listen, God Is Red,* and *Behind the Trail of Broken Treaties*—has emerged as the most prominent of the modern orators, inspired by the accomplishments of such illustrious native speakers as the Shawnee Tecumseh (whose people, he said, have vanished before the onslaught of the white man "as snow before a summer sun") and Chief Joseph of the Nez Percé, author of the famous "I will fight no more forever" surrender speech. Representative samples of the growing body of contemporary Indian oratory can be found in Stan Steiner's *The*

New Indians and an anthology compiled by Steiner and Shirley Hill Witt entitled *The Way*.

Problems relating to relocation and termination and the reaction to genocide are perhaps the first themes to which younger imaginative writers direct their attention, with somewhat predictable results. Often, native writers are overcome with the urgency of their message and forsake all concerns of craft in the effort to make a point, as in these examples:

> It was the land of the free,
> and of the first Americans.
> Where has it all gone?
>
> Look around and you will see
> bare eroded lands, damned rivers,
> discarded hungry people . . .[23]
>
> In my own country I'm in a far off land
> I'm strong but have no force or power
> I win yet remain a loser. . . .[24]
>
> I've often wondered why it is said
> that the Indian Spirit is broken and dead—
> why such balderdash fills the air
> when in their midst like a grizzly bear
> is the sleeping red-skinned giant now on the prowl
> an answer to a lone Kiowa's vengeful howl.[25]

Given some understanding of the problems referred to in these works, any reader would be sympathetic to the sentiments expressed, but most readers looking for artful use of the language are likely to be put off by the prosaic stridency. Such black writers as Albert Lee Murray and Ralph Ellison have seen their works criticized by some militants who seek more visible anger in the writing. But as Murray, in his *Omni-Americans*, and Ellison, in *Shadow and Act*, have made clear, forever reacting in rage to accusations only suggests the truth of the charges and prevents positive action along a course of self-determination: the poet's most important initial task is to develop his or her own voice. G. W. Haslam has called for the day "when Indian writers as a group forsake blatant protest and employ more imaginative—and probably more persuasive—forms; the pressure of their plight has tended to force Indian writers into desperate excoriations of conditions. Like Afro-Americans, who have found that subtlety is often a more effective social weapon than shrill anger, Native American artists are beginning to discover their own most moving modes of expression" (*Forgotten Pages*, p. 24). Examples of poems that do operate according to such principles of subtlety and yet maintain their social force are found today in the work of James Welch, Simon Ortiz, and Anita Endrezze-Probst, among others.

In this section of Endrezze-Probst's poem "The Week-End Indian," we find understatement and suggestion working despite the deceptive prosaic quality and the highly charged subject matter:

> In red wool jacket and earflaps
> you circle your camp three times
> before you realize you're lost.
> You deny it, squinting at moss
> growing on the north of trees,
> and thumb through your new copy
> of "Indian Lore and Camp Book."
> The pages are blank.
>
> Your compass, with its glowing digits,
> whirs spastically toward your feet.
> Fur-lined and waterproofed, your boots
> are, in case of emergencies, edible.
> Your fishing line has become knotted,
> clumped in a thick-leafed bush,
> like a small bird's nest.
> The redwoods gather above you,
> waiting like many-winged vultures
> . . . .
> Lost, on the night of your first day,
> you huddle against a deep cliff
> whispering into your palms,
> cupping them against your ears.
> They answer you in slow echoes.[26]

And clearly we see restraint working hand in hand with the same theme of loss and dispossession in this segment of Simon Ortiz' "Relocation":

> i see me walking in sleep
> down streets down streets grey with cement
> and glaring glass and oily wind
> armed with a pint of wine.

But Ortiz himself occasionally shifts to more direct statement, as in this excerpt from the same poem:

> the deadened glares
>   tear my heart
>   and close my mind
>
> who questions my pain
> the tight knot of anger
> in my breast.[27]

It is in the works of James Welch, however, that we find perhaps the most balanced and convincing blend of suggestion, dense imagery, and sociopolitical theme. Consider this excerpt from "The Man from Washington":

> The end came easy for most of us
> . . . .
> we didn't expect much more
> than firewood and buffalo robes
> . . . The man came down,
> a slouching dwarf with rainwater eyes
> . . . He promised that life would go on as usual
> that treaties would be signed, and everyone—
> man, woman and child—would be inoculated
> against a world in which we had no part,
> a world of wealth, promise and fabulous disease.[28]

Similarly, this quotation from "The Only Bar in Dixon":

> These Indians once imitated life.
> Whatever made them warm
> they called wine, song or sleep,
> a lucky number on the tribal roll.
>
> Now the stores have gone the gray
> of this November sky. Cars
> whistle by, chrome wind, knowing
> something lethal in the dust.[29]

Welch's approach is even more understated in "Dancing Man," where the poem works equally well as lament for a boy's loss of innocence and lament for the loss of the lyric cultural heritage of an entire people:

He swung gracefully into midnight
that man on the plains.
The stories he told were true enough
and we were young
to understand his beetle eye.
It wasn't till later
the dream broke
and we spun solid as a rock
back to the cold cactus ground,
winehappy and stubborn.[30]

    While such social and political concerns are easily enough discerned in Native American poetry, a more complex related theme underlies many works, one of a spiritual attachment to the land and an interrelationship with all things, organic and inorganic alike. While specific rituals differ from tribe to tribe, most commentators agree that traditional Indian religions stress a spiritual equality of all things: fish, trees, human beings, rocks, and rivers. Herbert Blatchford, one of the founders of the National Indian Youth Council and director of the Gallup Indian Community Center, explains the thinking that girds many traditional myths and legends and applies to modern works as well: "To fully understand these stories, which to my mind are designed to teach moral behavior, a person has to think in terms of Universal Life Continuity; that is, that there is a related continuity of life and well-being between all living matter, and that this life and well-being are dependent upon all organic and inorganic matter."[31]

    Blatchford asserts further that, because of the Indians' concern with maintaining harmony and thus disrupting the course of natural events as little as possible, traditionally oriented Indians do not project their goals far into the future ("Religion of the People," p. 176). Because Indians believe there is strength to be gained from maintaining this balance, their homeland and all its natural accoutrements become an integral part of their life, with the cliffs and grasses as important to them as their neighbors and themselves. N. Scott Momaday makes the concept clear in this passage from *House Made of Dawn*, where the grandfather takes his sons out on the land for their first important lesson:

    He made them stand just there, above the point of the low white rock, facing east. They could see the black mesa looming on the first light, and he told them there was the house of the sun. They must learn the whole contour of the black mesa. They must know it as they knew the shape of their hands, always and by heart. . . . They must know the long journey of the sun on the black mesa, how it rode in the seasons and the years, and they must live according to the sun appearing, for only then could they reckon where they were, where all things were, in time.[32]

According to this view, a lifetime is not a linear journey: the quality of existence is measured in terms of lateral expansion, not attenuation.

A similar attitude toward an integrated life force is seen in this untitled poem by Vance Iron Good, who describes the coming of spring, when the rains

> . . . awaken the earth
> as one would wake a dreamer
> or love a young girl
> gently at first.[33]

And in this segment from Momaday's poem, "Angle of Geese," we find also the sense of eternity in the moment, an emblem of the nonlinear concept of time:

> And one November
> It was longer in the watch,
> As if forever
> Of the huge ancestral goose.
>
> So much symmetry!
> Like the pale angle of time
> And eternity.
> The great shape labored and fell.
>
> Quit of hope and hurt
> It held the motionless gaze,
> Wide of time, alert,
> On the dark distant flurry.[34]

Without a knowledge of this necessary oneness with the land and its attendant convictions, readers might completely misunderstand a story such as Grey Cohoe's "The Promised Visit."[35] In this work, a young Navajo leaves his home on the reservation to journey to the tribal council headquarters for a scholarship interview. The boy has decided to leave his family and the reservation to study art, a decision that will also remove him from an atmosphere of primitive superstition he professes to disdain. At this point, most Anglo readers would applaud the boy's thinking as forward looking and properly goal oriented. Later, however, as a result of a mystical encounter with a beautiful spirit girl who embodies many of the traditional aspects of "Navajo-ness," the boy begins to question his earlier resolve and finally suggests that he may turn down the scholarship and stay on with the land and the tilling and his people. By this time, the Anglo reader might fault the boy's final indecision as whimsical, irresponsible, and based in superstitious fear. That judgment would constitute a misreading of the story, however. The key line exhibiting the Navajo point of view is this summary statement from the protagonist: "From that day I had proven to myself the truth of the Navajo superstitions" (p. 171). Through his fortuitous encounter with the strong spirit of his people, the boy has realized something of the absurdity of a Navajo totally renouncing his own heritage in order to learn art in the white man's school.

In Durango Mendoza's story, "Summer Water and Shirley,"[36] there exists the possibility of another kind of misunderstanding on the part of the non-Indian reader. The narrator is a twelve-year-old whose younger sister Shirley comes down with a sudden fever after taunting a *stiginee*, or witch/shaman, near the dry stream bed on their Oklahoma reservation. After the futile application of all traditional remedies for possession by evil water spirits and the equally useless visits from a white doctor, Shirley's mother and the rest of the community abandon hope. Everything possible has been done; the elders are resigned that the girl will die before the fourth sun rises.

The boy, however, is not content to sit by while his sister dies, and so he steals into the darkened room where she has been prepared for her passing. After a long night's vigil during which the boy directly confronts his fear of the dark unknown and prays for his sister's recovery, the dawn brings with it his sister's miraculous stirrings of recovery. This series of events could possibly confuse the reader unfamiliar with yet another pillar of the Indian American cosmos. After all, not only has the white man's medicine failed, but so has that of the native. Thus the story might remain murky, a tale describing a miracle, perhaps signifying the efficacy of pious prayer to some, unless one considers more carefully the passage describing the boy's most fervent efforts to take back his sister's life from the spirits of the dark:

> And then he spoke softly, saying what they had done, and how they would do again what they had done because he had not given up, for he was alive, and she was alive, and they had lived and would *still* live. And so he prayed to his will and forced his will out through his thoughts and spoke softly his words and was not afraid to look out through the window into the darkness through which came the coolness of the summer night (p. 504).

Here the key to understanding is the Native American concept of the great and inherent power of the *word*. Because the boy can force his will out through his thoughts and into words, he succeeds in his task. This sense of the power of the word derives from the thousands of years of the Native American oral literary tradition. From its labyrinthine and tenuous history the word arrives in the present with inestimable force. As Scott Momaday points out in his essay "The Man Made of Words," the oral form exists always just one generation from extinction and is all the more precious on that account.[37] And this sense of care engendered for the songs and stories and their words naturally leads to an appreciation of the power of the word itself.

Properly cared for, preserved intact, a story has the power to sustain an entire culture, as it literally did in the case of the Kiowa. Momaday recounts the beginnings of such a process at the conclusion of his retelling of the Kiowa myths in *The Way to Rainy Mountain*. Shortly after midnight on 13 November 1833, a spectacular meteor shower lit up the heavens above the Oklahoma camp of the Kiowa. Terrified, the people ran out upon the night, certain that the world was coming to an end. And in fact, it was only four years later that the Kiowa were forced to sign their first treaty with the government of the United States, an action that signaled the ensuing decline of one of the proudest tribes of the Plains culture.[38]

Momaday first heard of that fateful night from Ko-Sahn, a venerable Kiowa woman who had not seen the event but who spoke of it in such detail that she surely had lived it in her mind's eye. Further, Momaday explains, seeing the shower as an omen of disaster gave the Kiowa the strength to bear what befell them thereafter. Thus, his ancestors had invested the event with meaning and order, and it sustained them through chaos, as it in turn sustained Ko-Sahn (*Way to Rainy Mountain*, p. 105). For Momaday, our very being is a function of our idea of ourselves, and the richest, most enduring expression of that being is to be found in its timeless expression in literature–hence, his concept of man *made* of words.

This appreciation of the word's power to create and shape also accounts for the repetition found in much traditional Indian poetry, as we see in this excerpt from the Navajo "Voice of the Bluebird," a song to bring the rain and raise the corn:

> The corn grows up. The waters of the
>   dark clouds drop, drop.
> The rain descends. The waters from the
>   corn leaves drop, drop.

> The rain descends. The waters from the
>   plants drop, drop.
> The corn grows up. The waters of the
>   dark mists drop, drop.[39]

And this belief in the power of words in turn explains those portions of modern Native American poetry that might seem unnecessarily repetitive to the Anglo reader. Although it is difficult to perceive the rhythm of an entire poem from an excerpt, this portion of Janet Campbell's "Nespelim Man" exemplifies the attempt to call the needed ancestor into the barren present by means of an incantation. In the same fashion, his transitory nature and inevitable departure is underscored by the purposive echoes of the poet's grief:

> From the land of Nespelim he comes.
> His mother is the sky.
> His father is the earth.
> He is Nespelim Man.
> Oh, joy, he is Nespelim Man.
> Ya-che-ma, Nespelim Man.
>
> To Many Lakes he has come.
> Let our fields be fruitful.
> Let our game be plentiful.
> Ya-che-ma, he goes,
> Ya-che-ma, he goes.
>
> Over the mountains he goes
> Across the waters he goes.
> I weep, I weep, for he is gone.
> Ya-che-ma, he is gone—
>   He is dead![40]

Herbert J. Spinden, in his introduction to *Songs of the Tewa*, identifies such a device as "repetition with an increment,"[41] calling it the "outstanding feature of American Indian verse." Spinden, whose research turned up no evidence of the use of rhyme in traditional Indian poetry, proposes that this use of repetition was the Indian's counterpart to rhyme, giving the effect "not of rhyming sounds but of rhyming thoughts" (p. 58). And G. W. Haslam adds that, "Just as repetition may, despite all its variations, sound redundant and limited to Euro-Americans, the metrical and rhyming patterns of Euro-American poetry have the same effect on Amerindians. Each individual recognizes and enjoys the forms his culture trains him to favor; no poetic pattern is inherently superior to another."[42]

As a device in modern written poetry, of course, repetition must be muted and controlled, for the incantatory effect that is necessary in the transitory oral presentation can become overwhelming in the printed context. Nonetheless, the modern reader familiar with the Hebrew psalms can appreciate the similarity to Indian poetry in the repetition, free rhythm, and resultant loose stanzaic construction, an observation made by Mabel Major and T. M. Pearce.[43] William Brandon, in the preface to his collection of traditional poetry, *The Magic World*, describes the guidelines he employed in preparing his own translations of ceremonial works: "In the buffalo songs, for instance, it would not only be wearisome to follow faithfully all the magic numbers, but we might also, who knows, materialize a buffalo. We don't really want the buffalo. We only want the feeling of the earnest repetition, the feeling of the hypnosis, of the marvelous emerging, the feeling of the magic. All that we want from any of it is the feeling of its poetry."[44]

One final stylistic characteristic of contemporary Native American literature has been touched on before and also derives from the oral tradition. Because it was necessary to keep the literature intact and easily transmittable, the traditional poems and stories were constructed efficiently, with each word chosen to perform yeoman duty. The dense holophrastic nature of the language, in which we often see one word standing for an entire English phrase such as "fear-living-in-place-shakes-continually,"[45] and the close-knit nature of the tribal cultures contributed to the compactness of the literature. In turn, the character of the languages and cultures was intensified by the inherited literature. Writing in the *English Journal*, G. W. Haslam calls attention to the resultant "cryptic" nature of later traditional poems such as this Chippewa "Song of the Trees":

> The wind
> Only
> I am afraid of.[46]

Yet, as Haslam points out, if one realizes that here the wind represents divine power and the tree stands for man, we apprehend a more complex metaphorical statement than would at first be apparent (p. 711). Even without an intimate knowledge of the Chippewa cosmos, the realization that practically no Indian poem was without its ultimate application to human beings and their relationships to other *spirit*-ed things should illuminate such compressed lyrics. One needs only to be attuned to this embedding technique.

Mary Austin once claimed that "No Indian ever says all his thought,"[47] and she proceeded to share the remarks of Kern River Jim, who told her bluntly that white men's songs talk too much: "You see Piuty man singin' sometime and cryin' when he sing, [but] it ain't what he singin' make him cry." It's what he thinking about when he sing make him cry" (cited in *American Rhythm*, pp. 60–61). Austin developed the notion of the native poem as a "shorthand note to the emotions,"[48] with the poem's "inside song" as its most important component. She included in her remarks that prefaced George Cronyn's collection of songs and chants the observation that the native poems made the then current imagist movement seem primitive, adding that "the first free movement of poetic originality in America finds us just about where the last Medicine Man left off" (*Path of the Rainbow*, p. xvi).

In *American Rhythm*, Austin provides a direct example of this imagist construction. One of her correspondents, Washoe Charlie, had given his girl a grass green ribbon on her departure for Indian boarding school. A few days later, still mourning his loss, he caught a brief glimpse of another girl wearing the same kind of ribbon. According to Austin, Charlie expressed the incident perfectly in this compressed fashion: "The green ribbon when I saw a girl wearing it, my girl existed inside me" (*American Rhythm*, pp. 52–53).

Washoe Charlie's technique, so obviously similar to suggestive elements in imagism, deep imagism, and symbolism need not be explained further. Readers familiar with those aspects of Euro-American poetry are simply required to apprehend Native American use of those techniques in the same way they approach those of William Carlos Williams. They may consider, for instance, the reverberation of peace, personal loss, and cosmic regeneration in Joseph Concha's short poem that speaks of the snow, which

> . . . comes last
> for it quiets down everything.[49]

In Nancy Boney's "What This Poem Can Do," compression operates to kindle a wealth of social implications without the need for a traditional transition:

> Run through the woods like a deer eating
> sweet grass . . .
> . . . .

> Not caring about the thunder and the sound
>> of the whispering
> wind that blows through the trees and shakes
>> the autumn
> leaves that line the old gravel road or in a
>> back alley
> beat up and drunk.[50]

Because of an inability or unwillingness to understand such basic distinctions of Indian literature as those we have discussed, some otherwise able critics have done readers a grave disservice. Ignorance can result in a too hasty dismissal, as we see in the case of William James Smith's review of *House Made of Dawn*. "Something broken backed about that title to begin with,"[51] went Smith's introduction, immediately revealing his ignorance of a metaphor that suggests the central unity of nature, man, and life spirit, the very understanding that the protagonist Abel must finally accept. Smith goes on to say that Momaday's style "makes you itch for a blue pencil to knock out all the interstitial words that maintain the soporific flow. It is a style that gets in the way of content" (p. 636). Here again Smith misunderstands the concept of the power of the word and the use of repetition to suggest ritual, as in this passage describing Abel's symbolic reintegration with the Great Spirit: "The soft and sudden sound of their going, swift and breaking away all at once, startled him, and he began to run after them. He was running, and his body cracked open with pain, and he was running on. He was running and there was no reason to run but the running itself and the land and the dawn appearing" (*House Made of Dawn*, p. 211). Of course, one could trim that passage down to something like "The rest of them started to run before Abel did, so he hurried to catch up and felt the true meaning of life as he did," but it is obvious that the passage depends upon, actually requires, the repetition to make the reader *feel* the change taking place.

In a final complaint Smith says that the characters in the novel remain "bemisted" and that the protagonist Abel "does not come through at all" (p. 636). But Smith, it would seem, is asking for a hero in the existential mode, a man who stands alone, chin thrust out against the natural and manmade forces that assail him, a man apart, alone. Yet Abel's redemption in this novel lies in an opposite mode of being: he must become *a part of* his ancient and abiding world once again, or he will surely die, teeth kicked out, drunk, dead drunk, in some Los Angeles alley. As Carole Oleson puts it: "*House Made of Dawn* is not a short novel about Abel, but a long prose poem about the earth, about

the people who have long known how to love it, and who can survive
as a people if they will cling to that knowledge."[52]

Critics of modern Indian American imaginative works should heed
this advice from John Bierhorst. Although he refers to traditional works,
the principles remain applicable: "(1) that Indian literature, if symbolic,
is far from chaotic—each verbal element has a contributory meaning
and each element has its proper place—and (2) that this literature,
owing to its 'geometrical' bias, cannot be read for style in the usual
sense of the term; the ideas and images are there, but generally unwrapped
(and spread out) rather than neatly packaged."[53] In *House Made of Dawn*,
events and memories are chosen to suggest character and theme rather
than lay it out explicitly, while the language and phrasing, in like
manner, suggest the meaning of the events themselves, a welcome
subtlety. The sense of irrevocable loss is implicit in Ben Benally's
utterance, "Look! Look! There are blue and purple horses . . . a house
made of dawn . . ." (p. 114), and again in Abel when he struggles to
express the remembered beauty of geese rising into the moon above a
river of his childhood (pp. 118–19). The reader is not told exactly what
emotion or precisely what importance the visions have for the characters,
but the vividness, the breathlessness of their telling, the focus on the
re-creation of the events rather than on an explanation of them—this
nondirective approach—allows a reader the feeling and the meaning of
the experience in his or her own turn.

In the progression of the novel as a whole, Momaday's approach
suggests reality. Events important to the protagonist are reported in
the order that they recur in memory, outside strict chronology. Where
blocks of time have passed without meaningful incident, they have
fallen out of the novel in the way they naturally fade from the mind.
Momaday's is obviously a purposeful method, one tied to the Indian-
Oriental view of all experience as a continually flowing river where
chronological time loses significance, where events leap out of context
to recur and grow "in the mind's eye," where the seemingly concrete
quality of history proves illusory and relative to each perceiver. Here,
event freed from analysis and stasis easily carries supernatural significance
and cosmic reverberation, even becomes mythic in the way of the tradition
Momaday draws on.

While critics such as Reynolds Price and Roger Sale gave James
Welch's *Winter in the Blood* generally thoughtful consideration, both
mentioned a "flaw" that actually does not exist in the book's construction.
Shortly after the protagonist, who is a modern reservation farming
Blackfeet, discovers that his lineage is actually a proud one, untainted

with white blood, the novel ends, with this unnamed narrator deciding once again to try to bring home his indifferent love, "a Cree from Havre, scorned by the reservation people [Blackfeet]."[54] The two critics seem troubled by this apparently impractical decision, as if agreeing with the agency doctors that it would be wiser for the narrator to go to the white man's hospital for a lengthy knee reconstruction. The central events of the novel, Sale contends, "lead the hero only to the sense that his own life hasn't been good since his father and brother died."[55] The narrator's discovery of his grandfather's true identity "opens no vista on the past" (p. 22). And while the book is "unnervingly beautiful" for Sale, he concludes that just what it means to be an Indian is "never once offered us for summary or conclusion" (p. 20). Price is not quite so troubled by the conclusion, and he remarks that, while the true light in the novel comes when the narrator learns his heritage, still the novel does not forecast total triumph, and suggests that our protagonist remains essentially "frozen" at the book's end.

Both critics, however, overlook the information that comes at the same time that the narrator learns of his true background: his grandmother, who had become an outcast among her own people, the Blackfeet, was saved by the humane care and constancy that the man Yellow Calf rendered her in secret. Eventually they became lovers, and the narrator's mother was born. Without that care and constancy, his grandmother would not have lived past that first long winter, and he would not exist.

As he returns home, mulling this lesson, the narrator encounters a maverick cow stuck in a slough and has this initial reaction: "I wanted to ignore her. I wanted to go away to let her drown in her own stupidity, attended only by clouds and the coming rain. . . . She had earned this fate by being stupid, and now no one could help her. Who would want to?" (p. 166). And yet try to help her he does, all alone, with an aged horse, a bad leg, and no chance in hell. At the end of this heroic struggle, the narrator, still down in the mire himself, looks up into a rainstorm that has drifted upon him and says, "Some people . . . will never know how pleasant it is to be distant in a clear rain, the driving rain of a summer storm. It's not like you'd expect, nothing like you'd expect." (p. 172).

Yellow Calf's actions and the narrator's gradual realization of their meaning, of the essential relationship and ensuing responsibility between men and all other things, likewise accounts for the narrator's decision to go after that scorned Cree from Havre once again. He remembers well an earlier encounter where, "In her black eyes I could see the reason

I had brought her home that time before. They held the promise of warm things, of a spirit that went beyond her miserable life of drinking and screwing and men like me" (p. 113).

In this light, the narrator's final decision suggests that he has opened a great window on his past—and it could be argued that his triumph is as total as a human can expect. Shall we have overhauled knees or humanly functioning hearts?

It should be clear now that a certain reorientation can make a great deal of difference in appreciating a work fully. It is the purpose of all my remarks to begin the process of that reorientation; the paper does not intend to be exhaustive or constricting. While the comments that I have passed on are largely those of Indian Americans, those same commentators would caution that no definitive limits should be imposed on a developing literature. We all await tomorrow's news. Likewise, no Indian American writer would argue that any single discussion could completely explain or conjure up the "total Indian experience." We are left with the individual works to speak for themselves, ultimately. There is no substitute for a careful reading where one trusts the work itself and not a body of preordained criticism. If these remarks help readers divest themselves of certain inapplicable preconceptions, they serve as intended. But in every instance, attend first to the voice of the poet.

At this point, having considered the past and the present of Indian American literature, we might well speculate as to its future. As I mentioned at the outset, the appearance of contemporary, written, imaginative work by Indian Americans is a relatively new phenomenon and thus is sure to foster many more tribally oriented writers. The names I have mentioned include a number of young writers who have yet to publish book-length works but who surely will. The creation of projects such as the Department of Creative Writing of the Institute of American Indian Arts suggests that there will be a steady flow of young writers who understand both their own heritage and the artful use of poetic language. A wide-ranging survey of the program's results can be found in *Arrows Four*, edited by Terry Allen, director of the writing program, and published by Pocket Books (1974). Such respected journals as *Alcheringa: Ethnopoetics, A First Magazine of the World's Tribal Poetries*, edited by Dennis Tedlock and Jerome Rothenberg, and *Angwamas Minosewag Anishinabeg* ("Time of the Indian") edited by James L. White, provide outlets for Native American writers.

Moreover, the chances for survival of the Native American voice as a distinct force in American letters enjoy a special, if tenuous, advantage. So long as the policy of termination lies dormant, the center of the tribal cultural world will remain intact. Destroy the reservation and its attendant interlocking cultural network, and the voice of the Native American will likely lose its singularity and fade into an echo of things past. A. Grove Day, in discussing the representation of tribes in his collection of traditional songs and poems, *The Sky Clears*, suggests what termination would mean: "It is probable, for example, that the Algonkian tribes of the eastern regions had poetry no less rich than that preserved among the Pueblo groups; but as few of the eastern specimens have survived the long period of decline and decay resulting from the intrusion of white settlers, we can only guess what this 'lost' literature might have been."[56]

It seems a remarkable achievement that a written tradition so new as that of the Native American could in its first decade produce a Pulitzer Prize winner and another book deemed important enough to be discussed on the front page of the *New York Times Book Review*. Such accomplishments promise even greater contributions during the next ten years.

In fact, in the short time between the original publication of this article and its reappearance in this volume, at least three additional novels that merit serious attention have appeared: *Ceremony*, by Leslie Silko, *Wind from an Enemy Sky*, by D'Arcy McNickle, and *The Death of Jim Loney*, James Welch's second novel.

Speaking in David W. McCullough's "Eye on Books" column in *Book of the Month Club News*, Welch describes his recent work in this way: "You see people in small towns who are there and walking around but who never seem to be there at all . . . Jim Loney, who is half-Indian, is one of them. I tried to make him find his past so he could find his future, but he knew he wouldn't find either. He knew the days pile up faster than time recedes."[57] Elsewhere in that column, which deals with significant works *not* offered for sale by the club, McCullough mentions the laudatory reviews for *Winter in the Blood* and remarks that the recent book "deserves to be greeted with as much, or more, enthusiasm" (p. 20).

Other reviewers suggest that Welch's writing is well on its way to acceptance by the general reading public. A *Saturday Review* notice comments that "The specter of Hemingway hovered over . . . *Winter in the Blood*, but here Welch's lean prose is richer, while his dialogue retains the ache of overheard conversation."[58] And while the *Atlantic*'s review took note of Jim Loney's half-breed status, it concluded that the detail was "not of controlling importance." For that commentator, Loney could be any unfortunate soul adrift in a society indifferent to the mentally ill unless they create a nuisance.[59]

D'Arcy McNickle's *Wind from an Enemy Sky* is his third novel, in fact, and was published shortly after his death in 1977. While it received favorable notices from the major library review journals (*Publisher's Weekly* credited McNickle with portraying a "perfect understanding of the insoluble conflicts involved"[60]), this story of the Little Elk people's struggle against anthropologists and dam builders bent on usurping their sacred icons did not attract the widespread attention given other titles in Harper's Native American Publishing Program. For one thing, McNickle's characters lack the depth of those created by Welch or Momaday. This is partly because McNickle tends to intrude into his characters' consciousness: "Rafferty saw the fatal error of encouraging Adam to speak. But he knew he could not stop him."[61] It is also partly because McNickle's dialogue is more symbolic than literal: "I have to tell you that I admire you people, the great Indian race. Ever since my boyhood I have tried to learn about you, your great leaders, your skilled craftsmen—" (p. 253).

Still, if characters are somewhat leaden and sentimentally manipulated, McNickle's narrative skill is noteworthy. Witness the deftness of the novel's opening sentence: "The Indian named Bull and his grandson took a walk into the mountains to look at a dam built in a cleft of rock, and what began as a walk became a journey into the world" (p. 1). McNickle maintains this quick narrative pace throughout so that by story's end, he has drawn the reader's attention from the characters to the cultural conflict they serve to dramatize.

Leslie Silko's novel suffers no such bifurcation, for her characters are as memorably drawn as the intriguing story she tells. *Ceremony* is the story of Tayo, a half-breed Pueblo who returns home from World War II wracked with guilt after witnessing the death of his highly accomplished cousin during a combat mission. Tayo, who survives a Japanese prison camp and suffers a meaningless stay in a veterans' hospital, is finally discharged to New Laguna to face yet another struggle against the faceless confusion and malaise that a changing outside world has foisted on the reservation.

Beyond the initial premise of an exploited, disillusioned veteran unable to return "home," Silko has fashioned a truly original narrative, however. In portraying Tayo's lengthy "ceremony" to regain wholeness, Silko moves smoothly, almost imperceptibly, from a realism disturbed only by time fragmentation into a symbolic landscape blending traditional creation myth and contemporary story in a distinctive way.

As an illegitimate half-breed, Tayo has always lived on the fringes of Pueblo society. When he returns, feeling the blood of his cousin on his hands, his community regards him more with suspicion and fear than with understanding. Finally, a delegation of tribal elders determines that he must be sent to Betonie, an aged medicine man (and a half-breed himself) to undergo the ritual that may restore Tayo to useful life.

The night-long encounter that follows turns out to be only a preliminary, however. Betonie draws an unfamiliar constellation in the dawn-lit sand, warning Tayo, "Remember these stars . . . I've seen them and I've seen the spotted cattle; I've seen a mountain and I've seen a woman."[62] Ultimately, Betonie's vision becomes reality, a strange story that Tayo himself becomes a part of.

The speckled cattle are those from a Mexican herd brought to the family land many years before by Tayo's uncle, who hoped that their tolerance to drought would prove them adaptable to the harsh New Mexico range. The cattle proved wild and unmanageable, however, and long ago had broken their fences and disappeared. Guided by Betonie's star map and aided by a sensuous and mystical woman he encounters near the foot of a sacred mountain, Tayo eventually recovers the lost herd. His struggle is far from over, though, for the "evil witchery" that grips him can be exorcised only after he confronts its manifestation in his own people and ultimately in himself.

Watching from a hiding place as members of his own tribe torture a former friend, Tayo faces his final test of faith with the following result:

> He moved back into the boulders. It had been a close call. The witchery had almost ended the story according to its plan; Tayo had almost jammed the screwdriver into Emo's skull the way the witchery had wanted, savoring the yielding bone and membrane as the steel ruptured the brain. Their deadly ritual for the autumn solstice would have been completed by him. He would have been another victim, a drunk Indian war veteran settling an old feud (p. 253).

In this way, Silko carefully points out that the true enemy is an evil afflicting Tayo's people and whites alike. In fact, Tayo's understanding that fixed native ritual must give way to a continually developing "ceremony" matched to a changing world is central to the novel's theme. No autobiographical accident, *Ceremony* is a powerful work of art, a complex weaving of native oral tradition and evocative symbolic techniques from an American tradition dating back to Hawthorne.

It is clear, then, that Indian writers have already expanded the vision of American readers and writers alike who seek an alternative to the predominant Puritan heritage of the United States. Reynolds Price entitled his review of *Winter in the Blood* "When Is an Indian Novel Not an Indian Novel?" and went on to explain that while the subject matter is tied to the land and the reservation characters, its story "has as much to say of the bone-deep disaffection and bafflement, the famous and apparently incurable psychic paralysis of several million Americans now in their twenties and early thirties, as of any smaller group."[63]

Randall Ackley, who teaches writing on the Navajo reservation in Arizona, recently spoke of a distinction to be understood between poets who continue to speak out of and through the tribal voice and those opportunists of the stripe that Vine Deloria describes in *Custer Died for Your Sins*, who come looking to jump on an ethnic bandwagon with a suddenly discovered Indian grandmother in the family tree.[64] Still, one cannot manufacture the voice of the great spirit that moves all things, just as not everyone can hear it. I hope that these remarks will help in that regard, but as Sanders and Peek put it: "To listen for the voice out of Wah'Kon-tah that drifts through the English phrasings is to hear language enriched beyond its spiritual bounds. Unfortunately, the ear that cannot hear it in the Indian's line cannot hear it in Hemingway's or Lawrence's either" (pp. 449–50).

To invoke that voice once more before closing, then, let me quote from this Incan/Ayacucho "Dance Song":

> Wake up . . .
> Rise up . . .
> In the middle of the street
> A dog howls.
>
> May the death arrive,
> May the dance arrive,
>
> Comes the dance,
> You must dance,
> Comes the death
> You can't help it!
>
> Ah! what a chill
> Ah! what a wind. . . .[65]

Notes

[1] "Storytellers on Storytelling," *Friends of Thunder: Folk Tales of the Oklahoma Cherokees*, ed. Jack S. Kilpatrick and Anna G. Kilpatrick (Dallas: Southern Methodist Univ. Press, 1964), p. 5.

[2] Reynolds Price, "When Is an Indian Novel Not an Indian Novel?" rev. of *Winter in the Blood*, by James Welch, *New York Times Book Review*, 10 Nov. 1974, p. 1.

[3] Louis Untermeyer, "The Indian as Poet," *The Dial*, 8 March 1919, pp. 240–41.

4 "Correspondence," *The Dial*, 3 May 1919, p. 569.

5 Vine Deloria, Jr., *Custer Died for Your Sins* (New York: Macmillan, 1969), p. 94.

6 Gary Snyder, "The Yogin and the Philosopher," *Alcheringa: Ethnopoetics, A First Magazine of the World's Tribal Poetries*, 1, No. 2 (1975), 2–3.

7 Jerome Rothenberg, *Shaking the Pumpkin: Traditional Poetry of the Indian North Americans* (Garden City, N.Y.: Doubleday, 1972), p. xix.

8 William Kittredge, "The Snow Never Falls Forever," *Harper's*, Nov. 1972, p. 120.

9 G. W. Haslam, *Forgotten Pages of American Literature* (Boston: Houghton, 1970), p. 84.

10 Frances Densmore, *Chippewa Music*, Nos. 45–53 (Washington: Bureau of American Ethnology, 1910–13); rpt. in Rothenberg, p. 203.

11 Ray A. Young Bear, "One Chip of Human Bone," in *Voices from Wah'Kon-Tah*, ed. Robert K. Dodge and Joseph B. McCullough (New York: International, 1974), p. 133.

12 Letter received from N. Scott Momaday, 1 Dec. 1975.

13 A. Grove Day, *The Sky Clears* (Lincoln: Univ. of Nebraska Press, 1970), pp. ix–x.

14 Harold Fey and D'Arcy McNickle, *Indians and Other Americans*, rev. ed. (New York: Harper, 1970), p. 239.

15 Thomas Sanders and Walter Peek, eds., *Literature of the American Indian* (Beverly Hills: Glencoe, 1973), p. 10.

16 See Fey and McNickle, pp. 14–15; and Sanders and Peek, pp. 3–5 for summaries of the basic archaeological theory.

17 William Brandon, *The Magic World* (New York: Morrow, 1971), p. xi.

18 Dee Brown, *Bury My Heart at Wounded Knee* (New York: Holt, 1970), p. 170.

19 David F. Beer, "Anti-Indian Sentiment in Early Colonial Literature," in *The American Indian Reader: Literature*, ed. Jeanette Henry (San Francisco: Indian Historian, 1973), p. 207.

20 For a firsthand look at such government manipulation, see the records of the Republic of Texas' dealings with the Cherokee tribe, in *The Indian Papers of Texas and the Southwest*, ed. Dorman H. Winfrey and James M. Day (Austin: Pemberton, 1966), II, passim.

21 William Brandon, *The American Heritage Book of Indians* (New York: Dell, 1964), p. 373.

22 See *The American Heritage Book of Indians*, pp. 360–74, and Fey and McNickle, pp. 105–24 and 155–65, for accounts of the policy of termination and related matters.

23 Edmund Hendricks, "It Was Beautiful," *American Indian Reader*, p. 27.

24 David Reeves, "Loser," in *The Way*, ed. Shirley Hill Witt and Stan Steiner (New York: Vintage, 1972), p. 149.

25 Kenneth Kale, "Sorry about That," in *The Way*, p. 144.

26 Anita Endrezze-Probst, "The Week-End Indian," in *Voices of the Rainbow: Contemporary Poetry by American Indians*, ed. Kenneth Rosen (New York: Viking, 1975), pp. 110, 112.

27 Simon Ortiz, "Relocation," in *The Way*, pp. 84–85.

28 James Welch, "The Man From Washington," in *The Way*, p. 139.

29 Welch, "The Only Bar in Dixon," *Riding the Earthboy 40* (New York: Harper, 1976), p. 39.

30 Welch, "Dancing Man," *Earthboy 40*, p. 49.

31 Herbert Blatchford, "Religion of the People," in *The Way*, p. 176.

32 N. Scott Momaday, *House Made of Dawn* (New York: Harper, 1968), p. 197.

33 Vance Iron Good, in *The Way*, p. 138.

34 N. Scott Momaday, "Angle of Geese," in *Forgotten Pages*, pp. 59–60.

35 Grey Cohoe, "The Promised Visit," in *Myths and Motifs in Literature*, ed. David J. Burrows et al. (New York: Free Press, 1973), pp. 162–71.

36 Durango Mendoza, "Summer Water and Shirley," in Sanders and Peek, pp. 498–505.

37 N. Scott Momaday, "The Man Made of Words," in *Literature of the American Indian*, ed. Abraham Chapman (New York: Meridian, 1975), p. 108.

38 Momaday, *The Way to Rainy Mountain* (Albuquerque: Univ. of New Mexico Press, 1969), pp. 85–86.

[39] "Voice of the Bluebird," in *American Indian Reader*, p. 4.

[40] Janet Campbell, "Nespelim Man," in *Voices from Wah'Kon-Tah*, p. 36.

[41] Herbert J. Spinden, *Songs of the Tewa* (New York: Exposition of Indian Tribal Arts, 1933), p. 58.

[42] Haslam, *Forgotten Pages*, p. 19.

[43] Mabel Major and T. M. Pearce, *Southwest Heritage: A Literary History with Bibliography* (Albuquerque: Univ. of New Mexico Press, 1972), p. 16.

[44] Brandon, *The Magic World*, p. xiv.

[45] Mary Austin, *The American Rhythm* (Boston: Houghton, 1930), p. 60.

[46] Frances Densmore, *Chippewa Music*, No. 48; rpt. in G. W. Haslam, "American Oral Literature: Our Forgotten Heritage," *English Journal*, 60 (1971), 711.

[47] Austin, *American Rhythm*, p. 60.

[48] Mary Austin, Introduction, *The Path of the Rainbow: An Anthology of Songs and Chants from the Indians of North America*, rev. ed., ed. George Cronyn (New York: Liveright, 1934), p. xxv.

[49] *The Way*, p. 136.

[50] Nancy Boney, from "What This Poem Can Do," *Angwamas Minosewag Anishinabeg* (*Time of the Indian*), Winter 1974, n.p.

[51] William James Smith, rev. of *House Made of Dawn*, by N. Scott Momaday, *Commonweal* 88 (1968), 636.

[52] Carole Oleson, "The Remembered Earth: Momaday's *House Made of Dawn*," *South Dakota Review*, 11, No. 1 (1963), 160.

[53] John Bierhorst, ed., *Four Masterworks of American Indian Literature* (New York: Farrar, 1974), p. xvi.

[54] James Welch, *Winter in the Blood* (New York: Harper, 1974), p. 6.

[55] "Winters Tales," *New York Review of Books*, 12 Dec. 1974, p. 22

[56] *The Sky Clears*, p. xii.

[57] *Book of the Month Club News*, Feb. 1980, p. 20.

[58] William Logan, "Books in Brief," *Saturday Review*, 10 Nov. 1979, p. 54.

[59] Phoebe-Lou Adams, "PLA," *Atlantic Monthly*, Oct. 1979, p. 108.

[60] Review of *Wind from an Enemy Sky*, by D'Arcy McNickle, *Publishers Weekly*, 28 Aug. 1978, p. 388.

[61] D'Arcy McNickle, *Wind from an Enemy Sky* (New York: Harper, 1978), p. 253.

[62] Leslie Marmon Silko, *Ceremony* (New York: Viking, 1977), p. 152.

[63] Reynolds Price, p. 1.

[64] Randall Ackley, address before the Western Americana Folklore Symposium, Rocky Mountain Modern Language Association, Denver, 17 Oct. 1975.

[65] "Dance Song," *American Indian Prose and Poetry*, ed. Margot Astov (New York: Capricorn, 1962), p. 344, originally printed in 1948 as *The Winged Serpent*.

An Introduction to Chinese-American and Japanese-American Literatures

Jeffery Paul Chan, Frank Chin, Lawson Fusao Inada, and Shawn H. Wong

Asian-Americans are not one people but several. Chinese- and Japanese-Americans have been separated by geography, culture, and history from China and Japan for seven and four generations respectively. They have evolved cultures and sensibilities distinctly not Chinese or Japanese and distinctly not white American. Even the Asian languages as they exist today in America have been adjusted and developed to express a sensitivity created by a new experience. In America, Chinese- and Japanese-American culture and history have been inextricably linked by confusion, the popularization of their hatred for each other, and World War II.

Our essay deals with Chinese-Americans and Japanese-Americans, American born and raised, who got their China and Japan from the radio, off the silver screen, from television, out of comic books, from the pushers of a white American culture that pictured the yellow man as something that when wounded, sad, or angry, or swearing, or wondering whined, shouted, or screamed "aiiieeeee!" Asian America, so long ignored and forcibly excluded from creative participation in American culture, is wounded, sad, angry, swearing, and wondering, and this is its AIIIEEEEE!!! It is more than a whine, shout, or scream. It is fifty years of our whole voice.

Seven generations of suppression under legislative racism and euphemized white racist love have left today's Asian-Americans in a state of self-contempt, self-rejection, and disintegration. We have been encouraged to believe that we have no cultural integrity as Chinese- or Japanese-Americans, that we are either Asian (Chinese or Japanese) or American (white) or are measurably both. This myth of being either/or and the equally goofy concept of the dual personality haunted our lobes while our rejection by both Asia and white America proved we were neither one nor the other. Nor were we half and half or more one than the other. Neither Asian culture nor American culture was equipped to define us except in the most superficial terms. However, American culture, equipped to deny us the legitimacy of our uniqueness as American minorities, did so, and in the process contributed to the effect of stunting self-contempt on the development and expression of our sensibility that in turn has contributed to a mass rejection of Chinese and Japanese America by Chinese- and Japanese-Americans. The Japanese-American Citizens League (JACL) weekly, the *Pacific Citizen*, in February 1972, reported that more than fifty percent of Japanese-American women were marrying outside their race and that the figure was rising annually. Available statistics indicate a similar trend among Chinese-American women, though the fifty percent mark may not have been topped yet. These figures say something about our sensibility, our concept of Chinese America and Japanese America, our self-esteem, as does our partly real and partly mythical silence in American culture.

The age, variety, depth, and quality of the writing prove the existence of Asian-American sensibilities and cultures that might be related to but are distinct from Asia and white America. American culture, protecting the sanctity of its whiteness, still patronizes us as foreigners and refuses to recognize Asian-American literature as "American" literature. America does not recognize Asian America as a presence, though Asian-Americans have been here seven generations. For seven generations we have been aware of that refusal and internalized it, with disastrous effects.

Asian-American sensibility is so delicate at this point that the fact of Chinese or Japanese birth is enough to distinguish you from being American-born, in spite of the fact that you may have no actual memories of life in Asia. However, between the writer's actual birth and birth of the sensibility, we have used the birth of the sensibility as the measure of being an Asian-American. Victor Nee was born in China and came to the United States when he was five. Novelist Louis Chu came when he was nine. For both, Chinese culture and China are not so much matters of experience as they are of hearsay and study. Victor and his wife, Brett, have written the first Chinese-American history of Chinese America, *Longtime Californ': A Documentary Study of an American Chinatown* (1973). Louis Chu's *Eat a Bowl of Tea* (1961) is the first Chinese-American novel set in Chinese America. Here we get sticky, however, for the first novel published by an American-born Chinese-American is *Frontiers of Love* (1956), by Diana Chang, a Eurasian. She was born in America but moved to China before her first birthday, to be raised in the "European Compound" of Shanghai as an American in China. She writes of that experience, while Chu writes of Chinatown, New York. Between them so many questions are raised as to what is or is not Chinese-American that to save, and in another sense encourage, confusion (our criterion of Asian-American literature and identity is not a matter of dogma or party line), we have included them both. Chu's book honestly and accurately dramatizes the Chinese-American experience from a Chinese-American point of view, and not from an exclusively "Chinese or Chinese-according-to-white" point of view. Diana Chang's protagonists of mixed blood and their single-blooded parents provide us with a logical dramatic metaphor for the conflict of cultures. Her protagonist Sylvia cannot choose between her parents or identify her blood as one thing or the other. The question of choice is shown to be a phony one imposed on her by outside forces.

Sensibility and the ability to choose differentiate Asian-American writers from the Americanized Chinese writers Lin Yutang and C. Y. Lee. They were intimate with and secure in their Chinese cultural identity in an experiential sense, in a way we American-born can never be. Again, unlike us, they are American by choice. They consciously set out to become American, in the white sense of the word, and succeeded in becoming "Chinese-American" in the stereotypical sense of the good, loyal, obedient, passive, law-abiding, cultured sense of the word. It is no surprise that their writing is from whiteness, not from Chinese America. Becoming white supremacist was part of their consciously and voluntarily becoming "American." Lin Yutang's *A Chinatown Family* (1948) and C. Y. Lee's *Flower Drum Song* affected our sensibility but did not express it. They come from a white tradition of Chinese novelty literature, would-be Chinese writing about America for the entertainment of Americans in books like *As a Chinaman Sees Us, Chinaman's Chance,* and *A Chinaman Looks at America.* These travel books were in the tradition not so much of de Tocqueville as of *Gulliver's Travels.* Their attraction was comic. The humor derived from the Chinese mangling of the English language and from their comic explanations of American customs and psychology. These books appeared in the early twentieth century after almost fifty years of travel books on China written by Christian missionaries and "world travelers" who cited missionaries as authorities on China. The reversal of the form, books of American adventures by Chinese travelers, was a comic inevitability. During this period the exploitation of the comic potential of Asian dialect became forever a part of popular American culture, giving rise to Earl Derr Biggers' series of Charlie Chan novels and Wallace Irwin's Hashimura Togo stories. The Hashimura Togo stores were featured in *Good Housekeeping* magazine and described the adventures of a Japanese house servant who is both unintelligible and indispensable in an American household. A sample of the wit and wisdom of Hashimura Togo, from "Togo Assists in a Great Diamond Robbery" (*Good Housekeeping*, March 1917):

With occasional oftenness she approached up to me and report with frogged voice, "Togo where did you put my diamond broach and Mother Hubbard chamois ring when you stole it?"

The substance and imagery of these books and stories were reinforced by the whining, apologetic tone of books written by Chinese government officials giving the official explanations of Chinese culture and the nonthreatening, beneficial, humble motivations of the Chinese presence and immigration to America, books such as *The Real Chinese in America* (1923) by J. S. Tow, secretary of the Chinese Consulate at New York, with the rank of Consul-Eleven. The subservient character of the Chinese and the inferiority of China were major themes in works by Chinese converts to white supremacy and Christianity. Yung Wing's *My Life in China and America* (1909) is the outstanding example of early yellow white supremacy.

In 1925 Earl Derr Biggers, a distinctly non-Chinese, non-Chinese-American, and subtly racist writer, created the modern Chinese-American: Charlie Chan, the Chinese detective, who first appears in "The House without a Key" walking with "the light dainty step of a woman." The travel format, going from one nation to another, became, in Biggers' immensely popular Charlie Chan novels, an interior journey from one culture to another. Thus, the form that evolved into the Chinatown book reinforced and clearly articulated today's popular notion of being an Asian-American. The concept of the dual personality, of going from one culture to another, emerged.

Eleven years after the appearance of the fat, inscrutable, flowery but flub-tongued effeminate little detective, the first book by a Chinese-American about Chinese America was published. Leong Gor Yun's *Chinatown Inside Out* (1938) was a direct descendant of the Charlie Chan novels and became the prototype of what was to become the "Chinatown Book." The essence of the formula was "I'm an American because I eat spaghetti and Chinese because I eat chow mein." The Charlie Chan model of Chinese-Americans was developed in books like Pardee Lowe's *Father and Glorious Descendant*, Lin Yutang's novel *A Chinatown Family*, Jade Snow Wong's *Fifth Chinese Daughter,Inside Chinatown* by Garding Lui, and two books titled *Chinatown, U.S.A.*, one by Calvin Lee and the other by a white, Elizabeth Coleman.

Chinatown Inside Out was obviously a fraud. The author's name, "Leong Gor Yun," means "two men" in Cantonese. The book consists of items cribbed and translated from the Chinese-language newspapers of Chinatowns in San Francisco and New York tied together with Charlie Chan/Fu Manchu imaginings and the precise logic of a paranoid schizophrenic. Part exposé, part cookbook, the book was supremacist in its overlooking of the effect of racism on our psychology and its never missing a chance to brown-nose the white man with Charlie Chan-like observations:

> Like chop-suey, this [unofficial Chinatown] government is an American product. It uses racketeer methods and ingenuity but it depends for its continued and prosperous existence on Chinese psychology, in this connection more precisely called passivity.

Far from giving America a big yuk and from being celebrated as a classic of American humor, *Chinatown Inside Out* was accepted by everyone as the first book about Chinese America by a Chinese-American. No one, not even the scholars of Chinese America, noticed the awkward changes of voice and style, the differences between the outright lies and the rare facts. The clue of the author's pen name "two men" escaped all. *Chinatown Inside Out* was the source of Lin Yutang's 1948 novel *A Chinatown Family*. In 1962 S. W. Kung from China published *Chinese in American Life* and cited the work of another foreigner to Chinese America, Lin Yutang's *A Chinatown Family*. In 1965 Calvin Lee, a former assistant dean at Columbia University and the author of Chinese cookbooks, saw the light and testified to his successful conversion to utter white supremacy in *Chinatown U.S.A.*, in which he cited Leong Gor Yun and S. W. Kung. Betty Lee Sung loosed *Mountain of Gold* in 1967. She praised the "Chinese in America" for never being "overly bitter about prejudice." In this book, she told us, "If you make yourself obnoxious . . . that is a hindrance to acceptance." *Mountain of Gold* cited the gospel according to S. W. Kung, Lin Yutang, and Calvin Lee. In 1971 the gospel of Leong Gor Yun became hilarious self-parody in Francis L. K. Hsu's *The Challenge of the American Dream*:

> The Chinese in America, in common with other minority groups, will have a continuing problem of double identity. But the effective way of dealing with it is not to deny its existence but to face it squarely. The first step is to realize that the double identity of a minority group is not dissimilar to that of the professional woman. She is a woman and a professional. Some American professional women have tended to forget their sex identity but most have kept some sort of balance between it and their profession. In the latter case, their sex identity sometimes becomes an advantage rather than a disability.

Hsu's work may or may not give us insight into the mind of the first-generation upper-middle-class Chinese immigrant scholar, but in terms of the native Chinese-American sensibility, we can only note that, in the great tradition of Charlie Chan and Leong Gor Yun, his vision of Chinese America reinforces white racist stereotypes and falls short of the vision Malcolm X and other blacks had for their "minority."

The period from the late twenties through the thirties that spawned Charlie Chan, Fu Manchu, and Leong Gor Yun also produced a rash of popular songs, Charlestons, and fox-trots about "China boys" being stranded in America without their women. Such a song was "So Long Oolong (How Long You Gonna Be Gone)," which tells of a girl, "Ming Toy," pining for her sweetheart, "Oolong," stranded in America. Songs with titles like "Little Chinky Butterfly," "Hong Kong Dream Girl," and dozens of others appeared to be Tin Pan Alley's way of celebrating America's closing of the last loopholes in the Chinese Exclusion Act of 1923 by finding ways to exclude entry of Chinese women into the country. Also, a series of popular novels and movies involving passive Chinese men, worshiping white women but afraid to touch them, appeared in *Son of the Gods, East Is West,* and the Fu Manchu and Charlie Chan series.

In the meantime Japanese-Americans cranked up an underground press and literary movement in English, publishing their own poetry magazines, literary quarterlies, and newspapers that featured, as they still do, creative writing supplements in their holiday issues.

The "Inside Chinatown" books were done by American-born Chinese for the most part, but Chinese from China capitalized on the formula and played it for bucks and popularity. Secure in the Chinese identities and Chinese cultural values—both of which were respectable in America, in the Mandarin versions—these books were not as significant or personally affecting to them as they were to the American-born, for whom these books represented manifestos of Chinese-American identity and assimilation. The Chinese (not Chinese-American) writers Lin Yutang and C. Y. Lee refined the "spaghetti-chow-mein" form. In Arthur T. S. Chu's *We Are Going to Make the Lousiest Chop Suey in Town* (1966), the form takes its most ridiculous shape.

During World War II the inside books became more personal and more manipulated. Patriotic Chinese-Americans wrote anti-Japanese propaganda disguised as autobiography. Pardee Lowe's *Father and Glorious Descendant* was the first. Though *Fifth Chinese Daughter* was published in 1950, it fits the propaganda-as-autobiography mold perfectly. There is reason to believe work on it actually began during the war. Chapters of it appeared in magazines in 1947. America's "anti-Jap" prejudice, as indicated by the release of new anti-Japanese war movies, continued strong until the mid-fifties, when the first sign of a change in white attitude was an announcement disclaiming prejudice against loyal Japanese-Americans before the airing of World War II "anti-Jap" movies on television.

In travel books and in music, Japanese America was indiscriminately linked in confusion with Chinese America. In America's pop mind, Japan and China, as well as Japanese America and Chinese America, were one in exotica. China and Japan and Japanese America became distinguished from one another by hatred. That hatred was explained not in the terms of culture and politics but in the terms of the Hatfields and McCoys—we were all some kind of silly but civilized hillbillies feuding in the hills of jade. Chinese-Americans became America's pets, were kept and groomed in kennels, while Japanese-Americans were the mad dogs who had to be locked up in pounds. The editors and writers of the Japanese-American community papers were thrown ever closer to Japanese-American artists, poets, and storytellers. The Japanese-American writing in English that had been an activity was now welded into a movement.

The tradition of Japanese-American verse as being quaint and foreign in English, established by Yone Noguchi and Sadakichi Hartman, momentarily influenced American writing with the quaintness of the Orient but said nothing about Asian America, because, in fact, these writers weren't Asian-Americans but Americanized Asians like Lin Yutang and C. Y. Lee.

The first serious creative writing by an Asian-American to hit the streets was Mine Okubo's *Citizen 13660*, an autobiographical narrative in drawings and words, describing the relocation and camp experience from an artist's point of view. It was a remarkable book, given the time of its appearance, 1946, when anti-Japanese sentiment was still high. Toshio Mori's collection of stories, *Yokohama, California*, appeared in 1949. It had been scheduled for release in 1941, but World War II "anti-Jap" prejudice worked against Japanese-Americans appearing in print; however, it also spared their being shaped, used, and manipulated as Chinese-Americans were.

After the war, the best way to rehabilitate Japanese America, from the white point of view, was to link it up and get it inextricably confused with Chinese America again, so from *Fifth Chinese Daughter* came son of *Fifth Chinese Daughter*, Monica Sone's *Nisei Daughter*, a book remarkable for maintaining its Japanese-American integrity in spite of its being, in the publisher's eyes, blatantly modeled on Wong's snow job.

Asian-American writers are elegant or repulsive, angry and bitter, militantly antiwhite or not, not out of any sense of perversity or revenge but out of honesty. America's dishonesty—its racist white supremacy passed off as love and acceptance—has kept seven generations of Asian-American voices off the air, off the streets, and praised us for being Asiatically no-show. A lot is lost forever. But from the few decades of writing we have recovered from seven generations, it is clear that we have a lot of elegant, angry, and bitter life to show.

Asian-Americans have been writing seriously since the nineteenth century, and writing well. Sui Sin Far, an English-born Eurasian, wrote and published short fiction in the nineteenth century. She was one of the first to speak for an Asian-American sensibility that was neither Asian nor white American. And, interestingly enough, in her work, there is no cultural conflict between East and West. That is a modern invention of whites and their yellow goons—writers who need white overseers to give them a license to use the English language. In 1896 the California magazine *Land of Sunshine* said her stories ". . . are all of Chinese characters in California or on the Pacific Coast; and they have an insight and sympathy which are probably unique. To others the alien Celestial is at best mere 'literary material': in these stories he (or she) is a human being." Working within the terms of the stereotype of the Chinese as laundryman, prostitute, smuggler, coolie, she presents "John Chinaman" as little more than a comic caricature, giving him a sensibility that was her own.

Americans' stereotypes of "Orientals" were sacrosanct and no one, especially a "Chink" or a "Jap," was going to tell them that America, not Asia, was their home, that English was their language, and that the stereotype of the Oriental, good or bad, was offensive. What America published was, with rare exception, not only offensive to Chinese and Japanese America but *actively inoffensive* to white sensibilities.

World War II signaled the suppression of a Japanese-American writing movement that had been active since the late twenties and the sudden popularity of Chinese-Americans' writing to encourage America to "assimilate her loyal minorities," as the dust jacket of Pardee Lowe's *Father and Glorious Descendant* states. The implied worth of these first Chinese-Americans to reach mass print and enjoy a degree of popularity was that they mostly had patriotic virtues rather than literary ones. They were more manipulable. The autobiographies of Pardee Lowe and later Jade Snow Wong were treated less as works of art than as anthropological discoveries. Indeed, the dust jacket of Lowe's book said that he "enlisted in the U.S. Army shortly after delivering the manuscript of this book," as if this patriotic gesture affected its literary worth.

Much of Asian-American literary history is the history of a small minority being cast into the role of the good guy in order to make another American minority look bad. In World War II the Chinese were used against the Japanese. Today, Chinese and Japanese-Americans are used to mouth the white racist clichés of the fifties, as evidenced by a *Newsweek* magazine article (21 June 1971) entitled "The Japanese-American Success Story: Outwhiting the Whites" and the favorable reception of Daniel I. Okimoto's *American in Disguise* and Betty Lee Sung's *Mountain of Gold: The Story of the Chinese in America*.

Betty Lee Sung's *Mountain of Gold* (1967) went through two printings of 7,500 and in 1971 was issued in a paperback edition under the title *The Story of the Chinese in America*. It enjoys the distinction of being cited by scholars (in *Forgotten Pages of American Literature*, ed. Gerald Haslam) as an authoritative source, supporting the age-old stereotype of Chinese-Americans being culturally Chinese and only monetarily white.

"There is nothing wrong with autobiography," writes Kai-yu Hsu in his introduction to *Asian-American Authors* (1972), "except when one realizes that the perceptions of reality revealed through these works seem to continue to confirm rather than to modify a stereotyped image of the Chinese and their culture." Part One of Virginia Lee's novel *The House That Tai Ming Built* consists mostly of the retelling of the legend of "the house that Tai Ming built." This narration is supposed to be from the Chinese point of view, but we find that the point of view is surprisingly Western:

> Grandfather Kwong continued: "To know why Tai Ming wore a queue we must go back in Chinese history, to the time when the Mongol Emperor Kublai Khan and his successors ruled China for nearly a century in the Yuan Dynasty from the year 1230 until 1368 A.D., when they were driven out of power by the Chinese.

Virginia Lee is the victim, so completely brainwashed that she sees no discrepancy between an old man from China talking about China in reference to the white Christian calendar. Yet she would be the first to protest if John Wayne were to speak about Abraham Lincoln freeing the slaves in the Year of the Pig. In the early novels, confirming the education of the white reading audience became an obsession, to the point where writers such as Virginia Lee obviously had to do a lot of research into such things as Chinese history, Chinese-American history, Chinese art, and Chinese opera—all from the white point of view. And the white point of view was that Chinese were "culturally superior." That the cultural superiority of the Chinese served white supremacy by keeping Chinese in their place is clear in the work of Jade Snow Wong and Virginia Lee. They both respond to racism silently and privately, not with action but with an attitude of a noncommunicative cultural superiority that as a response is ineffectual. Virginia Lee in *The House That Tai Ming Built* illustrates this concept:

> The first thing Lin noticed as she stepped into the house of Mrs. Hayes was the wallpaper in the foyer. It was a lovely medallion design in pale yellow. She wondered if Mrs. Hayes knew that the ancient Chinese had invented wallpaper and that it was not until the fourteenth century that wallpaper was introduced into Europe.

This was not a firsthand knowledge of Chinese culture, but it was being passed off as such. Virginia Lee paraphrases Chinese history as written by white and Chinese scholars.

Kai-yu Hsu correctly states that "These largely autobiographical works tend to present the stereotype of Chinese culture as described in the connoisseur's manual of Chinese jade or oolong tea, and the stereotype of the Chinese immigrant who is, or should be, either withdrawn and stays totally Chinese, or quietly assimilated and has become unobtrusively American, exhibiting a model of the American ideal of the melting pot process."

An American-born Asian, writing from the world as an Asian-American who does not reverberate to gongs struck hundreds of years ago or snuggle into the doughy clutches of an America hot to coddle something ching chong, is looked upon as a freak, an imitator, a liar. The myth is that Asian-Americans have maintained cultural integrity as Asians, that there is some strange continuity between the great high culture of a China that hasn't existed for five hundred years and the American-born Asian. Gerald Haslam in *Forgotten Pages of American Literature* perpetuates this idea:

> . . . the average Chinese-American at least knows that China has produced "great philosophies," and with that knowledge has come a greater sense of ethnic pride. Contrasted, for example, with the abject cultural deprivation long foisted upon Afro-Americans, Asian-Americans have an inner resource: The knowledge that their ancestors had created a great and complex civilization when the inhabitants of the British Isles still painted their fannies blue.

Thus, fourth-, fifth-, and sixth-generation Asian-Americans are still looked upon as foreigners because of their dual heritage, or the concept of dual personality that suggests that the Asian-American can be broken down into an American part and an Asian part. This view explains Asian assimilation, adaptability, and lack of presence in American culture.

This sustaining inner resource keeps Asian-Americans strangers in the country in which they were born. They are supposed to feel better off than the blacks, whose American achievement is the invention of their own American culture. American language, fashions, music, literature, cuisine, graphics, body language, morals, and politics have been strongly influenced by black culture. They have been cultural achievers, in spite of white supremacist culture, whereas Asian America's reputation is an achievement of that white culture—a work of racist art.

The overthrow of the Manchus, the Sino-Japanese War, World War II, the success of the Communist Revolution, and the Cultural Revolution are five major events resulting in a China the Chinese of a hundred years ago, the ancestors of fourth-, fifth-, and sixth-generation Chinese-Americans, never saw and wouldn't understand. These new Chinese are emigrating to America. The assertion of distinctions between Chinese and Chinese-Americans is neither a rejection of Chinese culture nor an expression of contempt for things Chinese, as the whites and the Chinatown Establishment would make them out to be. It is calling things by their right names. Change has taken place in China, in American Chinatowns, and in the world generally—changes that have been ignored and suppressed to preserve the popular racist "truths" that make up the Oriental stereotype.

It is a racist "truth" that some nonwhite minorities, notably the Asians, have suffered less and are better off than the other colored minorities. It is generally accepted as fact that Asians are well liked and accepted in American society, that they have been assimilated and acculturated and have contributed to the mainstream of American culture. There is racist hate and racist love. That is, if the system works, the stereotypes assigned to the various races are accepted by the races themselves as reality, as fact, and racist love reigns. The minority's reaction to racist policy is acceptance and apparent satisfaction. Order is kept, the world turns without a peep from any nonwhite. One measure of the success of white racism is the silence of the minority race and the amount of white energy necessary to maintain or increase that silence. The Chinese-American is told that it is a matter not of being ignored and excluded but of being quiet and foreign. It is only recently that we have come to appreciate the consequences of that awful quiet and set out collecting Chinese-American oral history on tape. There is no recorded Chinese-American history from the Chinese-American point of view. Silence has been a part of the price of the Chinese-Americans' survival in a country that hated them. That was the trouble with the language. It was full of hate. Silence was love.

The failure of white racism can be measured by the amount and kind of noise of resistance generated by the race. The truth is that all the country's attention has been drawn to white racism's failures. Everything that has been done by whites in politics, government, and education in response to the failure of white racism, while supposedly antiracist, can be seen as an effort to correct the flaws, redesign the instruments, and make racism work. White racism has failed to convince the blacks that they are animals and failed to convince the Indians that they are living fossils. Nightriders, soldier boys on horseback, fat sheriffs, and all the clowns of racism did destroy a lot of bodies and leave among these minorities a legacy of suffering that continues to this day. But they did not destroy the literary sensibility and impulse to cultural integrity of these minorities. They could not produce races of people who would work to enforce white supremacy without having to be supervised or watchdogged.

In terms of the utter lack of cultural distinction in America, the destruction of an organic sense of identity, the complete psychological and cultural subjugation of the Asian-American, the people of Chinese and Japanese ancestry stand out as white racism's only success. The secret lies in the construction of the modern stereotype and the development of new policies of white racism.

The general function of any racial stereotype is to establish and preserve order between different elements of society, maintain the continuity and growth of Western civilization, and enforce white supremacy with a minimum of effort, attention, and expense. The ideal racial stereotype is a low-maintenance engine of white supremacy whose efficiency increases with age, as it becomes authenticated and historically verified. The stereotype operates as a model of behavior. It conditions the mass society's perceptions and expectations. Society is conditioned to accept the given minority only within the bounds of the stereotype. The subject minority is conditioned to reciprocate by becoming the stereotype, live it, talk it, believe it, and measure group and individual worth in its terms. The stereotype operates most efficiently and economically when the vehicle of the stereotype, the medium of its perpetuation, and the subject race to be controlled are all one. When the operation of the stereotype has reached this point, at which the subject race itself embodies and perpetuates the white supremacist vision of reality, indifference to the subject race sets in among mass society. The successful operation of the stereotype results in the neutralization of the subject race as a social, creative, and cultural force. The race poses no threat to white supremacy. It is now a guardian of white supremacy, dependent on it and grateful to it. In Monica Sone's *Nisei Daughter* the operation of the stereotype in the Japanese-American is clearly evident:

Although I had opinions, I was so overcome with self-consciousness I could not bring myself to speak. Some people would have explained this as an acute case of adolescence, but I knew it was also because I was Japanese. Almost all the students of Japanese blood sat like rocks during discussion period. Something compellingly Japanese made us feel it was better to seem stupid in a quiet way rather than make a boner out loud. I began to think of the Japanese as the Silent People, and I envied my fellow students who clamored to be heard. What they said was not always profound or even relevant, but they didn't seem worried about it. Only after a long, agonizing struggle was I able to deliver the simplest statement in class without flaming like a red tomato.

To operate efficiently as an instrument of white supremacy, the subjects are conditioned to live in and accept a state of euphemized self-contempt. This self-contempt itself is nothing more than the subjects' acceptance of white standards of objectivity, beauty, behavior, and achievement as being morally absolute and their acknowledgment that, because they are not white, they can never fully measure up to white standards. In *American in Disguise* (1971), this self-contempt is implicit in Daniel I. Okimoto's assessment of Japanese-American literary potential:

> . . . it appears unlikely that literary figures of comparable stature to those minorities like the Jews and Blacks will emerge to articulate the nisei soul. Japanese-Americans will be forced to borrow the voices of James Michener, Jerome Charyn, and other sympathetic novelists to distill their own experience. Even if a nisei of Bernard Malamud's or James Baldwin's talent did appear, he would no doubt have little to say that John O'Hara has not already said.

The stereotype within the minority group itself, then, is enforced by individual and collective self-contempt. This gesture of self-contempt and self-destruction, in terms of the stereotype, is euphemized as being successful assimilation, adaptation, and acculturation.

If the source of this self-contempt is obviously generated from outside the minority, interracial hostility will inevitably result, as history has shown us in the cases of the blacks, Indians, and Chicanos. The best self-contempt has its sources seemingly within the minority group itself. The vehicles of this illusion are education and the publishing establishment. Only five American-born Chinese have published what can be called serious attempts at literature. We have already mentioned Pardee Lowe, Jade Snow Wong, Virginia Lee, and Betty Lee Sung. The fifth, Diana Chang, is the only Chinese-American writer to publish more than one book-length creative work to date. She has published four novels and is a well-known poet. Of these five, Pardee Lowe, Jade Snow Wong, Virginia Lee, and Betty Lee Sung believe the popular stereotypes of Chinese-Americans to be true and find Chinese America repulsive and do not identify with it. They are "exceptions that prove the rule." In an interview taped by Frank Chin in 1970, Virginia Lee said, "so in other words, you want the white population to start thinking of Chinese other than being quiet, unassuming, passive, et cetera, right? That's what you want, huh?"

"I don't want to be measured against the stereotype anymore," answered Frank Chin.

"But," she said, "you've got to admit that what you call the stereotype does make up for the larger majority of Chinese-Americans; now I've seen that in school. [Virginia Lee is a schoolteacher.] I think it behooves all minorities, Blacks, Chinese, what not, not to feel so insulted so fast. It's almost a reflex action."

Frank asked her if she would continue to write about Chinese America. She said, "I wouldn't want to go on a Chinese, you know, American conflict like that again. I don't want to do another one."

"Why?" he asked. "Was it difficult?"

"It wasn't difficult," she said, "but very candidly now, this might not even . . . ." She took a deep breath. "I just don't think it's that interesting."

And Jade Snow Wong on Chinese America as it exists here: "The American-Chinese I grew up with, in high school, out of forty or fifty . . . none of them went to college. We're not friends now." Jade Snow Wong, Virginia Lee, Pardee Lowe, and Betty Lee Sung are all of the first generation to go completely through the public school system. The preceding generations were barred, by law, from attending public schools. Their parents went to segregated mission schools if they went to school at all. Diana Chang lived from infancy to her early twenties in China.

Of these five, four were obviously manipulated by white publishers to write to and from the stereotype. Of these four, three do not consider themselves to be serious writers and welcomed the aid of editors, as Jade Snow Wong describes in this interview:

"Elizabeth Lawrence was the one who asked me to write it. And the other one was Alice Cooper, who's dead now. She was my English teacher at City College."

Frank Chin asked her, "What did their help consist of?"

"Oh, Elizabeth Lawrence, you know, she said, 'I want a story,' or something. Then I wrote up maybe three times as long as what finally came out in the book. I sent it to her and she went through it and said, 'ten, twenty, thirty pages, this may be necessary for the writer to write, but it's not necessary for the reader to read.' So then she took parts out. And then I took what was left of the manuscript and went to Los Angeles to see Alice Cooper who helped me bind it together again."

"You think this is right? Are you happy with the book?"

"I finally got to read it the second time about two or three years ago. It reads all right. Some of the things are missing that I would have wanted in, then, you know, it's like selling to Gumps or sending to a museum. Everybody has a purpose in mind, in what they're carrying out. So, you know, you kind of have to work with them. If this is what they want to print, and it's the real thing. I mean they didn't fabricate anything that wasn't so."

This was the talk of a good businesswoman, not a serious or very sensitive writer. Chin asked, "But you feel things were left out?"

She matter-of-factly expressed an acceptance of her inferior status as if it were a virtue. "Oh, maybe they were too personal, you see. I was what? Twenty-six then. And, you know, it takes maturity to be objective about one's self."

The construction of the stereotype began long before Jade Snow Wong, Pardee Lowe, Virginia Lee, and Betty Lee Sung were born within it and educated to fulfill it. It began with a basic difference between it and the stereotypes of other races. The white stereotype of the acceptable and unacceptable Asian is utterly without manhood. Good or bad, the stereotypical Asian is nothing as a man. At worst, the Asian-American male is contemptible because he is womanly, effeminate, devoid of all the traditionally masculine qualities of originality, daring, physical courage, and creativity. The mere fact that four out of five American-born Chinese-American writers are women reinforces this aspect of the stereotype, as does the fact that four of these writers, the four autobiographers, completely submerge and all but eradicate all traces of their characters in their books. Sung, by writing almost exclusively about "cases I heard of" and what happened to "an acquaintance of mine," and Wong, by writing about herself in the third person, further reinforce the stereotypical unmanly nature of Chinese-American men. Virginia Lee's novel *The House That Tai Ming Built* depicts a Chinese-American girl, for instance, who is just too much for the wishy-washy boys of Chinatown and falls in love with an "American," meaning "white," man.

The Chinatowns of Jade Snow Wong, Virginia Lee, and Pardee Lowe differ starkly from the drab, even boring Chinatown described in Louis Chu's novel *Eat a Bowl of Tea*. In *Eat a Bowl of Tea* you have the

first Chinese-American novel set against an unexoticized Chinatown—
the kind of Chinatown that has been duplicated wherever large numbers
of Chinese emigrants settle. It was basically a bachelor society, replete
with prostitutes and gambling, existing as a foreign enclave where the
white world stands at an officially described distance, where Chinatown
and its inhabitants are tributaries to a faceless and apathetic authority.
Published in 1961, one can imagine the reception of such a work by a
public so fully grounded in the machinations of family associations,
picture brides, and a reminiscence of a China that no longer exists.
From Lin Yutang's euphemized portrait of Chinatown to C. Y. Lee's
imported apothecary of ginseng and tuberculosis, the white reading
audience has been steeped in the saccharine patronage of Chinatown
culture.

Chu's portrayal of Chinatown is an irritating one for white audiences.
The characters in this book are not reassured by the pervasive influence
of the kind of Chinatown that we see in the autobiographies and pseu-
donovellas of Wong, Lee, and Lin. The kind of Chinatown that the
characters are secure in is a Chinatown devoid of whites. It is a Chinatown
that we are familiar with—filled with vulgarity and white whores, who
make up for the scarcity of Chinese women. In the same way that Chu's
Chinatown holds the white reader at a distance, his characters speak a
language that is offendingly neither English nor the idealized conception
that whites have of a "Chinaman's tongue"—the pseudopoetry of a
Master Wang in *Flower Drum Song* or a Charlie Chan. Witness:

> "Go sell your ass, you stinky dead snake," Chong Loo tore into the barber
> furiously. "Don't say anything like that! If you want to make laughs, talk
> about something else, you troublemaker. You many-mouthed bird."

The manner and ritual of address and repartee is authentic Chinatown.
Chu translates idioms from the Sze Yup dialect, and the effect of such
expressions on his Chinese-American readers is delight and recognition.
Chu's unerring eye and ear avoid the cliché, the superficial veneer and
curio-shop expressions. He knows Chinatown people, their foibles and
anxieties, and at once can capture their insularity as well as their humanity.

This picture of a predominantly male Chinatown is not unique in
Chinese-American literature. As early as 1896, Sui Sin Far wrote about
the Chinese on the Pacific Coast. Like Louis Chu, she accurately portrayed
Chinatown's bachelor society. In the story "A Chinese Feud," she wrote:

> He saw therein the most beautiful little woman in the world moving
> about his home, pouring out his tea and preparing his rice. He saw a cot;

and kicking and crowing therein a baby—a boy baby with a round, shaven head and Fantze's eyes. He saw himself receiving the congratulations of all the wifeless, motherless, sisterless, childless American Chinamen.

Historically, Chinatowns were predominantly male. Chinese families like those described in Jade Snow Wong, Virginia Lee, and Pardee Lowe's books were rare. In these better known works, the frustrated bachelors, who make up the majority of the Chinatown population, are symbolically rejected or totally ignored.

Unlike Chinese-American literature, Japanese-American writing has only recently accepted the concept of the dual personality. Daniel Okimoto's *American in Disguise*, of all the Japanese-American book-length works, unquestioningly accepts the concept of the dual personality and makes it central to the work. Significantly, though Lawson Inada, who ignores the concept, also published a book in 1971, Okimoto's book has been favorably reviewed by the nation's press, while Inada's book of poetry *Before the War*, the first book of poetry published by an American-born Japanese-American, has been ignored, as is most poetry, and the reviews of his work submitted to metropolitan newspapers have been rejected. The works of Japanese-American writers Toshio Mori (1949), John Okada (1957), Mine Okubo (1946), and Lawson Inada (1971) all see through the phoniness of the concept of the dual personality and reject it. Even Monica Sone's *Nisei Daughter* (1953) rejects this concept in spite of the publisher's blatant attempt to emulate Jade Snow Wong's *Fifth Chinese Daughter* (1950) and capitalize on that book's success.

"Although a 'first person singular' book, this story is written in the third person from Chinese habit." Thus Jade Snow Wong, in her author's note, immediately gives herself to the concept of the dual personality. George Sessions Perry, on the book's dust jacket, both accepts the concept of the dual personality and accidentally hints at its debilitating effect on the individual, if not its phoniness:

> Here is the curious dissonance of a largely Americanized young lady seeing her purely Chinese family life from both her and their points of view.

The suggestion is that the "dissonance" arises from her being a "largely" but not completely Americanized "young Chinese girl." The "dissonance" that thrills, bewilders, and charms Perry is built into the concept of the dual personality that controls his perception of Asian America. That the concept does not arise naturally from the Asian-American experience is dramatized clearly in Monica Sone's account of attending public school in the daytime and Japanese school (Nihon Gakko) in the afternoon:

> Gradually I yielded to my double dose of schooling. Nihon Gakko was so different from grammar school I found myself switching my personality back and forth daily like a chameleon. At Bailey Gatzert School I was a jumping, screaming, roustabout Yankee, but at the stroke of three when the school bell rang and the doors burst open everywhere, spewing out pupils like jelly beans from a broken bag, I suddenly became a modest, faltering, earnest little Japanese girl with a small, timid voice.

This concept of the dual personality was forced on her from without. Social pressure and education make her both Japanese and American. From her own experience, she is neither:

> Mr. Ohashi and Mrs. Matsui thought they could work on me and gradually mold me into an ideal Japanese ojoh-san, a refined young maiden who is quiet, pure in thought, polite, serene, self-controlled. They made little headway, for I was too much the child of Skidrow.

She declares herself a "child of Skidrow" and a "blending of East and West." For the Nisei author this was a fatal mistake, in terms of sales and popularity. The concept of the dual personality and conflict between the two incompatible parts are central to Wong's work, as it is with the work of all Chinese-Americans except Diana Chang. *Fifth Chinese Daughter* has gone through several paperback editions in the United States and England. It has been published in several languages and is critically and financially the most successful book ever produced by a Chinese-American.

Unlike Chinese America, Japanese America produced serious writers who came together to form literary-intellectual communities. As early as the twenties, Japanese-American writers were rejecting the concept of the dual identity and asserting a Nisei identity that was neither Japanese nor white European American (according to a 1934 essay by Toyo Suyemoto in *Hokubei Asahi*).

Through the thirties and forties Japanese-American writers produced their own literary magazines. Even in the internment period, Japanese-American literary journals sprang up in the relocation centers. During this, one of the most trying and confusing periods of Japanese-American history, their writing flourished. In the pages of *Trek* and *All Aboard* and the magazines and newspapers of camps around the country, Japanese-American English was developed and the symbols of the Japanese-

American experience codified by writers like Toshio Mori, Globularius Schraubi, poet Toyo Suyemoto, artist Mine Okubo, and Asian America's most accomplished short story writer, as of this writing, Hisaye Yamamoto. In spite of the more highly developed literary skills of Japanese-American publications, many of them commissioned by Japanese-American community organizations, more books by Chinese-Americans have been published than by Japanese-Americans.

No-No Boy (1957) is the first and, unfortunately, the last novel by John Okada. At the time of his death in 1971, he was planning a new novel on the Issei and their immigration from Japan to America. As it stands, this novel is the first Japanese-American novel in the history of American letters and the second book to be produced by a Seattle Nisei in the fifties (the other was Monica Sone's *Nisei Daughter*). Some scholars of Asian-American literature have said that *No-No Boy* has no literary value but is worth reading as a fairly accurate representation of the emotional and psychological climate of Japanese-Americans at a certain period in history. Okada is worth reading as a social history, not as literature, these critics say. The distinction between social history and literature is a tricky one, especially when dealing with the literature of an emerging sensibility. The subject matter of minority literature is social history, not necessarily by design but by definition. There is no reference, no standard of measure, no criterion. So, by its own terms, Okada's novel invented Japanese-American fiction, full-blown, self-begotten, arrogantly inventing its own criteria.

Minority writers work in a literary environment of which white writers have no knowledge or understanding. White writers can get away with writing for themselves, knowing full well they live in a world run by people like themselves. At some point minority writers are asked for whom they are writing, and in answering that question they must decide who they are. For Okada, being Japanese or American would seem the only options, but he rejects both and works on defining Nisei in terms of an experience that is neither Japanese nor American. Okada's hero, embodying his vision of the Japanese-American, cannot be defined by the concept of the dual personality that would make a whole from two incompatible parts. The hero of the double and hyphenated "No" is both a restatement of and a rejection of the term "Japanese-American"— "No" to Japanese and "No" to American.

Point of view is only partially stylistic in minority writing: it has immediate and dramatic social and moral implications. As social history, the mere gesture of Japanese-American writing is significant. Then the question of control follows; that is, what forces are operating and influencing writers and how aware of these forces are they? Specifically, how do writers cope with and reflect prevalent white and nonwhite attitudes of the period? How are they affected by the concept of the dual personality? By Christianity? How do they define the relationship among their own race, the other minorities, and the white race? How seriously committed to writing and a point of view is this writer? And if, as is too often the case, the writer is no writer at all, by self-admission, the question of white publisher and editor manipulation is raised, usually after the answer has become obvious.

So the serious Asian-American writer, who like any other minority writer works with the imperatives and universals of minority experience and applies them to a literary work, is treated as a quack, a witch doctor, a bughouse prophet, an entertaining fellow, dancing the heebie-jeebies in the street for dimes. Okada wrote his novel in a period all but devoid of a Japanese-American literary tradition above ground. There were only three predecessors: a book of short stories, Toshio Mori's *Yokohama, California*; an autobiography, *Nisei Daughter*; and the short stories of Hisaye Yamamoto. Okada's novel was an act of immaculate conception, it seemed, producing from nowhere a novel that was by any known criterion of literature so bad that Japanese-American literary critics ignored the book or dumped heavily on it, loaded up again and dumped on it again. *No-No Boy* became an instantly forgotten work: fifteen years after its publication the first edition of 1,500 copies had not sold out.

The critics have forgotten that the vitality of literature stems from its ability to codify and legitimize common experience in the terms of that experience and to celebrate life as it is lived. In reading Okada or any other Asian-American writer, the literary establishment has never considered the fact that a new folk in a strange land would experience the land and develop new language out of old words. Strangely, the critics accept this change in science-fiction stories of new planets in the future. Even the notion that the cultural clash produced by future overdoses of mass media will make new folks and new languages is accepted, as shown by the critical success of Anthony Burgess' *A Clockwork Orange* in the sixties, funny-talking Flash Gordon in the fifties, Buck Rogers and *The Wizard of Oz* in the thirties.

The critics were wrong in calling Toshio Mori's language "bad English," as William Saroyan did in his introduction to Mori's book *Yokohama, California*:

> Of the thousands of unpublished writers in America there are probably no more than three who cannot write better English than Toshio Mori. His stories are full of grammatical errors. His use of English, especially

when he is most eager to say something very good, is very bad. Any high
school teacher of English would flunk him in grammar and punctuation.

The critics were also wrong in ignoring or being too embarrassed by
Okada's use of language and punctuation to deal with his book at all.
The assumption that ethnic minority writers think in, believe they write
in, or have ambitions toward writing beautiful, correct, and well-punc-
tuated English sentences is an expression of white supremacy. The
universality of the belief that correct English is the only language of
American truth has made language an instrument of cultural imperialism.
The minority experience does not yield itself to accurate or complete
expression in the white man's language. Yet, minority writers, specifically
Asian-American writers, are made to feel morally obligated to write in
a language produced by an alien and hostile sensibility. Their task, in
terms of language alone, is to legitimize their, and by implication their
people's, orientation as white, to codify their experience in the form of
prior symbols, clichés, linguistic mannerisms, and a sense of humor
that appeals to whites because it celebrates Asian-American self-contempt.
Or their task is the opposite—to legitimize the language, style, and
syntax of their people's experience, to codify the experiences common
to their people into symbols, clichés, linguistic mannerisms, and a sense
of humor that emerges from an organic familiarity with the experience.

The tyranny of language continues even in the instruments designed
to inject the minority into the mainstream. Virtually every anthology
of Third World writing containing Asian-American sections confuses
Chinese from China with Chinese-Americans, conveniently ignoring the
obvious cultural differences. C. Y. Lee and Lin Yutang, born and raised
in China, are secure in their Chinese culture, and unlike Chinese-
Americans, are Chinese who have merely adapted to American ways
and write about Chinese America as foreigners. Their work inevitably
authenticates the concept of the dual personality. However, their being
Chinese precludes their ability to communicate the Chinese-American
sensibility. The other Chinese-American writers collected in this new
splash of anthologies most often include Jade Snow Wong and Pardee
Lowe, who also reinforce the stereotype. Lowe's book, *Father and Glorious
Descendant*, came out in 1943. The dust jacket revealed the racist function
of the book, saying that *Father and Glorious Descendant* "is a timely
document at a moment when America must learn how to assimilate its
loyal minorities."

The deprivation of language in a verbal society like this country's
has contributed to the lack of a recognized Asian-American cultural
integrity (at most, native-born Asian-Americans are "Americanized"

Chinese or Japanese) and the lack of a recognized style of Asian-American manhood. These two conditions have produced "the house nigger mentality," under which Chinese- and Japanese-Americans accept responsibility for rather than authority over the language and accept dependency. A state of dependency is encouraged by the teaching of English and the publishing establishment. This state of dependency characterizes the self-consciously grammatical language of Jon Shirota's first two novels, *Lucky Come Hawaii* (1966) and *Pineapple White* (1970). Shirota's communication of his Nisei orientation is handicapped by a language he seems to feel is not his own, unlike Toshio Mori and John Okada, who write strong in a language that comes from home. Mori and Okada demonstrate, as did Claude McKay, Mark Twain, and N. Scott Momaday, that new experience breeds new language.

John Okada writes from an oral tradition he hears all the time, and talks his writing onto the page. To judge Okada's writing by the white criterion of silent reading of the printed word is wrong. Listen as you read Okada or any other Asian-American writer. Okada changes voices and characters inside his sentences, running off free form but shaping all the time. These voice changes grate against the white tradition of tonal uniformity and character consistency, but more accurately duplicate the way people talk: "a bunch of Negroes were horsing around raucously in front of a pool parlor." There is a quick-change act here among "horsing around" and "raucously" and "pool parlor." The style itself is an expression of the multi-voiced schizophrenia of the Japanese-American compressed into an organic whole. It's crazy, but it's not madness.

John Okada's work is new only because whites aren't literate in the Japanese-American experience, not because Okada has been up late nights inventing Japanese-American culture in his dark laboratory. And though he presents an ugly vision of America in which Japanese-Americans wander stupefied with self-contempt, then overcompensate with despairing wails of superpatriotism, his book cannot honestly be dismissed as an operatic cry of self-pity or a blast of polemic. Yet the book has been ignored, if not by whites, then by Japanese-Americans fearful of being identified with Okada's work. Charles Tuttle, the publisher of *No-No Boy*, writes in a letter, "At the time we published it, the very people whom we thought would be enthusiastic about it, mainly the Japanese-American community in the United States, were not only disinterested but actually rejected the book."

Depression, despair, death, suicide, listless anger, and a general tone of low-key hysteria closed inside the gray of a constantly overcast and drizzling Seattle pervade the book. Definitely not the stuff of a musical. There is at the same time something genuinely uplifting and inspiring about this book—at least for Asian-American readers. The book makes a narrative style of the Japanese-American talk, gives the talk the status of a language, makes it work and styles it, deftly and crudely, and uses it to bring the unglamorous but more commonly lived aspects of Japanese-American experience into the celebration of life. The style and structure of the book alone suggest the Japanese-American way of life of a specific period in history. All in all, there is nothing arcane or mysterious about why this book satisfies and, through all its melodramatic gloom, cheers the blood to running warm. This is new literature, one for which the experience and the people have already been tried and want nothing but the writing and the reading. This isn't an attempt to appeal to old values, translate life into a dead language, or drive whites into paroxysms of limpid guilt, or an effort to destroy the English language.

Ichiro, the no-no boy of the title, is a Nisei who refused to be inducted into the armed forces during the war and chose prison instead. The novel opens with Ichiro's arrival in Seattle, home from two years in prison. He has come home to a mother who is so convinced that Japan has won the war that she refuses to send money or goods from the family store to relatives writing from Japan, begging for help. Ichiro's father is an alcoholic; his younger brother, Taro, drops out of high school to join the army to make up for the shame of Ichiro's being a "no-no boy." Other "no-no boys" fade into easy booze and easy women and out of Ichiro's life. His best friend turns out to be Kenji, a war hero with a medal and without a leg, whose heroism has cost him his leg and by the end of the book his life. Kenji, the admirable war hero, dying of a progressive creeping crud that repeated amputations of his leg have failed to check, seems to have the divinity of the suffering. He gives Ichiro an understanding woman, an abandoned wife whose husband, rather than coming home, reenlists and stays in Europe. Kenji makes Ichiro himself a symbol of goodness and strength.

Ichiro has come home to a world in which everything he touches and loves dies, is killed, or goes mad. All offers of life, the love of a woman, a job by an understanding Mr. Carrick, are refused because he is unworthy, because he must somehow prove himself worthy by himself. He has been spat on, rejected by his brother, lost his good and his bad friends and his parents. Ichiro seems to be a pathological loser. What he does is wrong, and what he doesn't do is wrong. He is full of self-contempt, self-pity, and yet is governed by an innate sense of dignity, if not a coherent sense of humor. He is not Stephen Dedalus out to forge the unformed conscience of his race in the smithy of his soul, but he is searching for something more than his identity. It is the nature

of the language itself, this embryonic Japanese-American English language
that can only define the Japanese-American who is neither Japanese nor
American, in anything but negative terms, that makes every attempt
at positive expression an exercise in futility and despair. "Think more
deeply and your doubts will disappear," Ichiro's mother says. "You are
my son," she says, triggering a spinning, running internal monologue
and one of the most powerfully moving passages in the book:

> No, he said to himself as he watched her part the curtains and start into
> the store. There was a time when I was your son. There was a time that
> I no longer remember when you used to smile a mother's smile and tell
> me stories about gallant and fierce warriors who protected their lords with
> blades of shining steel and about the old woman who found a peach in
> the stream and took it home, and, when her husband split it in half, a
> husky little boy tumbled out to fill their hearts with boundless joy. I was
> that lad in the peach and you were the old woman and we were Japanese
> with Japanese feelings and Japanese pride and Japanese thoughts because
> it was all right then to be Japanese and feel and think all the things that
> Japanese do even if we lived in America. Then there came a time when
> I was only half Japanese because one is not born in America and raised
> in America and taught in America and one does not speak and swear and
> drink and smoke and play and fight and see and hear in America among
> Americans in American streets and houses without becoming American
> and loving it. But I did not love enough for you were still half my mother
> and I was thereby still half Japanese and when the war came and they
> told me to fight for America, I was not strong enough to fight you and
> I was not strong enough to fight the bitterness which made the half of
> me which was bigger than the half of me which was America and really
> the whole of me that I could not see or feel. Now that I know the truth
> when it is late and the half of me and the half that remains is enough to
> know why it was that I could not fight for America and did not strip me
> of my birthright. But it is not enough to be only half an American and
> know that it is an empty half. I am not your son and I am not Japanese
> and I am not American. I can go someplace and tell people that I've got
> an inverted stomach and that I am an American, true and blue and Hail
> Columbia, but the army wouldn't have me because of the stomach. That's
> easy and I would do it, only I've got to convince myself first and that I
> cannot do. I wish with all my heart that I were Japanese or that I were
> American. I am neither and I blame you and I blame myself and I blame
> the world which is made up of many countries which fight with each
> other and kill and hate and destroy again and again and again. It is so
> easy and simple that I cannot understand it at all. And the reason I do
> not understand it is because I do not understand you who were the half
> of me that is no more and because I do not understand what it was about
> the half of me which was American and the half which might have become

the whole of me if I had said yes I will go and fight in your army because that is what I believe and want and cherish and love.

This passage is central to the book in suggesting the wholeness that Ichiro contains and is searching for. His whole life is contained in the paragraph, beginning with childhood and Japan in the form of his family moving from the first "no" through the samurai defending their lords to Ichiro refusing to defend America and ending on a hypothetical positive chord ringing with "yes" and "cherish and love."

A sign of Ichiro's strength, of his sense of despair, and of the truth of his being neither Japanese nor American is the fluid movement into the sick joke about the inverted stomach that recalls simultaneously draft-dodger humor and the stereotype of Japanese being slant-eyed, sideways, doing things backwards. His being not Japanese is subtly underscored by his avoidance of Japanese terms: "gallant and fierce warriors" instead of "samurai."

Okada's *No-No Boy* is an exploration of the universe of racial self-contempt. At one point, through Ichiro, Okada suggests that self-contempt based on your physical and cultural difference from other more favored races produces a contempt for all who are like you:

> . . . I got to thinking that the Japs were wising up, that they had learned that living in big bunches and talking Jap and feeling Jap and doing Jap was just inviting trouble, but my dad came back . . . I hear there's almost as many in Seattle now as there were before the war. It's a shame, a dirty rotten shame. Pretty soon it'll be just like it was before the war. A bunch of Japs with a fence around them, not the kind you can see, but it'll hurt them just as much. They bitched and hollered when the government put them in camps and put real fences around them, but now they're doing the same damn thing to themselves. They screamed because the government said they were Japs and when they finally got out, they couldn't wait to rush together and prove that they were.

The literature of Japanese America flourished through the thirties, into the war years and the camp experience. Those were years of tremendous literary and journalistic output. The question of Japanese-American identity, the conflicts between Issei and Nisei, yellow and white relations, black, white, and yellow relations, and the war were all examined and reexamined in camp newspapers, literary magazines, diaries, and journals. The result of the camp experience was a literate Japanese America that had encompassed broad areas of American experience. Highly skilled writers came from camps, like Bill Hosokawa and Larry Tajiri, who became editors of the Denver *Post*, and fiction writers and poets like

Iwao Kawakami, Hiroshi Kashiwagi, Paul Itaya, Jack Matsuye, Toshio Mori, Toyo Suyemoto, and Hisaye Yamamoto. The journalists got recognition, but the writers of fiction and poetry, all native to their brand of English, with rare exceptions remained confined to the pages of the Japanese-American Citizens League paper, the *Pacific Citizen*. To preserve the illusion of our absence, many Asian-American writers have been asked to write under white pseudonyms. C. Y. Lee was told a white pseudonym would enhance his chances for publication. To his credit, he kept his name.

The first novel published about the camp experience was predictably written by a white, non-Japanese woman, Karen Kehoe. The appearance of *City in the Sun* in 1947 led the *Pacific Citizen* to wonder why a Japanese-American had not written a work of fiction or nonfiction about the camp experience. The editors then went on to speculate that perhaps the experience had been too traumatic. The truth is that the camp experience stimulated rather than depressed artistic output. The Japanese-Americans did write of the camp experience, but they were not published outside the confines.

Blacks and Chicanos often write in unconventional English. Their particular vernacular is recognized as being their own legitimate tongue. Only Asian-Americans are driven out of their tongues and expected to be at home in a language they never use and a culture they encounter only in books written in English. This piracy of our native tongues by white culture amounts to the eradication of a recognizable Asian-American culture here. It is ridiculous that a non-Japanese woman should be the one and only novelist of the Japanese-American camp experience. And it is a lie.

As in the work of John Okada, there is nothing quaint about Lawson Inada's poetry, no phony continuity between sigh-inspiring Oriental art and his tough, sometimes vicious language. No one, not even William Saroyan trying hard, can make Inada out to be quaint or treat his work as a high school English paper. "Inada's poem is lean, hard, muscular, and yet for all that it has gentility, humor and love," Saroyan says on the jacket of Inada's first book, *Before the War*. Inada is a monster poet from the multiracial ghetto of West Fresno, California, where he ran with blacks, grew up speaking their language, playing their music. But his voice is his own, a Japanese-American, Sansei voice afraid of nothing. It is as distinct from the blacks now as country-western is from soul.

In an anthology of Fresno poets, *Down at the Santa Fe Depot*, Inada wrote of hatreds and fears no Asian-American ever wrote of before. Inada is tough enough to write about self-contempt. He took the names white folks called Chinese and Japanese and used them to violate the holy word of the English language. The result is not death but magic and a new American truth:

CHINKS

Ching Chong Chinaman
sitting on a fence
trying to make a dollar
chop-chop all day.

"Eju-kei-shung! Eju-kei-shung!"
that's what they say.

When the War came
they said, "We Chinese!"

When we went away,
they made sukiyaki,
saying, "Yellow all same."

When the war closed,
they stoned the Jap's homes.

Grandma would say:
"Marry a Mexican,
a Nigger, just don't
marry no Chinese."

The Chinese were contemptible for being actively "not Japanese." In *No-No Boy*, Kenji tells Ichiro, essentially, to be not Japanese. "Go someplace where there isn't another Jap within a thousand miles. Marry a white girl or a Negro or an Italian or even a Chinese. Anything but a Japanese. After a few generations of that, you've got the thing beat."

Inada echoes *No-No Boy*. The similarity is and is not accidental. Inada is bound to Okada by a common sensibility and not by any real knowledge of his predecessor. Inada did not learn of the existence of Okada's work until ten years after he had written "West Side Songs." Both articulated the belief common among Japanese-Americans that one remedy for being a contemptible, self-hating Japanese-American is to leave that society, associate oneself with whiteness of some kind, and rise in the world.

As in "Chinks," "Japs" ends with the formal name of the race, and it, not Chinks or Japs, is the dirty word.

JAPS

are great imitators
they stole
the Greek's
skewers,
used them
on themselves.
Their sutras
are Face
and Hide.
They hate
everyone else
on the sly.
They play
Dr. Charley's
games—bowling,
raking
growing forks
on lapels.
Their tongues
are yellow
with "r's"
with "l's."
They hate
themselves
on the sly. I
used to be
Japanese.

Inada confronts his own experience. Everything in his life is in his deceptively simple and humorous poems that have the feel of having been written in the guts of a juke box. He tears himself apart exposing all the symbols of Asian assimilation—education, the preservation of Oriental culture—as acts of desperation, terrific efforts to buy a little place in the country. It is the fear of America, not the fear of assimilation, that motivates him.

A constant theme in Asian-American literature, from Pardee Lowe's *Father and Glorious Descendant* through *No-No Boy* to Frank Chin's play *The Chickencoop Chinaman* (1972), is the failure of Asian-American manhood to express itself in its simplest form: fathers and sons.

"There is nothing good about being a son," says the unnamed narrator in Wallace Lin's "Rough Notes for Mantos." "I know; I am a son. When you have to admit that you have a father, allowing people to think that you are a father and son, as if any relation existed between those two terms, when there is really nothing to say."

What exists in these works is that mutual self-contempt. In Pardee Lowe's *Father and Glorious Descendant*, Father names his "Glorious Descendant" after Governor Pardee of California not to inspire his son with an American identity but to offer his son up as a sacrifice to white supremacy. Inspired by his American name, young Pardee has childhood visions of becoming the first Chinese-American President of the United States. The true meaning of his name comes home when his father tells him to forget his dream, not only because it is impossible but because it is, by implication, immoral. The book seems to celebrate a healthy relationship between father and son. Set in the context of Asian-American literature and history, this relationship is thinly disguised mutual contempt. In *No-No Boy*, the most sympathetic emotion Ichiro can muster for his father is pity. The dominant emotion is contempt. The perpetuation of self-contempt between father and son is an underlying current in virtually every Asian-American work. "Chinamans do make lousey fathers. I know. I have one," says Tam Lum, the main character of *The Chickencoop Chinaman*. He suggests that he is "a lousey father" himself when he says, "I want my kids to forget me." As the comic embodiment of Asian-American manhood, rooted in neither Asia nor white America, Tam is forced to invent a past, mythology, and traditions from the antiques and curios of his immediate experience. In an effort to link himself with the first known Chinese-Americans, he states, "Chinamen are made, not born, my dear. Out of junk-imports, lies, railroad scrap iron, dirty jokes, broken bottles, cigar smoke, Cosquilla Indian blood, wino spit, and lots of milk of amnesia."

In white writing there is a tradition of communication breaking down between father and son. The son rebels against the accepted past, strikes out for the future to dare the unknown. In *The Chickencoop Chinaman* the past is the unknown. Tam breaks with the past by trying to find it, define it, and identify with it. At the end of the play he links himself with the railroad, Chinese restaurants, and the future:

> Now and then, I feel them old days, children, the way I feel the prowl of the dogs in the night and the bugs in the leaves and the thunder in the Sierra Nevadas however far they are. The way my grandmother had an ear for trains. Listen, children. I gotta go. Ride Buck Buck Bagaw with me . . . Listen in the kitchen for the Chickencoop Chinaman slowin on home.

Chin, if not Tam Lum, is saying that an Asian-American sensibility is not a recent invention.

Language is the medium of culture and the people's sensibility, including the style of manhood. Language coheres the people into a community by organizing and codifying the symbols of the people's common experience. Stunt the tongue and you have lopped off the culture and sensibility. On the simplest level, a man in any culture speaks for himself. Without a language of his own, he no longer is a man. The concept of the dual personality deprives the Chinese-American and Japanese-American of the means to develop their own terms. The tyranny of language has been used by white culture to suppress Asian-American culture and exclude it from operating in the mainstream of American consciousness. The first Asian-American writers worked alone within a sense of rejection and isolation to the extent that it encouraged Asian America to reject its own literature. John Okada and Louis Chu died in obscurity, and Toshio Mori lives in obscurity. In the past, being as Asian-American writer meant that you did not associate with other Asian-American writers. Emulating the whites, we ignored ourselves. Now we seek each other out.

Postscript

It has been eight years since the first publication of our Preface and Introduction to *AIIIEEEEE! An Anthology of Asian-American Writers.* It remains, after all this time, the definitive critical work on Chinese-American and Japanese-American literature. The Modern Language Association requested that we update our original essay with new literature as well as with rediscovered poetry and prose. The result is 150 years of Asian-American literary tradition instead of the original "Fifty Years of Our Whole Voice." This new critical work grew from an essay into a book and, unfortunately, is too long for inclusion in this collection. That work, *The Big Aiiieeeee! Chinese-American and Japanese-American History in Literature*, is to be published by Howard University Press in 1982.

We still consider our original effort, eight years ago, an excellent primary source for any study of Asian-American literary traditions. Our new work is a much more personal statement than the original essay. We are not critics. We are—as playwright, poet, novelist, and short story writer—a major part of the Asian-American literary tradition of the 1980s. We obviously have the necessary critical skills to evaluate our own tradition but not really to evaluate our own place in that tradition. Our first book was intended, in part, to educate an audience in Asian-American literature and publish at least a representative collection of that literature. We challenged critics to write about Asian-American literature so that we could get on with our own creative work. When the challenge for the seventies went more or less unanswered, we felt, as artists not critics, the need to make our statement for the eighties more personal.

The new challenge for the eighties reads, in part:

> One measure of a healthy and thriving literature is the health of its critics. Asian-American literature, as yet, has no critics. Dorothy Ritsuko McDonald is moving toward serious Asian-American literary criticism, one careful essay at a time. Asian America suffered a charlatan, a failure in every school of American hobnob from beat to revolutionary, stooping into Asian-American literature to messiah the writers and begin our history.
>
> We are not critics. Chinese-American and Japanese-American writing is woefully uninhabited by critics, critical theories of Asian-American writing, schools, postures, and movements. Instead we are infested with

sociologists and holy Joes, picking at the bones of our poetry and tearing the lids off our prose looking for a mastodon frozen stiff in a block of ice.

We have done our scholarly homework haphazardly and reluctantly after the first *AIIIEEEEE!* essay. But no matter how careless, lazy, and serendipitous our method of searching the past for the works, and the works for the past, what we've found to read was stuff that hadn't been read for years, stuff our people had written and our people had forgotten. As Asian-American writers, we respond as much to the search for and discovery of our literary tradition as to the voices of Wong Sam, Nagai Kafu, Kyo Koike, Sui Sin Far, James Y. S. Sakamoto, the writers and word magicians we knew wrote in the past, because we wrote like them in the distant present, and knew we were not the beginning. These are the voices of Chinese-American and Japanese-American writers bound by visions of Chinaman and Nikkei integrity in the face of inevitable if not imminent racial extinction. In our search we discovered the sweet morbidity of aching epitaphs of the doomed.

The historians, the sociologists, the yellow practitioners of the white sciences said they knew nothing about Asian-American literature because there was nothing to know. In *AIIIEEEEE!* with nothing up our sleeves we produced proof of a Japanese-American and Chinese-American literature that the sociologists and historians said did not exist. This proof that had eluded the massed expertise training and instrumentation of the great white sciences was simply books, the works themselves. Sung says we were working too hard to write; Kung says we were too low class to write; Okimoto says we were too full of self-contempt to write and that if we could write we would have nothing to say. All three had obviously let their library cards lapse. We found John Okada on the shelf of a grocery store; Louis Chu we found in the card catalog of the Oakland Public Library; Toshio Mori we found on the shelf of a used book store we'd gone into seeking shelter on a rainy day in Berkeley. Our method was not scientific. We tried the scientific sociological method, and using that method, we couldn't find them either. No longer able to deny the existence of an Asian-American cultural sensibility, sociologists spent thousands of dollars of grant money to prove it didn't exist, was never there. They grudgingly acknowledged the fact of the works we had found, but would deny that between the works is a link of vision, cultural integrity, history, and literary ambition. Chinese America and Japanese America are not metaphors for white America.

We outlined this tradition and its sensibilities in the first *AIIIEEEEE!*

An Introduction to Frank Chin's
The Chickencoop Chinaman and *The Year of the Dragon*

Dorothy Ritsuko McDonald

I

"I was born in Berkeley, California in 1940, far from Oakland's Chinatown where my parents lived and worked," begins Frank Chin in his own profile.[1] "I was sent away to the Motherlode country where I was raised through the War. Then back to Chinatowns Oakland and San Francisco," where he stayed until he received a fellowship in 1961 from the State University of Iowa Writer's Workshop. "I was the first Chinese-American brakeman on the Southern Pacific Railroad, the first Chinaman to ride the engines," he continues. "Fine riding but I left the rails" to spend an apprenticeship as a television writer in Seattle.

"Chinatown," "Motherlode country" (the Sierra Nevada), "railroad," "Chinaman"—these are key words for this fine Asian-American writer, for they denote his sense of Chinese-American history as a valiant, vital part of the history of the American West, a history he believes his own people, under the stress of white racism, have forgotten or wish to forget in their eagerness to be assimilated into the majority culture. But the price of acceptance has been high, especially for the Chinese male who is trapped by a stereotype designed to keep him in an inferior place in American society: he supposedly lacks assertiveness, creativity, and aggressiveness; instead, he is passive, obedient, humble, and effeminate. But for Chin the Chinese men (the "Chinamans," as distinguished from the assimilated Chinese-Americans) who left their families for the New World in the nineteenth century were masculine like other "pioneers . . . the explorers of the unknown—seekers after gold, the big break, the new country."[2] They encountered a systematic racism, however, whose violence and overtness were angrily deplored by Mark Twain in his account of his experiences in the West, *Roughing It*:

> Any white man can swear a Chinaman's life away in the courts, but no Chinaman can testify against a white man. Ours is the "land of the free"—

nobody denies that—nobody challenges it. (Maybe it is because we won't let other people testify.) As I write, news comes that in broad daylight in San Francisco, some boys have stoned an inoffensive Chinaman to death, and that although a large crowd witnessed the shameful deed, no one interfered.

. . . .

In California [a Chinaman] gets a living out of old mining claims that white men have abandoned as exhausted and worthless—and then the officers come down on him once a month with an exorbitant swindle to which the legislature has given the broad, general name of "foreign" mining tax, but it is usually inflicted on no foreigners but Chinamen.

. . . .

They are a kindly disposed, well-meaning race, and are respected and well treated by the upper classes, all over the Pacific coast. No Californian *gentleman or lady* ever abuses or oppresses a Chinaman, under any circumstances, an explanation that seems to be much needed in the East. Only the scum of the population do it—they and their children; they, and, naturally and consistently, the policemen and politicians, likewise, for these are the dust-licking pimps and slaves of the scum, there as well as elsewhere in America.[3]

Chin believes that Chinatowns are also the products of racism. The notion that the Chinese themselves clustered together to preserve their alien culture is, Chin believes, a myth: "The railroads created a detention camp and called it 'Chinatown.' The details of that creation have been conveniently forgotten or euphemized into a state of sweet confusion. The men who lived through the creation are dying out, unheard and ignored. When they die, no one will know it was not us that created a game preserve for Chinese and called it 'Chinatown.' "[4]

Given this historical perspective, is it any wonder that echoes of the West would resound in the work of this rebellious fifth-generation American, imbued with the aborted dreams of the hardworking, manly gold miners and railroad builders of his past? In Chin's first play, *The Chickencoop Chinaman* (Seattle: Univ. of Washington Press, 1981), his hero Tam Lum tells his children of their old American Dream:

. . . grandmaw has an ear for nothing but ancient trains in the night, and talks pure Chinamouth you understood only by love and feel. She don't hear what a boy hears. She's . . . livin to hear one train, once more. . . . And grandmaw heard thunder in the Sierra hundreds of miles away and listened for the Chinaman-known Iron Moonhunter, that train built by Chinamans who knew they'd never be given passes to ride the rails they laid. So of all American railroaders, only they, sung no songs, told no jokes, drank no toasts to the ol' iron horse, but stole themselves some iron on the way, slowly stole up a pile of steel, children, and hid there in the granite face of the Sierra and builded themselves a wild engine to take them home. Every night, children, grandmaw listened in the kitchen, waiting, til the day she died. (p.31)

Chin's grandfather worked as a steward on the Southern Pacific and owned a watch with a train engraved on it. "I took my grandfather's watch and worked on the Southern Pacific," says Chin elsewhere. "I rode in the engines up front . . . I rode in the cabooses where no Chinaman had ever ridden before. I was hired with the first batch of blacks to go braking for the SP, in the 60's when the fair employment legislation went into effect. (Ride with me grandpa, at least it's not the steward service. You get home more often now.)" ("Confessions," p. 62).

He begins his essay "Confessions of the Chinatown Cowboy" by describing poet and labor organizer Ben Fee, one of that rare breed, the modern-day Chinaman. Note how Chin compresses the western theme with his sense of historical loss:

His hometown, Chinatown San Francisco has forgotten the name of Ben Fee and the man he was, for its own good. In New York he's what he was in Frisco, but more so, a word of mouth legend, a bare knuckled unmasked man, a Chinaman loner out of the old West, a character out of Chinese sword-slingers, a fighter. The kind of Chinaman we've been taught to ignore, and forget if we didn't want America to drive Chinatown out of town. (p. 58)

It was Ben Fee who called Chin the "Chinatown Cowboy" (p. 59) for the way he was dressed during their first meeting—"a Chinaman dressed for a barndance," says Chin of his younger self ironically: "My hair was long, parted in the middle. My beard was long and as effective as a beard as needles are at making cactus look hairy, but it was me then, a kind of topping for me all in black, black from my cowboy boots, black denims, black leather belt with a tough, but not flashy two fanged buckle instead of the standard one prong job, a black western shirt with phoney pearl snaps, a silver vest [,] a toothpick in my mouth and a Chinese wiseass beard making me solid affectation" (p. 58).

Despite the irony, the black-garbed, two-fang-buckled Chin is obviously no assimilated Chinese: he is declaring his aggressive masculinity and claiming the history of the American West as his own. For the unwary reader, then, who rigidly associates Asian-Americans with Asian culture and not American history or culture, some passages in Chin's plays can be disconcerting if not downright incomprehensible or offensive. To such a reader, the meaning of Tam's lyrical monologue on the Iron Moonhunter would be lost. And what of the Lone Ranger metaphor that dominates the balance of the play? Aware that Asians were excluded from the ranks of American heroes, Tam Lum during his boyhood had idolized the black-haired Lone Ranger whose mask, he thought, hid his "slanty" eyes. One farcical scene occurs, during which the Ranger is revealed to be a broken-down white racist. A train whistle sounds, and the young Tam recognizes it as that of the Iron Moonhunter for which his grandmother had listened until she died. But the Ranger protests to Tam and his friend: "Hear no evil, ya hear me? China boys, you be legendary obeyers of the law, legendary humble, legendary passive. Thank me now and I'll let ya get back to Chinatown preservin your culture!" He admonishes them in the end to keep their place in the American Dream:

> Don't move! . . . Keep your asses off them long steel rails and short cross ties, stay off the track, don't be a followin me, stop chasin me, or you'll be like me, spendin your whole lifetime ridin outa your life into everybody's distance, runnin away from lookin for a train of sullen Chinamans, runaways from their place in the American dream, not thanking me . . . not thanking the masked man . . . the West ain't big enough for the both of us! But, say, ya speak good English, China Boy. . . . (pp. 37-38)

He bids them farewell, and at the beginning of the next scene, Tam is "dressed dark, trim and slim. No hat. Cowboy boots." But more of this later.

Chin's historical perspective is also found in his next play *The Year of the Dragon* (Seattle: Univ. of Washington Press, 1981), set in San Francisco's Chinatown. Ross, the white liberal, well-meaning husband of Mattie Eng, the sister of Fred Eng, the hero, has "always admired the superiority of Chinese culture." He does not realize his exclusionary preconception of Asian-Americans when he says of Fred who has wearily returned home after a day as a Chinatown tour guide: "Oh, don't be silly, Mattie. Why shouldn't he want to talk about his culture with a sincerely interested student of all things Chinese?" (p. 79). Sensing the tension in the air, he later continues, "I'm trying to say, I am not totally insensitive to Chinese like most whites are. . . ."

"Listen Ross," says Fred, informing him of his condescension and the assimilative thrust of Chinese Americans, "it's the rule not the exception for us to marry out white. Out in Boston, I might even marry me a blonde. We're yours. Hell, Chinatown's your private preserve for an endangered species, and you're the park ranger" (p. 85).

The theme of the West is sounded by Mattie, or "Sis," in her greetings to her brother Fred after their many years of separation. Her comments show that they had shared a childhood enhanced by movie Westerns. The somewhat dotty Ma Eng hums or sings cowboy tunes; and in trying to persuade Fred to leave Chinatown, Sis later says, "We're pioneers. You and me, Junior Texas Rangers," afterwards crying out, perhaps in exasperation, "The Chinatown Cowboy rides again!" In the climactic last scene after Pa Eng dies suddenly while struggling with him, Fred says, "I woulda liked to have packed him up into the Sierras and buried him by the railroad . . . I was saving that one for the last. . . ."

That this ritual haunts Chin's imagination in search of its historical meaning is revealed in a yet unfinished manuscript (*Gee, Pop!*) in which the hero's father, who considers the Sierras the Plymouth Rock for Chinamen, tells his dead wife: "I'll bury you by the railroad in the Sierra. I put a railroad spike and gold in your hands for precious metal. I bury you in the earth for dirt. I plant a tree over you for wood. I water it for water." When his son is killed at the end, after being twice outdrawn by "John Wayne," the dead hero speaks through an older Chinaman to his younger self:

> Gum. Mook. Faw. Sur. Toe. Gold. Wood. Fire. Water. Dirt. A Chinaman's Elements. We'll bury El Chino the Chinatown Cowboy deep, here. Put a railroad spike in his hands, cuz it's precious metal. Plant a tree on him for wood and fire. Water him. Cover him in dirt. Those things make Chinamans. And they make trains. . . . This is about us, kid.

II

If Chin seeks to preserve the history of the first pioneering Chinamen, he nonetheless looks forward in time and sees, as does Fred Eng, the Chinese-Americans as an endangered species. Not only are Chinese women like Mattie "marrying out white" at a rapidly increasing rate, in part no doubt because of the present "sissy" image of the Chinese male, but in Chinese America women have always been outnumbered by men. Historically, the series of discriminatory exclusion laws (1882–1924) made it difficult, then impossible, for both alien and American Chinese to bring in their wives from China. The Chinatowns were therefore essentially bachelor societies. In addition, an American-born woman lost her citizenship when she married a person ineligible for citizenship; and under the Exclusion Act of 1882, immigrant Chinese could not be naturalized: "That hereafter no State court or court of the United States shall admit Chinese to citizenship." These laws were repealed in 1943 during World War II when China was an ally of the United States.[5]

In *The Year of the Dragon*, it is mainly through the American-born Ma Eng that the reader discerns this historical discrimination. She tells Ross: "My grandmother, Ross . . . she used to tell me she used to come home oh, crying like a sieve cuz all she saw was blocks and blocks of just men. No girls at all. She was very lonely." Moreover, she says of her daughter: "You know . . . my Sissy is a very limited edition. Only twenty Chinese babies born in San Francisco in 1938." When she discovers that the mysterious visitor in her home is her husband's first wife who had to be left in China because of the Exclusion Act of 1924 and now could enter America because of its repeal, she says: "I coulda been deported just for marrying your pa. The law scared me to death but it make your pa so thrilling to me. I'm American of Chinese descent."

Had Ma Eng, by some stretch of the imagination, desired to marry a white American, it would have been illegal at that time, for in California such an intermarriage was forbidden in 1906 by a law that was not nullified until 1948.[6] But at present not only are the women marrying out white; so are the males. Thus, as stated above, Fred tells Ross, albeit ironically, "Out in Boston, I might even marry me a blonde." It is apparent, moreover, from other statements he makes that because of his self-hatred, his casual sexual encounters are with white women. Also, while trying to urge his juvenile-delinquent brother, Johnny, to leave Chinatown for Boston and college, he adds as a way out of the racial dilemma: "Get a white girl while you're young. You'll never regret it."

This urge toward assimilation and extinction is similarly found in *Chickencoop Chinaman* in which Tam Lum, though a loner in the play, is revealed to have been previously married to a white woman who had deserted him, leaving with his children Sarah and Jonah for a white husband. He recalls talking to a member of the aging bachelor society who advised him on how to survive in a hostile America:

> And all our men here, no women, stranded here burned all their diaries, their letters, everything with their names on it . . . threw the ashes into the sea . . . hopin that that much of themselves could find someplace friendly. I asked an old man if that was so. He told me it wasn't good for me to know such things, to let all that stuff die with the old. . . . He told me to forget it . . . to get along with "Americans." Well, they're

all dead now. We laugh at 'em with the "Americans," talk about them saying "Buck buck bagaw" instead of "giddyup" to their horses and get along real nice here now, don't we? (pp. 26–27)

His assimilated counterpart, Tom, is eager to marry out white and is taken aback when he learns that Lee, his former wife, who appears to be white, may be part Chinese. At the play's end, Lee, in turn, will probably marry Kenji, Tam's friend and a Japanese-American.

In his essay "Yellow Seattle," Chin repeats his conviction that not only Chinese America but Asian America in general is historically doomed. "Nationally, between 60 and 70 per cent of Japanese Americans are marrying out white. They're abandoning the race, giving up on a people they feel has no history, identity, culture, or art. Chinese Americans aren't far behind. . . . The process of marrying out faster than we can reproduce seems irreversible."[7]

This conviction casts a veil of tragedy over his work. In fact, one can see chronologically from *Chickencoop Chinaman* to *Gee, Pop!* an increasing disintegration of both family and self. "Seven generations of suppression under legislative racism and euphemized white racist love," he had said earlier, "have left today's Asian Americans in a state of self-contempt, self-rejection, and disintegration."[8] His heroes, like so many other American heroes, are isolated and wounded. They are articulate but incapable of taking the action necessary to fulfill the hope and promise of the past.

There are nonetheless humorous scenes and muted, positive moments in his work; and Chin is a Chinaman. "But when we're all gone," he says, "the greatness that was Asian America will be seen in the works and stories and art of the Japanese and Chinese Americans who happened here" ("Yellow Seattle," p. 11).

III. Chickencoop Chinaman: *The Search for an Ideal Father*

Chin is a developing artist, and this first play, which won the East West Players playwriting contest in 1971 and was produced by the American Place Theatre of New York in 1972, shows the clarity and coherence of vision of his later plays and essays in their formative stage. This play is nonetheless important to Asian-American literature for its definition of the problems facing its writers.

In *Aiiieeeee!*, edited by Chin and his group, the hero Tam Lum is described as "the comic embodiment of Asian-American manhood, rooted in neither Asia nor white America." He is thus, they say, "forced to invent a past, mythology, and traditions from the antiques and curios of his immediate experience. In an effort to link himself with the first known Chinese-Americans, he states, 'Chinamen are made, not born, my dear. Out of junk-imports, lies, railroad scrap iron, dirty jokes, broken bottles, cigar smoke, Cosquilla Indian blood, wino spit, and lots of milk of amnesia' " (*Aiiieeeee!*, pp. 34–35).

What is interesting here for the American scholar is that Tam's speeches in the first scene deny the stereotype of the Asian-American dual personality: he is neither Chinese nor assimilated American but a new breed created by the American experience. Thus he declares to the Dream Girl his historical derivation: "My dear in the beginning there was the Word! Then there was me! And the Word was CHINAMAN. And there was me. . . . I lived the Word! The Word is my heritage." He affirms that he was never born: "Born? No! . . . Created! Not born. No more born than heaven and earth. No more born than nylon or acrylic. For I am a Chinaman! A miracle synthetic! Drip dry and machine washable. For now, in one point of time and space, as never before and never after, in this one instant of eternity, was focused that terrific, that awesome power of the universe that marks a moment divine."

One would guess that here is another American Adam with infinite potentiality at the start of history, ready to create a new world. But these words are sheer bravado, for even in this initial scene, Chin shows Tam to be enmeshed in history by the very name of the Dream Girl, whom he describes as a "dream monster from a popular American song in the twenties," a song called "Hong Kong Dream Girl," which parodies the womanless bachelor society:

> China boy is very sad because he went away,
> From his little China maiden,
> China boy feel very sad and only yesterday
> He wrote a note to her to say:

> My little Hong Kong Dream Girl
> In every dream you seem, girl,
> Two almond eyes are smiling,
> And my poor heart is whirling like a big sail round my pigtail
> I dream of you till dawning,
> But early in the morning
> Oriental dream is gone,
> China boy is so forlorn,
> Hong Kong Dream Girl goodbye. ("Confessions," p. 62)

The ensuing scenes reveal, moreover, that Tam has a deep sense of his own emasculation, his inability to achieve. As noted in the previous section, he had already tried to obliterate his Chinese-American identity by marrying a white woman and forgetting the history of his people. During his confrontation with Lee, his friend Kenji's guest whose many husbands had included a Chinese-American, she describes him as "no kind of man" and "like those little vulnerable sea animals born with no shells of their own so he puts on the shells of the dead." Later on she says, "I knew you hated being Chinese. You're all chicken! Not an ounce of guts in all of you put together! Instead of guts you have . . . culture! . . . You couldn't even get one of your own girls, because they know . . . all about you, mama's boys and crybabies, not a man in all your males . . . so you go take advantage of some stupid white girl who's been to a museum, some scared little ninny with visions of jade and ancient art and being gently cared for."

In his efforts to discover a more heroic past and identity, the young Tam had, as previously stated, idolized the Lone Ranger who, he discovered, was not a Chinaman after all, but a white racist denying him a just place in the American Dream. Tam also rejects his father (whom he nonetheless loved), a dishwasher in the kitchen of a home for the aged, who used to bathe with his underpants on, for fear of being peeked at by old white ladies. "Chinamans do make lousey fathers," Tam says later, "I know, I have one." He similarly rejects himself. Divorced from his white wife who had deserted him, he says of his children: "I don't want 'em to be anything like me or know me, or remember me. This guy they're calling 'daddy' . . . I hear he's even a better writer than me."

Tam believes his destiny as a writer is "to talk to the Chinaman sons of Chinamans, children of the dead." But the problem of an appropriate language in which to represent their experience disturbs him: in fact, during the opening scene, the stage directions note that "His own 'normal' speech jumps between black and white rhythms and accents." Ironically Tam says: "I speak nothing but the mother tongues bein' born to none of my own, I talk the talk of orphans." Chin explains in *News of the American Place Theatre*:

> Our condition is more delicate than that of the blacks because, unlike the blacks, we have neither an articulated organic sense of our American identity nor the verbal confidence and self-esteem to talk one up from our experience. As a people, we are pre-verbal, pre-literate—afraid of language as the instrument through which the monster takes possession of us. For us American born, both the Asian languages and the English language are foreign. We are a people without a native tongue. To whites, we're all foreigners, still learning English. . . . And to Asians born to

Asian culture—Asian by birth and experience and American by choice—
our Chinese and Japanese is a fake.

. . . .

We have no street tongue to flaunt and strut the way the blacks and
chicanos do. They have a positive, self-defined linguistic identity that can
be offended and wronged. We don't. With us, it's dangerous to say
anything, dangerous to talk because every time you open your mouth you
run the risk of being corrected. The tongue-tying notion that everything
out of your mouths is mimickry has been built into our psychology in
our seven generations here. And if our basic means of expression is mimickry
and ventriloquism, then our art and culture is mimickry and ventriloquism
too. Such is our self contempt. ("Back Talk," pp. 4–5)

In this context, Tam's self-characterization as a linguistic orphan is
made understandable, as is his exchange with Lee concerning the way
he speaks. Lee derides Tam's varying black and white accents and
rhythms: "What'sa wrong with your Chinatown acka-cent, huh?"
   Tam replies, "I got tired of people correcting it. They were even
telling me I was 'mispronouncing' my name . . . kept telling me it
was pronounced 'Tom.' "
   The truth is that a Chinaman language was developing as the result
of the new American experience, but, say the editors of *Aiiieeeee!*, "the
literary establishment has never considered the fact that a new folk in
a strange land would experience the land and develop new language out
of old words" (p. 22). White America's "tyranny of language," continue
the editors, has contributed to "the lack of a recognized style of Asian-
American manhood" and hobbled its literary creativity (p. 24).
   This denial of manhood has also placed Asian Americans in an
equivocal position among the minorities. Unlike the more manly—and
therefore more threatening—blacks and Chicanos, the stereotype of the
effeminate Asian-American has become, says Chin,

   a comfortable part of the American subconscious. White America is as
   securely indifferent about us as men as plantation owners were about their
   loyal house niggers. House niggers is what America has made of us,
   admiring us for being patient, submissive, esthetic, passive, accommodating,
   essentially feminine in character . . . what whites call "Confuciusist,"
   dreaming us up a goofy version of Chinese culture to preserve in becoming
   the white male's dream minority. ("Confessions," p. 67)

In *Chickencoop*, Chin attacks this racist love by satirizing Helen
Keller—who could not see, speak of, or hear the evils of white racism—
as the role model for Asian-Americans. She is supposedly the "Great

White goddess," the inarticulate mumbler and squeaker, who "overcame her handicaps without riot! She overcame her handicaps without looting! She overcame her handicaps without violence! And you Chinks and Japs can too."

Tam's emasculation by white culture is symbolically portrayed when at the beginning of their encounter, the Lone Ranger shoots the innocent young Tam—the future writer—in the hand. In the dialogue that follows, Tam repeatedly asks the hero for the reason for his action: "Why'd you shoot me in the hand, old man? I ain't no bad guy."

"I curse ya honorary white!" replies the Ranger. "In your old age, as it were in your legendary childhood, in the name of Helen Keller, Pearl Buck, and Charlie Chan, kiss my ass, know thou it be white, and go thou happy in honorary whiteness forever and ever, preservin your culture, AMEN." (Similarly, in *Gee, Pop!*, the Chinaman's leg is sawed off in one sequence, and he dies in another while being derided for his awkward shooting style by "John Wayne" and "Charlie Chan.")

Perhaps because he was also conscious of his own emasculation, of being symbolically shot in the hand, Tam's father idolized boxers; one of the duties of the young Tam was to escort his father out of Chinatown to fights and training bouts. Tam himself admires boxers and, for all his self-rejection, still hopes he might somehow make his children remember and be proud of him. He is filming a documentary about the hero of his youth, a black fighter named Ovaltine Jack Dancer, a former light-heavyweight champ. The Dancer had filled him with tales of his heroic father, and Tam's purpose in flying from California to Pittsburgh is to meet Charley Popcorn, the ostensible father. Tam stays at the home of his childhood friend "Blackjap" Kenji, a research dentist who lives by choice in the Oakland black ghetto for reasons obvious by his epithet. Tam enthusiastically looks forward to meeting Charley: "This trip's going to make me well. I'm going to see again, and talk and hear." Kenji himself is eager to accompany Tam: "Father of a champion, man."

Chin's own sympathy for blacks and his acknowledgment of their pioneering efforts in civil rights are revealed in the encounter between the two Asian-Americans and Charley, who is puzzled by the appearance of Chinaman Tam after hearing a black voice over the telephone. Charley denies that he is Ovaltine's father and asserts that the Dancer's wonderful tales of an ideal father-son relationship are pure fabrications—assertions that the hero-and-father-seeking Tam cannot accept. Charley becomes sympathetic to Tam's dilemma, although blacks, Charley says, "don't particularly favor Chinese." He chastises Tam for rejecting his own father: "I just know it's wrong to turn your back on your father however old you be." The exhausted Tam takes a swing at Charley and falls: "My punch won't crack an egg," says Tam, "but I'll never fall down."

The next scene finds Tam in Limbo, symbolically being carried on the black man's back. But in the ensuing scene Charley is on Tam's back as he staggeringly reenters Kenji's apartment. "I'm gonna throw up," says Popcorn. "Put me down."

Lee's former Chinese-American husband Tom—who appropriately plays Tonto in the Lone Ranger scene—is there in an attempt to get Lee to remarry him. Tom mistakes Tam for Kenji; and Tam, knowing full well that he has an assimilated Chinese-American before him, drops a wad of gum foil in his hand, saying, "Here, this silver bullet should tell you who I am!" During their angry exchange, Tom gives the standard rationalization for his assimilation: "I don't know what you're trying to prove, brother. But you'd better face facts. . . . I wondered why we didn't speak up more. Then I saw we don't have to. We used to be kicked around, but that's history, brother. Today we have good jobs, good pay, and we're lucky. Americans are proud to say we send more of our kids to college than any other race. We're accepted. We worked hard for it. I've made my peace."

Kenji as host is angered by Tam's rudeness to Tom and calls Tam vicious—like a rogue elephant. "You were my silent pardner," Tam says regretfully. "We used to run together." The conflicts are finally resolved. Kenji assumes an authoritative, fatherly role over Lee's child and declares that he and Lee will have a baby. Tam says he will make a straight, professional fight film without a fake father in it. Accepting his aloneness, he goes into the kitchen to cook dinner for all.

In his final monologue, addressed to his own children, he recalls again their family history, the stories of grandmaw and the Iron Moonhunter of the Old West. He adds how her father, broken and frostbitten while working on the granite face of the Sierras, was rescued and raced home by other "Chinamans, nobodies' fathers." He dies in his home, "comfortable, comforting a little girl rolling counterfeit Spanish cigars." Tam deeply feels this history and wishes his children would share it with him:

> Now and then, I feel them old days, children, the way I feel the prowl of the dogs in the night and the bugs in the leaves and the thunder in the Sierra Nevadas however far they are. The way my grandmother had an ear for trains. Listen, children. I gotta go. Ride Buck Buck Bagaw with me. . . . Listen in the kitchen for the Chickencoop Chinaman slowin on home.

IV. The Year of the Dragon: *The Disintegration of the Chinese-American Family*

The Year of the Dragon was first produced in 1974 by the American Place Theatre in New York. A PBS version for *Theater in America* was videotaped in 1975. In the spring of 1977, Chin directed and starred in a San Francisco production. To a theater critic of a city newspaper he wrote:

> The play is set in Frisco, because this city is known as the place our history began. Frisco is the soul of Chinese America. The play is set in the Year of the Dragon because the Dragon was the Bicentennial year. The play sums up where I see Chinese America in the Year of the Dragon: 1976. Chinese New Year's because . . . obvious reasons, including the war imagery and sounds that dominate Chinatown during New Year's.[9]

What are these "obvious reasons" and the "war imagery and sounds"? We are, in fact, hearing the voice of Frank Chin, Chinaman, protesting what is happening to Chinese America. He is aware of the white fear of the "Yellow Peril," the threat of Asian expansion at the turn of the century, and of Jack London's "The Unparalleled Invasion," in which, because of this peril, "the celebration of the Second Centennial of American Liberty was deferred." In London's story, China had been awakened to Western mechanization by Japan, but the "real danger lay in the fecundity of her loins" and the resultant outnumbering of the whites of the world. To obviate this danger America began on 1 May 1976 to drop on China glass vials of diseases from airplanes, and in the ensuing summer and fall the country became an "inferno." London tells us, however, that not until the cold of February did the first expeditions enter China. They found a "howling wilderness" and roving bandits: "All survivors were put to death wherever found."[10]

Chin, who believes that the eventual extinction of Chinese-Americans is inevitable, must have found London's Bicentennial story curiously prophetic of white intentions. But he feels that it is not nine months of germ warfare but the Chinese-Americans' loss of history and "soul," or integrity—the price of white acceptance—that will wipe them out eventually.

> On the West Coast and specifically Frisco, where we began, yellow culture that is not imported fresh from some real China or Japan is ignored and suppressed. The place is a goddamned Hollywood set. I mean it. . . .

Frisco's Chinatown is Shangri la built by Hollywood and stocked from a Chinese-American farm run by white Christians. Virtually all of the influential Chinatown establishment and showcase Orientals are first, second and third generation Christian converts. And the most respected powers in Chinese America are Hollywood bit players, who play Orientals who die, are goofy servants, and make Confucius sound like Rod McKuen.[11]

The mission schools undertook the education of Chinese Americans because of continuing public efforts to segregate or ignore them. Chin believes that they nonetheless became political instruments by fostering the ideal of the passive, nonaggressive male who recognizes the superiority of whites and by eradicating the memory of the bold, pioneering Chinamen of old. The schools also denied Chinese-American history: ". . . we were indoctrinated into forgetting the names of every burned down or wiped out Chinatown, [into becoming] gah gah for the little town of Bethlehem instead." But despite this indoctrination, there was a tacit assumption of their alien identity: "I was raised by whites I knew to be a foreigner. I'm fifth generation here and white clergymen pat me on the head and hope I'll become president of China" (Kirby, p. 15).

Of this condescension, Chin says elsewhere that

A Chinese can take being told he speaks English pretty good and that he's pretty "Americanized and aggressive" as compliments, as English and being American for him are the results of conscious effort. The same things said to a Chinaman are insults. It's putting him in his place, not in the Chinatown a Chinese could see today, but in the Chinatown that's in the blood of all *juk sing*, the deathcamp Chinatown. ("Confessions," p. 65)

It is the "deathcamp Chinatown" that's in the blood, not a Hollywood Shangri-la, that we glimpse in the Eng family of *The Year of the Dragon*. In a moment of compounding, encircling frustrations, the hero Fred Eng cries out: "I am shit. This family is shit. Chinatown's shit. You can't love each other around here without hating yourself."

The play, with its theme of disintegration, begins with the imminent death of the father during the Year of the Dragon. Having lived in America since 1935, he is now the respected "mayor" of Chinatown, probably by virtue of his presidency of the Christian-dominated Chinese Benevolent Society. Realizing his impending death, he is anxious about the future of his family outside Chinatown's confines because of his dislike and suspicion of whites. Although he is at times brutally autocratic and selfish, his children and wife love him, and the family thus has a semblance of unity.

He married Ma Eng when she was but fifteen. Through her carefully recited clichés, she shows that she has been mission educated: "I always told you to be proud to be the best of the East, the best of the West" and "Miss Thompson, she said, 'Talking two completely incompatible languages is a great asset.' " Unconsciously she sings repeatedly an American-written "Chinese Lullabye" that tells of the selling of "slave girls" (purportedly saved by the missions):

> Sing song, sing song, so hop toy
> Allee same like China Boy.
> But he sellee girl with joy,
> Pity poor Ming Toy.

She loves her home and family, and she fears change. She is nonetheless aware of the slow disintegration of her family: her husband is dying; her forty-year-old unmarried son Fred rarely sleeps at home; Johnny is on probation for carrying a gun; Mattie has married a white and has returned to Chinatown only at her father's request. Ma Eng attempts to escape moments of stress by going to the bathroom or bursting into song. But she spiritedly objects to the unexpected appearance of Pa Eng's first wife, brought over from China so that he would be "happy families when I die." Nevertheless, in the uproar that follows, when the family threatens to disintegrate even more, she accepts China Mama's presence to preserve as best she can her family's integrity. She even adheres to Pa's request that she instruct China Mama in some English by teaching her the "Chinese Lullabye."

Unlike her mother, Mattie has escaped entirely: she hates Chinatown and asserts that her home is now in Boston with her white husband, Ross. She had made clear her intention to leave forever when she left for college by saying to a friend of Fred's, who cared for Chinatown and later died of a stabbing, that "it didn't matter where I was born or what color I was . . . especially being a Chinese girl." Apprehensive upon her return to Chinatown, she says, "all of a sudden I feel like just another yellow girl on the arm of a Caucasian."

Her brother Johnny brings forth an undercurrent of violence in Chinatown that destroys the image of the strong, law-abiding Chinese-American family. Before his entrance in the first act, we are informed that his friend has been shot and killed. Vigorously hostile to Ross, Johnny is an alienated youth, preferring his criminal escapades with immigrant hoodlums whose language he cannot understand to college and his sister's Boston and her loss of identity. Aware of the deterioration in her mother and brothers, Sis urges that they all leave for Boston after Pa Eng's death: "Out there we'll be able to forget we're Chinamen, just forget all this and just be people and Fred will write again." Johnny replies coldly: "You have to forget you're a Chinatown girl to be just people, Sis?"

Chinatown is flooded by white tourists during New Year's, especially for the famed parade whose festive sounds serve as an ironic background for the tragic last scenes of the play. Fred, who despises whites, says after the conflicts of the first act, which augur his family's dissolution: "There are twenty-five thousand tourists out there right now and more every day until the parade. . . . You'll look out of the window and see so many white people's faces and hair, it'll look like a sparkling gravel path and I feel I can go take a walk on bok gwai's faces . . . it'll be like making wine."

Fred, the head of Eng's Chinatown Tour 'n Travel, hates Chinatown, regarding it, as stated before, as the whites' private preserve for an "endangered species." But as Chinatown's top guide, with an inimitable spiel, he hates himself even more for his artistic corruption: he has lost sight of his dream of being a writer. His job, moreover, forces him to conform to the American stereotype of the Chinese-American. According to Chin, a tourist guide is by definition "a Chinaman, playing a white man playing Chinese. A yellow in cultural whiteface playing a white man in yellowface. A minstrel show. The tourist guides of Chinatown are traditionally the despised and perverted" (Weiner, p. 2).

Thus Fred and his brother Johnny present their spiels in the language and manner that the white tourists expect. The prototype for these expectations is Charlie Chan, a character invented by a white man in 1925 and invariably played by white men in the movies and on television. Chin finds the date of Chan's appearance macabre, for by coincidence "1925 marked the first Chinese American Christian Fellowship Conference at Lake Tahoe" (Kirby, p. 15). Though intelligent, Chan has the expected Asian-American qualities: he is humble, passive, polite, self-effacing, and effeminate, and he has difficulty with English. In his 1971 interview with Roland Winters, the last of the movie Charlie Chans, Chin asked why NBC chose Ross Martin, a white, to play the TV detective. Winters replied: "I don't know. The only thing I can think of, if you, uh, if you want to cast a homosexual in a show, and you get a homosexual, it'll be awful. It won't be funny. If you get a man, a normal man, playing a homosexual, it's funny. And maybe there's something there." Confucianisms were also part of Chan's humor, as was his use of humble language: in the denouement of every movie when "the stupid police lieutenant said, 'Well, okay, I'll arrest Charlie,' " Chan, said Winters, "always said, 'Uh torn with grief to disagree but Charlie not murderer. Real murderer is so and so.' " Chin noted the slight accent used. Winters replied that he used "more of an accent than that really. *And a slightly higher voice*" [italics added]. When asked about his Chan mannerisms, Winters replied:

> Well, actually, they're very few! Because uh, the only Orientals that I've ever dealt with, I've found very reserved of gesture. They don't wave their arms around like Italians or Frenchmen. They're very very contained people.
>
> And the only thing that uh that stands out in the mind when you're playing an Oriental of, I mean of *education*, is that number one, his manners are very good. And he's very simple, and very courteous. That's about it. So you do a lot of bowing, rather than saying "Right on" or "You know," "Yeah!" or something. And uh. And uh, I've deliberately kept my hands at my side. I very rarely used any gestures unless they were absolutely important, in some way or other.

Although he kept his hands at his sides, Winters said he believed that Chan was physically courageous, and he (Winters) would have been willing to do "any physical stuff." But "they said, 'Oh, no, no, Chan never does anything like that. And he rarely ever even uses firearms.' " Winters, however, told of a scene in an undertaking parlor when a disguised lighter, flicked on accidentally, "came like a flame thrower. . . . I jumped back. And I said, 'Great, let's do that. Let's keep it, that's funny,' you know. Chan snooping around, and he doesn't know what this is, and he hits this thing and [it] goes on in a great burst of flame and scares the hell out of him! 'No' he says, 'Oh, no no no!' "[12]

Contends Chin, "Charlie Chan is not trivia or a mere stereotype to us. Charlie Chan is the name of the epoch of history we now inhabit" (Weiner, p. 4). Ross, Mattie Eng's white husband, shows the prevalence of the Chan stereotype by reciting Confucianisms and suggesting that Pa Eng, as mayor of Chinatown, add a Charlie Chan joke to the speech he is to give after the parade. Therefore, before Pa leaves for the occasion, he greets Fred with "You got dah case solve yet?" and insists that Fred, his "Nummer One Son," call him "Pop": "Gosh, Pop!" "Gee, Pop!"

That Pa would accept the Chan stereotype himself shows the effect of Chinese America's loss of cultural integrity. Ma Eng herself, in preparation for the event, appears with her hair "done in a style too young for her." To Ross's approval, significantly, "She's dressed in a tight cheongsam, and is playing the part of a Chinese woman as authentically as she can, which means she's Susie Wong and *Flower Drum Song.*" Of the influence of movies on the behavior of Asian Americans, Chin says: "Yellows take the making of movies about yellows as historic events. Chinese America marks its epochs by *The Good Earth, The Charlie Chan Series . . . Flower Drum Song, Kung Fu* on TV. . . . The movies about us are as serious and momentous in our history as great battles are in European history. Even from reading the autobiographies and the letters to the editor columns of the *New York Times,* while *Kung Fu* was hot on ABC, you can tell we take movies and TV about us as a sign of white approval and a list of suggestions for character and behavior changes" (Kirby, p. 28).

Fred's own perception of Chan is found earlier in a scene with China Mama, his real mother, who has recently arrived from China. He responds to her question, asked, of course, in Chinese: "You want me to be Chinese too, huh? Everybody does. . . . You know how the tourists tell I'm Chinese? No first person pronouns. No 'I,' 'Me,' or 'We.' I talk like that lovable sissy, Charlie Chan, no first person personal pronouns, and instant Chinese culture . . . ha, ha, ha."

He teaches her these pronouns and, when she learns them, he declares: "You are now a citizen, congratulations." To her uncomprehending ears, moreover, he declares himself to be a Chinaman:

> I'm not Chinese. This ain't China. Your language is foreign and ugly, so how come you're my mother? . . . I mean, I don't think I'm quite your idea of a son, either. . . . You hear all my first person pronouns, China Mama. They're glistening in my natural talk like stars. Me and Ma and Sis get together and we're talking a universe, and sing. . . . You're just another tourist wanting me to be Chinese, China Mama. Just because we're born here don't mean we're nobody and gotta go to another language to talk. I think Chinatown Buck Buck Bagaw is beautiful.

The use of the first person pronouns is for Fred the declaration of his American individualism and individual rights. He had wanted to become a writer, "someone special," not just his father's son. But because he was born in China and entered America illegally as an infant, he is torn between his desire to live his own life and his duty to fulfill his responsibilities to his own family. The mixture of the old and the new may be seen in some of Fred's small gestures. In the first scene of Act II, for instance, he twice lights some incense for the ancestral shrine before lighting up a "joint." More important, ten years before, while yet in college pursuing his dream of being a writer, he—as the eldest son—was called home by his father, who was suffering from a lung complaint. His father, an immigrant, expected him to be obedient, to earn money, and to be responsible for his younger siblings. As for the last, Fred is belabored by his father for Johnny's delinquency, and Sis recalls that in the past it was Fred who was beaten for her misbehavior. But perhaps in acknowledgment of Fred's manliness, Pa assigned Ma to do the beating because he knew Fred would not strike back at her.

Despite his hatred of his job, Fred is proud of having successfully shouldered his family responsibilities. He has enabled Mattie to go away to college, and when Mattie and Ross arrive, he gives them the traditional envelopes full of money to present to Pa Eng on New Year's. He sees Boston, where their Mama FuFu business is prospering, as a place where Johnny can escape from his hoodlum friends and, after Pa's death, as a refuge for Ma Eng and a place of fulfillment for himself. Almost nightly he attends his father in the bathroom when he is sick. For all his fidelity and success, he expects some gratitude and respect from his father. Consequently he is enraged when Pa imports China Mama without consulting him and also when he realizes that Pa truly considers him a "flop," unable to care for the family outside Chinatown's confines.

Chin says of the Cantonese family:

> Sons were raised to one purpose, survive and support the family in the parents' old age. Cantonese had lots of kids and hoped for boys cuz few kids lived to adulthood. . . . The youngest son and daughter became the rebel heroes of pop fiction and art. It seemed to be understood that the first son was doomed from the start and never rebels. He was broken in childhood. The younger sons and daughters break away and adventure, but not the first son. Sometimes the eldest surviving son goes amok. (Kirby, p. 24)

Pa Eng, for all his Chinese roots, has taken on the values of this American Chinatown. Though demanding unquestioning obedience from Fred, he ironically selects a tourist guide business for him, a business despised by the people of Chinatown. Furthermore, as a person of consequence, he has never acknowledged his children in print and once, while lunching with Fred when fellow dignitaries approached, did not bother to introduce him. Although it was he who removed Fred from college, he disdains Fred's ambition to be a writer, valuing only the more lucrative and traditional professions—which require a college degree. In preparing his New Year's speech, he thus hurts Fred by asking Ross, a "real" American, for help, but in his own insecurity with English he asks Fred privately to edit his speech so that Ross will not discern his ineptness.

When Pa Eng brings China Mama to America so that he can die "Chinese," Fred asks him why he did not return to China instead. Pa replies that he has lived in America for many years and regards Chinatown as his home. This for Chin is significant as he believes most Chinese came here not as sojourners who would eventually return to China but as immigrants, like their European counterparts, with their own vision of America.

Pa, in this bathroom scene, is aware that the family line has probably come to an end and attempts to exact from Fred a promise that he will always remain in Chinatown. Of his daughter he says, "Sissy go colleges what happening? Bok gwai low! [White devil!] And no more blood. No more Chinese babies born in a family. No Merican Chinese babies, nutting doing and flop." He derides Fred's desire to write a cookbook for the Mama FuFu enterprises. Fred is also forty, balding, and unlikely ever to marry. Johnny's criminal escapades will probably kill him eventually.

During the last scene of the play, before the entire family leaves for the parade ceremonies, Fred asks his father to look at him for once as an individual and not as his obedient eldest son. Aware of Ma's psychological deterioration, Johnny's descent into criminality, and his father's power over them, Fred promises to remain in Chinatown if Pa will tell Ma and Johnny to leave for Boston with Mattie. But Pa remains adamant, and during their physical struggle, Pa dies. At the beginning of his aborted speech, Pa was to have introduced Fred as his heir: "dah one who're teck obber solve dah case. My's Nummer One Son, allaw time, saying 'Gee, Pop!' Fred Eng!"

At first afraid to leave Chinatown and become a "nobody" or discover that his writing ability has vanished, Fred is further crippled by his father's inability to the very end to see him as an individual. As the lights fade before his final spiel, Fred, his father's heir, "dressed in solid white, puts on a white slightly oversized jacket, and appears to be a shrunken Charlie Chan, an image of death. He becomes the tourist guide."

V. *Kwan Kung: The Ideal Discovered*

Ross, in his attempt to placate Fred, says that he will hang on the walls of the Mama FuFu restaurants parts of Fred's tourist spiel translated into Chinese calligraphy along with the quotation, "A good son is neither an actor nor a soldier." Chin believes that this statement by Confucius was fostered by white Christians to help create the stereotype of the "sissy," meek, and mild Chinese male. He believes, in fact, that the Cantonese—who became the first Chinamans—revered the masculine god Kwan Kung: "the god of war to soldiers, the god of plunder to soldiers and other arrogant takers, the god of literature to fighters who soldier with words, the god patron protector of actors and anyone who plays him on stage" (Kirby, p. 2). Because of his scholarly and military duality, Kwan Kung is often portrayed wearing a costume that is half scholar's robes and half general's uniform.

But though the Cantonese revered Kwan Kung, they never worshiped him as the Christians did their God; only the individual's self, according to Chin, is that important, and the Cantonese saw themselves in their hero: "We were all soldiers, plunderers, natural badmouths, showoffs, actors, loyal friends and avenging enemies" (Kirby, p. 3). Despite his loyalty and vengefulness, Kwan Kung was selfish and individualistic.

> The Chinese used to say the Cantonese were so individualistic, they didn't get along with or trust anyone, not even each other. You could never get close to a Cantonese cuz he either told you everything endlessly and entertainingly and you couldn't sort out what counts—or he told you nothing. Every CANTONESE IS WHOLE UNTO HIMSELF AS A PLANET and trusts no other living thing. (Kirby, p. 3)

Because actors were an outcast and distrusted group, Kwan symbolized their famed loyalty to one another. "Many of the folk tales . . . involve actors playing him on stage," wearing his red mask. They consequently *become* Kwan Kung, and his name "breaks all magic, good or bad" (Kirby, p. 3a). Because of his popularity among both actors and audience, his was the most popular of the Cantonese operas that traveled to America with the immigrants.

The opera's popularity was such that "Once there were three opera houses in Chinatown Frisco hot and heavy with hundred night, five hours a night, free for all versions of . . . *The Romance of the Three Kingdoms*. Kwan Kung was played by the strongest young men in Chinatown." Like the novel on which it is based, the opera is sprawling and complex in form: it seems "a collection of documents, various story tellers' cheat sheets, doggerel and repeats of folk hearsay by different people writing at different times about the same historical event." It disdains the Western neoclassical unities and is the result "of thousands of years of literate storytelling wordhappy culture." Both the novel and opera "pose as raw documentary history. The form contains the notion of destroying a people by destroying their history" (Kirby, p. 5a).

The opera also contains the famed Oath in the Peach Garden:

It's a soldier's blood oath of loyalty and revenge. Nothing charitable, necessarily honorable, in any Western sense, passive or timid about it. . . . It encouraged an aggressive self-reliance and trust nobody, watch out killer's sense of individuality that reached a peak in China with the Cantonese, took to the image of what the Chinamans scratching out mountains for gold thought of themselves, grew roots in California and sprouted a Kwan Kung happy race of people who wanted to hear, read, and rewrite, only one story, and sing and sit through and pass with one opera only. (Kirby, p. 11)

But, says Chin, the imported Cantonese opera became "purely Chinaman" in expression "as it adjusted language, style, detail, event, and setting to the changing world of the Chinamans at work on a new experience, making new language to define the new experience, and made new history." Such were the changes made that, for "Chinamans in mining and railroad camps and Chinatown," the opera became "a one man medicine show done by traveling kung fu fighters selling their personal kung fu brew." Whole families of such fighters "traveled by wagon from camp to camp selling tonic, breaking chains, and doing flash versions of *Three Kingdoms*" (Kirby, p. 11).

It is to this Chinaman version of Cantonese opera that Chin owes his artistic origins: "I write from links with the original whoremothers of our people and through my mother, ties to the most popular hero of the most popular novel and opera in Chinatown history. . . . I have a piece of old Chinatown opera living with me. The Kwan blood from my mother meant I was chosen to write theater like making war, throw everything away and get even" (Kirby, pp. 33–34).

Chin therefore says: "I am not any white writer. I'm Frank Chin, Chinaman writer. White reviewers like Julius Novick and Clive Barnes stuck in their Christian esthetic of one god, one good, one voice, one thing happening, one talk at a time get so dizzy in the atmosphere of Chinaman word strategy they gotta cancel out every white writer they know to make sense of my simple Chinaman backscratch" (Kirby, p. 8). He believes that artists should be judged on their own terms and that, if their intention is not considered, the traditional Western criteria become irrelevant and unfair. Act I of *The Year of the Dragon* has been especially confusing to viewers who have not previously studied the play.

Yet, in his conception of a New Man (a Chinaman) and a new language wrought out of the new American experience, he shows his awareness of the early nineteenth-century American struggle for cultural and linguistic freedom from Britain. He wrote in 1976: "Americans, especially white Americans, remember this Bicentennial year, especially this year, the day when white people in America wondered if they were British subjects or American Colonials, til they discovered and said they were neither, and declared themselves Americans." Further, "As British received standard became a distinctly new English . . . so spoken and written Cantonese became Chinaman Cantonese" (Kirby, pp. 27, 6).

Moreover, to counter the effeminate, Christianized, Charlie Chan image of the post-1925 era, he has restored the immensely masculine Kwan Kung, whose strength of mind and body, whose individuality and loyalty, whose capacity for revenge, and whose essential aloneness are reminiscent of the rugged Western hero of American myth. The interested reader might wish to contrast this rugged individualism with the perception of Chinese character in Francis L. K. Hsu's *Challenge of the American Dream.*[13] Hsu is an immigrant Chinese.

Kwan Kung's opera also, as stated before, contains the idea that haunts Chin's work: the destruction of a people by destroying their history. He is well aware of the white fear of such destruction: one of his more amusing insights is of James Hilton's Shangri-la as a place for the preservation of white culture where whites with low self-esteem can be worshiped and serviced by yellows. He regrets, however, that most members of his own generation have forgotten their past and their old hero: "There was a statue of Kwan Kung in every Chinese American home I was ever in," he says, "til my generation moved into houses of their own, and hadn't known 'Chinaman' is what we called ourselves in the English we spoke and made our own for three generations now" (Kirby, p. 11).

Acknowledging the eventual extinction of Asian America, Chin in his own life and work has maintained the heroic stance of the old Chinaman god. He mentions Kwan Kung in his still unfinished *Gee, Pop!* in which the immigrant father directly associates himself with him:

> Kwan Kung was a plunderer, King of the resourceful men. So I live here Gum Sahn [the Sierras] forever anyhow I can. I was a cowboy! My father come here before and lay down duh Chinaman crosstie celebrate we build duh railroad. My pa one dah four hundred Chinamans spike down track for lay dah record, of the transcontinental original. . . . Him [Kwan] God for writers! So, when I paralyze, no can talk, I begin write down in my memory, dah story of humanity in Gum Sahn.

He had come to America "to fight for the survive the human race agains the people who make us forget the whole Motherlode Sierra Nevada mountain full of gold is the Chinaman Plymouth rock. . . .

But bok gwai white people catches up allwa Chinaman kid doy chillun and nebbuh teach'em remember what exactly Gum Sahn is. And we fight gains' dose non-human white people makin us forget who build dah railroad." He admonishes his sons: "You nonk destroy nobody's history. You fight 'em. Dat's war! But no matter what! You nonk destroy nobody's history. Only sissy do dat. . . . When I get Naturalize, learn American citizenship history, you think I taught to forget the Alamo in order become citizen?"

A few years ago in a restaurant in Seattle, Chin (who avows he dislikes broken men) was revolted by an aging, embittered no-no boy of World War II who felt his life had been ruined by his imprisonment. The no-no boy ought to have felt that he was on Seattle's conscience; moreover, "He'd lost all sense of Seattle as a Japanese-American city, all sense of vision":

> "You say the Chinese came here with a vision too?" he whined, and I had to move or melt into a pool of boo-hoo and booze and give up with the old man.
>
> "Get up! Come with me right now!" I said and was walking to the front of the restaurant.
>
> If he had caught up with me, I'd have collared him and dragged him to the poster of Kwan Hung [sic] sitting on his tiger throne with his squire at his right hand, holding Kwan's knife, and his son at his left, holding Kwan's seal. Kwan's left side robed him like a scholar and his right side armored him like a soldier. "That's the vision of ourselves when we first came over," I said. ("Yellow Seattle," p. 11)

Notes

[1] Frank Chin, "Frank Chin Profile" (unpub. ms.), p. 1.

[2] Frank Chin, "Back Talk," *News of the American Place Theatre*, 3 (May 1972), 2.

[3] Mark Twain, *Roughing It* (Berkeley: Univ. of California Press, 1972), pp. 350, 351, 355.

[4] Frank Chin, "Confessions of the Chinatown Cowboy," *Bulletin of Concerned Asian Scholars*, 4 (Fall 1972), 60; hereafter cited in text.

[5] Thomas W. Chinn, ed., *A History of the Chinese in California: A Syllabus* (San Francisco: Chinese Historical Society, 1975), pp. 26–39. For an extended study of the bachelor society, see Victor G. Nee and Brett de Bary Nee, *Longtime Californ': A Documentary Study of an American Chinatown* (New York: Pantheon, 1973).

[6] H. Mark Lai and Philip P. Choy, *Outlines: History of the Chinese in America* (San Francisco: Lai and Choy, 1971), p. 99.

[7] Frank Chin, "Yellow Seattle," *The Weekly: Seattle's Newsmagazine*, 1–7 Feb. 1976, p. 11.

[8] Frank Chin, Jeffery Paul Chan, Lawson Fusao Inada, and Shawn Wong, eds., *Aiiieeeee!*

An Anthology of Asian American Writers (Garden City, N.Y.: Doubleday, 1975), p.-x.

9 Letter to Bernard Weiner, 12–13 April 1977, p. 2.

10 Jack London, "The Unparalleled Invasion," in *The Strength of the Strong* (New York: Macmillan, 1914), pp. 71–100.

11 Frank Chin, Letter to Michael Kirby, ed., *Drama Review*, 22 Oct.–23 Nov. 1976, p. 34.

12 Frank Chin, "Interview: Roland Winters," *Amerasia Journal*, 2 (Fall 1973), 1–19. Chin adds in the preface, "In the days when Charlie Chan was a bit part two Japanese actors Shojnin and George Kuwa briefly were thrown to light on the screen."

13 Francis L. K. Hsu, *The Challenge of the American Dream: The Chinese in the United States* (Belmont, Calif.: Wadsworth, 1971).

Of Place and Displacement:
The Range of Japanese-American
Literature

Lawson Fusao Inada

I. Toshio Mori

I envied him the places that he had not been

—William Stafford

Food for thought; thought for food. Here. This is mine; I made it for you. I love to do what I do. I hope you enjoy it too.

This is the essence of the old woman in Toshio Mori's story, "The Woman Who Makes Swell Doughnuts," and it can be said to be the essence of the book itself, *Yokohama, California*.[1]

The woman, like the community, is certainly worth her salt:

> Her face of today is coarse with hard water and there is no question that she has lived her life: given birth to six children, worked side by side with her man for forty years, working in the fields, working in the house, caring for the grandchildren, facing the summers and winters and also the springs and autumns, running the household that is completely her little world.

It is a privilege to visit her, to join her world:

> It is one of the experiences I will long remember—perhaps the only immortality that I will ever be lucky to meet in my short life—and when I say experience I do not mean the actual movement, the motor of our lives. I mean by experience the dancing of emotions before our eyes and inside of us, the dance that is still but is the roar and the force capable of stirring the earth and the people.

So we come in, make ourselves comfortable, and before we can "turn a page of a magazine she is back with a plateful of hot doughnuts." Now, what is there about these doughnuts? Obviously, it isn't simply the recipe: "It is a doughnut, just a plain doughnut just out of oil but it is different, unique." No, it has to do with the rest of the ingredients: the woman, the context, the community, and, of course, our involvement in all this. The doughnuts, then, are the center of an event in a place to come to when our "spirit wanes, when hell is loose," and we therefore "sing gratefully that such a simple and common experience becomes an event, an event of necessity and growth."

And the woman herself, what about her? "All her friends, old and young, call her Mama. Everybody calls her Mama. That is not new, it is logical. I suppose there is in every block of every city in America a woman who can be called Mama by her friends and the strangers meeting her." This woman "isn't a mama but is," and when we are with her we "do not need to know Plato or the Sacred Books of the East or dancing" and we "do not need to be on guard," but we are "on guard and foot-loose because the room is alive."

Her grandchildren—Mickey, Tadao, and Yaeko—are playing in the yard. She tells them to "play, play hard, go out there and play hard. You will be glad later for everything you have done with all your might." Trains go by. Sometimes the room is simply full of silence. She nods and seems to be saying "that this, her little room, her little circle, is a depot, a pause, for the weary traveler, but outside, outside of her little world there is dissonance, hugeness of another kind, and the travel to do. So she has her little house, she bakes the grandest doughnuts, and inside of her she houses a little depot."

So what we have, then, is an anonymous old woman in a very short, uneventful story in a modest collection by an obscure author— or a classic piece of poetic fiction by an American master that concludes thus:

> Most stories would end with her death, would wait till she is peacefully dead and peacefully at rest but I cannot wait that long. I think she will grow, and her hot doughnuts just out of the oil will grow with softness and touch. And I think it would be a shame to talk of her doughnuts after she is dead, after she is formless.
>
> Instead I take today to talk of her and her wonderful doughnuts when the earth is something to her, when the people from all parts of the earth may drop in and taste the flavor, her flavor, which is everyone's and all flavor; talk to her, sit with her, and also taste the silence of her room and the silence that is herself; and finally go away to hope and keep alive what is alive in her, on earth and in men, expressly myself.

Toshio Mori was born (1910), raised, and died (1980) in San Leandro, California—a one-time semirural community now all but an unidentifiable part of the urban sprawl of the Oakland–San Francisco area. Here is Mori's description of the community of "Yokohama, California":

> In Lil' Yokohama, as the youngsters call our community, we have twenty-four hours every day . . . and morning, noon, and night roll on regularly just as in Boston, Cincinnati, Birmingham, Kansas City, Minneapolis, and Emeryville.
>
> When the sun is out, the housewives sit on the porch or walk around the yard, puttering with this and that, and the old men who are in the house when it is cloudy or raining come out on the porch or sit in the shade and read the newspaper. The day is hot. All right, they like it. The day is cold. All right, all right. *Here, here,* they cry with their presence just as the youngsters when the teachers call the roll. And when the people among people are sometimes missing from Lil' Yokohama's roll, perhaps forever, it is another matter; but the news belongs here just as does the weather.[2]

Mori's parents were immigrants from Japan who, on arrival in America, worked in the nursery business—a profession that he took as his own. Toshio Mori, then, was a man of the soil, a husband, a father, and a citizen of good standing in the community. He is also "the first real Japanese-American writer,"[3] and to encounter his work is to encounter several major assumptions.

The first assumption is that he knows who he is: he has his own identity. The second is that he knows where he is: he has a sense of community. The third is that he knows he needs no justification. Thus, it is crucial to note that these are not "minority" stories in the negative sense but "majority" stories told from the perspective of the full self and self-determining community. To the people of "Yokohama, California," even their problems are their own. And these positive assumptions permeate and radiate from the stories in such a matter-of-fact way as to be taken for granted, which is only natural.[4]

That Toshio Mori is an original stylist is readily apparent and can be taken for granted; it is what he does with his style that really matters. William Saroyan, in his sincere introduction, dubs Mori a "natural-born writer" (p. 7). He is and isn't, and to imply that he is a primitive is to diminish his achievement. Rather, here is a master craftsman at work, an innovator, even, one who has, most certainly, despite the "natural" fluidity of his plots and prose, worked consciously to achieve his effects, even to the extent of employing subtle self-mockery through literary humor: the hapless, aspiring young writer in "Akira Yano" reads *Winesburg, Ohio* and produces a collection called *The Miserable Young Man*, which includes the story, "The Eighty Days through the Second Story Window" (Mori, pp. 65–70). This is Mori's way of acknowledging tradition, for Sherwood Anderson was a major influence on Mori's American contemporaries, including his fellow Californians, Steinbeck and Saroyan.

In another sense, though, it would be appropriate to consider Mori a "natural": there is a "spoken" quality to these stories, tales of the community incorporating local gossip, humor, and legend; thus, it could be said that Toshio Mori is a true storyteller, a "folk" artist in the finest sense—a conveyor of culture, of the people.

So, through the voice and words of Toshio Mori, before we know it, we are living in a Japanese-American community of the late 1930s and early 1940s, at one with the people, and, of course, depending on the occasion, "speaking" Japanese, which is only natural. Without gimmickry or delineation, he captures the language of his place and time—including the warmth and sweetness of colloquial Japanese—in the language of his own, the American English of Japanese America, and in this way *Yokohama, California* becomes immediate for and accessible to us all. Toshio Mori, through his judicious use of language, reveals the core.

And the core is the community. The context is the content: *Yokohama, California* is about Yokohama, California. To be sure, the rest of the world exists, but mainly in relation to this frame of reference—a place to be, to start from. And though *Yokohama, California* is fiction, it nevertheless "documents" the essence of Japanese America before World War II. These were vital, creative communities of families and clans, of spirit and celebration; these were real homes where people earned their keep, where people belonged.[5]

Mori gives us Motoji Tsunoda, the "Seventh Street philosopher"; Ishimoto-san, a grocer who delivered pride and trust; Teruo, the young idealist in the flower shop; Hatsuye, the plain girl dreaming of Clark Gable; Satoru Doi, dreaming of the stock market; Sessue Matoi, the heavy drinker; Hashimoto and his trees; the Sasakis, the Yamadas, the Moris, getting together to talk about old times in the old country while the young ones played and made their way in the world; and in the midst of all this is Toshio Mori, with a vision, working all day with plants and the land, making his way across the page at night, planting; Toshio Mori, of the people, living the life and writing it with love and conviction:

Tomorrow is a school day, tomorrow is a work day, tomorrow is another twenty-four hours. In Lil' Yokohama night is almost over. On Sunday nights the block is peaceful and quiet. At eleven thirty-six Mr. Komai dies of heart failure. For several days he has been in bed. For fourteen years he has lived on our block and done gardening work around Piedmont, Oakland, and San Leandro. His wife is left with five children. The neighbors go to his house to comfort the family and assist in the funeral preparations.

Today which is Monday the sun is bright again, but the sick cannot come out and enjoy it. Mrs. Koike is laid up with pneumonia and her friends are worried. She is well known in Lil' Yokohama.

Down the block a third-generation Japanese American is born. A boy. They name him Franklin Susumu Amano. The father does not know of the birth of his boy. He is out of town driving a truck for a grocer.

Sam Suda, who lives down the street with his mother, is opening a big fruit market in Oakland next week. For several years he has been in Los Angeles learning the ropes in the market business. Now he is ready to open one and hire a dozen or more men.

Upstairs in his little boarding room, the country boy has his paints and canvas ready before him. All his life Yukio Takaki has wanted to come to the city and become an artist. Now he is here; he lives on Seventh Street. He looks down from his window, and the vastness and complexity of life bewilder him. But he is happy. Why not? He may succeed or not in his ambition; that is not really important.

. . . .

Something is happening to the Etos of the block. All of a sudden they turn in their old '30 Chevrolet for a new Oldsmobile Eight! They follow this with a new living-room set and a radio and a new coat of paint for the house. On Sundays the whole family goes for an outing. Sometimes it is to Fleishhacker Pool or to Santa Cruz. It may be to Golden Gate Park or to the ocean or to their relatives in the country. . . . They did not strike oil or win the sweepstakes. Nothing of the kind happens in Lil' Yokohama, though it may any day. . . . What then?

. . . .

Today which is Wednesday we read in the *Mainichi News* about the big games scheduled this Sunday. The San Jose Asahis will travel to Stockton to face the Yamatos. The Stockton fans want to see the champs play once again. At Alameda, the Sacramento Mikados will cross bats with the Taiiku Kai boys.

And today which is every day the sun is out again. The housewives sit on the porch and the old men sit in the shade and read the papers. Across the yard a radio goes full blast with Benny Goodman's band. The children come back from Lincoln Grammar School. In a little while the older ones will be returning from Tech High and McClymonds High. Young boys and young girls will go down the street together. The old folks from the porches and the windows will watch them go by and shake their heads and smile.

The day is here and is Lil' Yokohama's day. (Mori, pp. 73–76)

San Leandro, California, through the soul of Toshio Mori and Japanese America, becomes *Yokohama, California*, the embodiment of a people.

Mama and her doughnuts just out of oil. Welcome.

II. John Okada

From my mother's sleep I fell into the State

—Randall Jarrell

In Toshio Mori's story, "Lil' Yokohama," which offers scenes in the regular life of the community, a young man is being seen off to college:

> Today which is Tuesday Lil' Yokohama is getting ready to see Ray Tatemoto off. He is leaving for New York, for the big city to study journalism at Columbia. Everybody says he is taking a chance going so far away from home and his folks. The air is a bit cool and cloudy. At the station Ray is nervous and grins foolishly. His friends bunch around him, shake hands, and wish him luck. This is his first trip out of the state. Now and then he looks at his watch and up and down the tracks to see if his train is coming.
>
> When the train arrives and Ray Tatemoto is at last off for New York, we ride back on the cars to Lil' Yokohama. Well, Ray Tatemoto is gone, we say. The folks will not see him for four or six years. Perhaps never. Who can tell? We settle back in the seats and pretty soon we see the old buildings of Lil' Yokohama. We know we are home. . . . So it goes. (Mori, p. 75)

In several important respects, the fictional Ray Tatemoto is similar to the real John Okada and to Ichiro Yamada, the protagonist in Okada's novel *No-No Boy*:[6] all three are second-generation Japanese-Americans of college age in the late 1930s and early 1940s, and all are from prominent Japanese-American communities. For America in general, this was a period of hope and growth following the depression, but for Japanese America it was a particularly promising time because the immigrant generation had established solid communities with fruitful interchange among them in the form of cultural, religious, and social activities, and the young were "real" Americans: natural-born citizens speaking English, going to school, and reaching out to the world. This was a time of trust and optimism. This was a time now referred to as "before the war."

John Okada was born in Seattle in 1923, where his parents ran a boarding hotel in the Asian-American community; he received B.A. degrees in English and in library science from the University of Washington and earned a master's degree in English from Columbia University. During World War II, while his family was "interned" in Idaho, he served as a sergeant in the U.S. Army. After the war, he worked as a librarian in Seattle and Detroit, and as a technical writer in Detroit and Los Angeles. *No-No Boy* is his only published work; he died in obscurity in 1971.

In terms of chronology, John Okada is a contemporary of James Baldwin and Norman Mailer, and *No-No Boy* takes place in the period immediately following World War II.[7] With the rest of America, Japanese America had contributed to the war effort, suffering casualties and winning distinctions, but it had also been "warred upon" by its own government: whole communities of American citizens were forcibly removed to concentration camps in isolated areas of America. In retrospect, it could be said that this act was not out of keeping with previous policies, laws, and actions directed toward Japanese-Americans and American minority groups in general, but it nevertheless came as a great shock and irrevocably altered the course of Japanese-American history: the camp experience has been termed "the great betrayal" by Japanese-Americans and non-Japanese-Americans alike.[8]

In the turmoil and uncertainty of the camps, the very strength of a people—their sense of identity and community, their sense of worth—was called to question and became subject to doubt by the people themselves. For the older generation, what had been second nature—maintaining Japanese tradition—now became a wrong; for the American born, being American was no longer taken for granted. In the "double war," they were all "aliens." It was as if the term "Japanese-American" no longer signified a viable whole but denoted an either/or situation, a double bind.

In short, the people were called on to confront, define, and justify their own existence, to themselves and to their government, and the camps fragmented into factions of "wrong" and "right" with more "ifs" than answers, for no matter what the people did—and most adjusted remarkably well to the rigors of camp life, a testament to spirit developed before the war—they were still behind barbed wire in the country that used to be home.

It is in this emotionally charged atmosphere, then, that *No-No Boy* is set, for though the war is over and much resettlement has taken place, and the people are eager to start over, the feelings of outrage and pain nevertheless remain, and though the barbed wire is gone, it has been sublimated.

Thus, it is as if the expansive community of Yokohama, California has contracted into itself with a victim's vigilance and become a place of *re*action instead of action, a place of blame and shame, with the people trying to prove something, to make things right again. The woman who made doughnuts is dead and buried somewhere in Idaho; her husband has come home but lost his business; her older son was wounded in Germany and is recuperating at home; her other son was stationed in Minneapolis and refuses to return to California; her daughter, the mother of Mickey, Tadao, and Yaeko, is running the household while her husband, an engineer by training, works as a gardener; Mickey, Tadao, and Yaeko seem to be doing all right in school but are called "Jap" by the "Americans," and last night some kids came and threw rocks through the living-room window. Ray Tatemoto was killed in Italy.

So Ichiro Yamada comes home to Seattle and thus begins the first Japanese-American novel and one of the great works of our time:

> Two weeks after his twenty-fifth birthday, Ichiro got off a bus at Second and Main in Seattle. He had been gone four years, two in camp and two in prison.
>
> Walking down the street that autumn morning with a small, black suitcase, he felt like an intruder in a world to which he had no claim. It was just enough that he should feel this way, for, of his own free will, he had stood before the judge and said that he would not go in the army. At the time there was no other choice for him. That was when he was twenty-three, a man of twenty-three. Now, two years older, he was even more of a man.
>
> Christ, he thought to himself, just a goddamn kid is all I was. Didn't know enough to wipe my own nose. What the hell have I done? Best thing I can do would be to kill some son of a bitch and head back to prison.
>
> He walked toward the railroad depot where the tower with the clocks on all four sides was. It was a dirty looking tower of ancient brick. It was a dirty city. Dirtier, certainly, than it had a right to be after only four years. (p. 1)

He is immediately spat on by a former friend—Eto Minato, in an

Eisenhower jacket—and, as he makes his way toward the Japanese-American section, blacks on the street call him "Jap" and tell him to "Go back to Tokyo." His parents are running a small grocery store and living in the back: "He knew what it would be like even before he stepped in. His father had described the place to him in a letter. . . . The Japanese characters, written simply so that he could read them, covered pages of directions as if he were a foreigner coming to the city for the first time" (p. 6).

Ichiro finds his father a broken man, a drunk, and his mother on the verge of insanity. She refuses to accept Japan's defeat and the fact that her family there is suffering. His younger brother, Taro, feels compelled to join the army to atone for Ichiro's behavior. Whatever plans Ichiro had before the war—earning a college degree, living the good life in America—seem like delusions now as he confronts the consequences of his actions; in the midst of collective confusion and his own self-doubt, he must make his way again and say yes to life.

"No-no boys" were those few men, in contrast to the thousands who complied or volunteered, who refused to be drafted into the army from the camps. Needless to say, the situation was an extremely complicated and confused one, not entirely resolved to this day, and since Okada does not dwell on the specifics, his intention is obviously to focus on the post-War present of the plot and the resulting ramifications:

> For each and every refusal based on sundry reasons, another thousand chose to fight for the right to continue to be Americans because homes and cars and money could be regained but only if they first regained their rights as citizens, and that was everything.
>
> And then Ichiro thought to himself: My reason was all the reasons put together. I did not go because I was weak and could not do what I should have done. It was not my mother, whom I have never really known. It was me, myself. It is done and there can be no excuse. (p. 34)

What is important is that Ichiro assumes responsibility for himself. As he says earlier, what he did was "of his own free will." Surely, however, other forces must have been at work on him to influence his decision—his domineering mother, for one—but the crucial point is that he assumes the blame in an effort to regain control of his life.

It is also important to note Okada's choice of a no-no boy as a protagonist instead of a common figure, perhaps a veteran like himself. A greater dramatic intensity is certainly achieved, but there is more to it than that. Though the no-no boy's refusal to serve can be interpreted as a negative act, an act of defiance, it can also be seen as a positive act: taking a stand. And though it was against the law, it was also *for* a matter of principle and not necessarily anti-American or pro-Japanese. Given the conditions of the camps, then, it might be said that joining the military was actually taking the path of less resistance, the way of compromise.

The point is, under those conditions, either way was both "wrong" and "right," and though most eligible men went into the army, distinguished themselves, and were acclaimed as a "credit to their race," their actions did not necessarily invalidate the position of the no-no boy any more than defeat discredited the Japanese people. And though the no-no boy was openly reviled as a "Jap lover," the vehemence of that reaction often masked something else—namely, self-doubt and a nagging sense of respect, not necessarily because the no-no boy *was* right but because he *had* a right to do what he did. The no-no boy was thus a threat to the smug and the complacent, for he was a reminder, not of the victories of war but of the defeats of camp. The image of the no-no boy was not to be easily exorcised by the people, no matter how completely "American" they thought they had become; the no-no boy was the "Jap" inside all of them, the part they had to accept to be whole again, to be Japanese-American.

Thus, the seemingly minor figure of the no-no boy in Japanese-America is actually a critical one. Suppose there had not been any no-no boys at all. Numbers are not significant; there need have been only one. The no-no boy is the underground, the resistance. The no-no boy is the conscience of Japanese America.

And this is what the novel is all about: the quest by Japanese-America to be whole again. Ichiro, the prototypical no-no boy for "all the reasons put together," in his quest for self exemplifies the quest of Japanese America for its own self. Though Ichiro cannot reconcile all the facets of himself, and though he is his own worst enemy, he is also a person of uncommon strength and integrity. Though Ichiro's quest is not completed, his determination to be whole remains, and one thing is certain: he is capable of loving and being loved in return:

> They didn't say much either in the car or after they found a sizable roadhouse and started dancing to a smooth six-piece orchestra. He was enjoying it and he felt that Emi was too. This is the way it ought to be, he thought to himself, to be able to dance with a girl you like and really get a kick out of it because everything is on an even keel and one's worries are only the usual ones of unpaid bills and sickness in the family and being late to work too often. Why can't it be that way for me? Nobody's looking twice at us. Nobody's asking me where I was during the war or

what the hell I am doing back on the Coast. There's no trouble to be had without looking for it. Everything's the same, just as it used to be. No bad feelings except for those that have always existed and probably always will. It's a matter of attitude. Mine needs changing. I've got to love the world the way I used to. I've got to love it and the people so I'll feel good, and feeling good will make life worth while. There's no point in crying about what's done. There's a place for me and Emi and Freddie here on the dance floor and out there in the hustle of things if we'll let it be that way. I've been fighting it and hating it and letting my bitterness against myself and Ma and Pa and even Taro throw the whole universe out of perspective. I want only to go on living and be happy. I've only to let myself do so. (p. 209)

No-No Boy is a testament to the strength of a people, not a tribute to oppression. Ichiro emerges as a loving person and in so doing determines the direction of his life. Even his internal difficulties are a sign of health, for he does not allow the power of blame to be usurped by anyone else, even the most deserving; rather, he keeps it for himself, to work with, and in this way the gift of self-determination is his own. Thus, in spite of the camps and prison, the death and destruction he experiences, Ichiro emerges as a positive person saying yes to life:

> He walked along, thinking, searching, thinking and probing, and, in the darkness of the alley of the community that was a tiny bit of America, he chased that faint and elusive insinuation of promise as it continued to take shape in mind and in heart. (p. 251)

"In mind and in heart." Once again, we have the work of a "majority"—the mind and the heart. The spirit of *No-No Boy* was nurtured in the soul of *Yokohama, California*. This literature, by its very nature—its range, its direction, its humaneness—embodies the soul and spirit of America.

Notes

[1] Toshio Mori, "The Woman Who Makes Swell Doughnuts," in his *Yokohama, California* (Caldwell, Id.: Caxton, 1949), pp. 22–25.

[2] Mori, p. 71.

[3] William Saroyan, Introd. *Yokohama*, p. 8. The term "Japanese-American writers" as used in this paper refers to writers in the continental United States; the vital body of literature developed by Japanese-Americans in Hawaii deserves its own discussion. Suffice it to say that Kazuo Miyamoto's novel, *Hawaii: The End of the Rainbow* (Rutland, Vt.: Tuttle, 1964) is an epic work of major importance.

[4] The publication of *Yokohama, California* was delayed from 1942 to 1949. Two stories— "Tomorrow Is Coming, Children," which attempts to justify the camp experience, and the one with the startling title "Slant-Eyed Americans," which takes place after the war begins—are obvious additions to the original manuscript and should be regarded as such: additions to an already intact work.

[5] For a closer look at this era, see Bill Hosokawa, *Nisei: The Quiet Americans* (New York: Morrow, 1969), a history of Japanese America; and Monica Sone, *Nisei Daughter* (Boston: Little, 1953), an autobiography centered on the war years. For a literary overview of this period, see Frank Chin, et al., eds., *Aiiieeeee! An Anthology of Asian-American Writers* (Garden City, N.Y.: Doubleday, 1975).

[6] John Okada, *No-No Boy* (1957; rpt. Seattle: CARP, 1976).

[7] While this discussion focuses on the Japanese-American context of the work, it is imperative to note that, above all, *No-No Boy* is a major novel of great depth and dimension and as such must be accorded the treatment it commands. Therefore, all the standard approaches to serious literature apply to *No-No Boy*—detailed analysis of structure, style, symbolic elements, characterization, and so forth—and the astute reader will recognize that the novel belongs to several major traditions, of its time and otherwise; the study of *No-No Boy* can contribute to any number of serious literature courses.

[8] For a detailed study of the camp experience, see Michi Weglyn, *Years of Infamy: The Untold Story of America's Concentration Camps* (New York: Morrow, 1976).